ALSO BY
DANIEL PATRICK MOYNIHAN

COUNTING OUR BLESSINGS

Daniel Patrick Moynihan

An Atlantic Monthly Press Book
Little, Brown and Company — Boston — Toronto

COUNTING OUR BLESSINGS

Reflections on the Future of America

Second Printing

Portions of this book, sometimes in a different form, have
previously appeared in *The American Scholar, The Atlantic,
The Center Magazine, Commentary, Harper's, The New Re-
public, The New Yorker* ("Cold Dawn, High Noon: Salt I and
Salt II" under the title "Reflections: The Salt Process"), and
The Public Interest.

LIBRARY OF CONGRESS CATALOGING IN PUBLICATION DATA

Moynihan, Daniel Patrick.
Counting our blessings.

"An Atlantic Monthly Press book."
Includes index.
1. United States—Politics and government—20th
century—Addresses, essays, lectures. 2. United
States—Constitutional history—Addresses, essays,
lectures. I. Title.
E743.M69   973.9   80–13371
ISBN 0–316–58702–8

Atlantic-Little, Brown Books
are published by
Little, Brown and Company
in association with
the Atlantic Monthly Press

BP
Designed by Susan Windheim
*Published simultaneously in Canada
by Little, Brown & Company (Canada) Limited*

Printed in the United States of America

For Nathan Glazer

Acknowledgments

From among essays that first appeared in the middle and later years of the 1970s I present here those that would seem worth preserving. They were written in a variety of circumstances and settings: the first from a villa tucked away among the flowering trees at the bottom of the Ambassador's garden in New Delhi; most in my beloved schoolhouse at Pindars Corners, New York; the last and longest composed at least in part at my desk on the floor of the Senate in the midst of the preliminaries to what was to have been a great debate on strategic arms limitation, one still to come.

I mention this variety of circumstances for the purpose of making a quite different point. As with the essays in my earlier collection, *Coping,* almost all of the work presented here was urged upon me, edited, and then published by a handful of men to whom my debt grows ever greater. Norman Podhoretz edited the first article; Robert Manning the second; Joseph Epstein the third; Irving Kristol the bulk of those that follow next; Robert Bingham the last. (As it happens, the first major essay I was to publish appeared some twenty-one years ago in the old

Reporter magazine. Irving Kristol was then senior editor, and Robert Bingham, who took responsibility for my work, was his assistant.) In a swirling world these men have been fixed points of craft and competence without which I should have long since lost direction.

None is more dear to me than Nathan Glazer, who invited me to join him in my first book (his, really) written at about the time of that first essay. We called it *Beyond the Melting Pot* and the reception was, well, mixed. We seemingly had raised rather an impolitic subject; at all events the Harvard University Press chose not to publish the book and that task fell to the more daring imagination of the M.I.T. Press. It has thus been a special joy to see the book win acceptance over the years. (And for that matter, to remain in print!) This month there came to my desk a splendidly turned-out volume (*from* the Harvard University Press) which I opened to find is a case study based on the hypotheses Glazer and I set forth in those distant years. And so we may have been of some use to social science. I dare to think we have been of other uses also. Just days ago I returned from a visit to Puerto Rico, where a senior official of the government there gave me a paper he had written a while back asserting with great force and *élan* the right of the Puerto Rican people both to be Americans and to be themselves and to see no conflict between these identities. His paper began:

Twenty years ago, a couple of visionaries wrote an epochal book, *Beyond the Melting Pot*. Their study brought about a change in attitudes, in theories which subverted some of the basic tenets of our Nation. That we did not indeed melt into a national melange. That there were distinguishable characteristics even in groups which were thought to have disappeared into the Nation, and even more damning, that the Melting Pot should not be a national goal. It was possible then to postulate that the uniqueness of our Nation lay precisely in these differences and that perhaps our greatness lay there too.

If this be so, then it is singularly to the credit of Nathan Glazer that it was discovered. *Maître.*

I have been assisted in various of these efforts by a number of younger associates, among them Elliott Abrams, Chester E. Finn, Jr., Charles Horner, Penn Kemble, and Abram N. Shulsky; I thank them all.

DANIEL PATRICK MOYNIHAN

Washington
March 3, 1980

Introduction

In 1973 I published a collection of papers written over a long period, giving it the title *Coping: Essays on the Practice of Government*. My purpose was didactic; to argue that a modest foresight was possible in public affairs. I offered examples. I was not arguing the existence of any exact technique; the extent of my assertion was that it is possible to "see a little way ahead in the fog."

In the last entry in *Coping* I made a bet with the reader. Most of the essays had been in print long enough for events in the main to have sustained their forecasts. But the reader might well ask how selective the author had been. As the Southerners say, "Even a blind hog finds an acorn sometimes." And so as the book went to press I added an essay entitled "Peace," based on a lecture I gave Andover Academy in early 1973, just as I was leaving to become United States Ambassador to India. I proposed that the social turmoil, especially among youth, that began in the 1960s was over. We would now enter a period of relative social peace. ". . . Most of the events that tore American society almost apart, or so it seemed in the 1960s, arose from conditions unique to the decade in which they occurred. They will not ever exist again."

I was not in the least asserting that the ills of American society, its injustices and imbalances, had been resolved. Rather to the contrary, with the turmoil passing, it might prove yet more difficult to bring them to the level of collective action. Still I put down my bet.

The essential facts were demographic. During the 1960s the cohort of persons aged fourteen to twenty-four years that begins in childhood and ends, presumedly, with a person settled in society increased more than it had ever done in the past or conceivably could in the foreseeable future. In the seven decades from 1890 to 1960 the size of this age group grew by 12.5 million persons. Then in the single decade of the 1960s it grew by 13.8 million persons. It would grow by 600,000 in the 1970s, and decline in the 1980s. This cohort explosion, combined with political events which, if not unique were nonetheless rare, produced in a synergistic mode the tumult of that decade with its particular prominence of persons of the young, soon-to-be-adult category. This had persuaded many that something like a permanent revolution had commenced, and of those persuaded, a good portion chose to align themselves with such a future. My message was that that future was now past.

There was another, more internal message. I had been no great friend of the 1960s, a period Richard Hofstadter described as "The Age of Rubbish." I said of him in the Andover lecture:

A man of the democratic left, he was depressed by the rise of a vulgar — but "irresistibly chic" — radicalism among the well-educated and well-to-do. He found "Almost the entire intellectual community . . . lost in dissent." There was almost no dialogue left "between those who are alienated from society and those who are prepared to make an intelligent defense of it."

The rubbish would now cease to be produced in such overpowering quantity. But what of a political society living on a rubbish heap? For that inevitably would be the aftermath of so much misinformation and misformation. What use would we make of the "peace" to come? It would be a different period, the one just commencing, and those who would attempt "an intelligent defense" of American society would face different questions.

Settled in India, living in the political ruins of the vast demi-raj Americans had constructed there, reading the bad news from home, I wondered what these new questions would be. A year passed. I was invited to give the address at the Woodrow Wilson International Center for Scholars on the occasion in February 1974 of the fiftieth anniversary of Wilson's death, and returned to Washington for this purpose. The paper, which I entitled "Was Woodrow Wilson Right?" is the basis in a slightly revised form of the first essay in the present volume. I took for my theme Wilson's concept of patriotism. "Patriotism, properly considered," he had said in 1907, "is not a mere sentiment; it is a principle of action, or rather is a fine energy of character and of conscience operating beyond the narrow circle of self-interest." I went on to ask in what respect one could say Wilson was right about the large issues of his presidency.

The essays that follow put similar questions. The first group deals with American values in foreign affairs; the second with issues in social science that touch upon questions of law and government; the third with political issues of the present; the fourth with arms control.

In the main these are *not* matters easily forecast. Outcomes are determined more by values and will than by objective circumstances, and in consequence outcomes are obdurately indeterminate. This adds interest, surely, and commands attention. We are a blessed people, but not invincibly elect. We must make our future as we did our past.

And so let us count our blessings, and look to them.

Contents

ONE

It has for some time seemed to me that among the more important separations of powers in the American political system is that which divides, or divided, functions between New York City and Washington. It is not strictly speaking constitutional, but it has its origin in the era of constitution-making, and arose from an agreement between Hamilton and Jefferson which resolved what were in their respective viewpoints matters of high constitutional principle. Hamilton desired an active and enterprising national government, and accordingly wished it to assume the debts incurred by the several states during the Revolution. Jefferson's view was just the opposite, but he agreed to Hamilton's proposal concerning the debt in return for Hamilton's agreeing to move the capital of the new government away from New York, the center of activity and enterprise in the nation, to a swamp on the banks of the Potowmac, which turned malarial in April such that any congressman who dallied into May might not be back in December.

As with much else, or so we are told, the balance of things has been tipping toward Washington of late. It was accordingly a special pleasure that the great visual spectacle of the Bicentennial was the flotilla of the Tall Ships sailing into New York

*Harbor. More narrowly observed, perhaps, but not less spectac-
ular, was the essay of the late Martin Diamond, that quintessential New York intellectual, which appeared in a Bicentennial
issue of* The Public Interest, *that quintessential New York
journal. It was entitled "The Declaration and the Constitution:
Liberty, Democracy and the Founders." Diamond, following the
lead of Leo Strauss, observed that the men of the Declaration of
Independence and of the Constitution were implementing, as
they saw it, what Hamilton called the "new science of politics."
There had been a crucial turn in political thought away from
the earlier Greek assumption that the virtue of its citizens was
the foundation of the state, and that society accordingly ought to
focus on the inculcation of such virtue, and its further elucida-
tion. Civic philosophy was the core intellectual discipline of
such a society, and this was the view that persisted thereafter for
two thousand years, with generally indifferent results. Then
came Locke and Montesquieu and others with a quite different
view. They saw the object of society as the attainment of liberty
for the individual, and judged that society accordingly ought to
focus on the practicable arrangements that would establish and
preserve that liberty. Diamond describes the Declaration as
expressing the "political science of liberty" of that age, a science
subsequently, and for the first time, fully elaborated in the
Constitution.*

*In the year of the Bicentennial I happened to ask a friend who,
rather late in life, had turned to the full-time study of the
classics, and especially of Aeschylus, what he had learned. He
thought a moment and replied: "I have learned that if you do not
know your future, you will never understand your past." This
set me to wondering about our two centuries of experimenting
with liberty.*

*For in a sense we know our future. However persistent and
durable our ideas should prove, there is no longer any foreseeable future in which they will prevail in the world at large.
There was such a time, the long second half of the nineteenth*

century, when, as Lord Bryce put it, America sailed a "summer sea." The apogee came under Woodrow Wilson, followed by the appearance of competing totalitarian systems.

Increasingly thereafter democracy in the twentieth century has attained to the condition of monarchy in the nineteenth: a form of government more to be associated with the past than the future, an arrangement largely peculiar to a handful of North Atlantic countries, and a few of their colonies, as the Greeks would have understood that term.

This says nothing whatsoever about the relative merits.

Nor yet of the energy and spirit that might be released if indeed we do turn, in Hofstadter's phrase, to an "intelligent defense" of liberal society as it had come to be in the West, and especially in the United States. Scarcely perfect, it has the elemental advantage of being so manifestly preferable to any available alternative. In his essay "Politics and the English Language," Orwell wrote: "In our time, political speech and writing are largely the defense of the indefensible." It seems to me this is no longer so. Not, given the ferocity, the vulgarity, of the attacks upon the West by despotisms new and old. There is another Orwellian maxim: the first duty of an intelligent man is to state the obvious.

1.
The Legacy of
Woodrow Wilson

I T IS MORE THAN FIFTY YEARS since Woodrow Wilson died, but it does not seem that: more like two hundred fifty. We are uncomfortable with Wilson in the twentieth century; he seems more the kind of man who came early rather than late in our national life when of a sudden we were to find that, far from being the youngest of governments, we had become virtually the oldest. Yet few would disagree that Wilson shaped this century as no other American has done. Herbert Hoover in his last book, *The Ordeal of Woodrow Wilson* (they were very alike, Wilson and Hoover, though Hoover was the more prolific author), put it fairly:

For a moment at the time of the Armistice, Mr. Wilson rose to intellectual domination of most of the civilized world. With his courage and eloquence, he carried a message of hope for the independence of nations, the freedom of men and lasting peace. Never since his time has any man risen to the political and spiritual heights that came to him.

There was no one like him, then; there has been none since. Except perhaps Lenin. (That case could be made. Men alike primarily in the way they both differed from their own people and were nonetheless able to inspire and to mobilize them as no leaders before or since.) But as an American figure, he is singular.

If we do not quite know what to make of Wilson, this is not least because it is still so uncertain what he made of us. The American people, the object of his highest hopes, his strongest passions, were not somehow part of his being. The apocrypha have it that he once began an address to a peace conference occasion saying that when he thought of mankind he did not think of men in dinner jackets. Which only extends the mystery from what he thought of Americans to what he thought of mankind. It is clear enough that once he entered politics he came more and more to think about the working masses, sweaty in those days and scarcely Calvinist, whose party he was soon to lead. (The International Labor Organization, established by the Versailles Treaty, was by no means, to his thinking, the least of the organizations of the League system. He had contrived for Samuel Gompers to head the commission at Paris which drew up its Charter. The speeches on his great trip through the West in 1919 are remembered as explanations and defenses of the Covenant of the League. But he also spoke repeatedly of the ILO, asking that more heed be paid to the charter of rights for the workingman embedded in the peace settlement. In turn the inclusion of the ILO had more to do with the defeat of the treaty in the Senate than standard histories are so far wont to record.) He came to think, surely, of mankind as including persons who spoke languages other than English (although not necessarily with an Irish accent). In his Western speeches he would say so with a candor — engaging and unashamed — now quite foreign to American public life.

"Do you know where Azerbaijan is?" he asked his audience, in San Francisco on September 18, 1919, speaking of the peace. conference:

Well, one day there came in a very dignified and interesting group of gentlemen from Azerbaijan. I did not have time until they were gone to find out where they came from, but I did find this out immediately, that I was talking to men who talked the same language that I did in respect of ideas, in respect of conceptions of liberty, in respect of conceptions of right and justice. . . .

It is at such points, of course, that one inclines to quarrel with Wilson: How can he ask us to believe that he believed such things? Worse: What if indeed he did? And for a new generation influenced, if at all, by Wilson, then at most by what I should suppose is now an attenuated Wilsonianism, there are vastly greater difficulties with his concluding assertion:

And I did find this out, that the Azerbaijanis were, with all the other delegations that came to see me, metaphorically speaking, holding their hands out to America and saying, "You are the disciples and leaders of the free world; can't you come and help us?"

We have since, as a nation, learned well enough where Azerbaijan is. But for the rest . . . no, we fall back in disbelief — even such as I, taught, if anything, to move forward in acceptance.

What then does it matter what he thought of mankind? It matters because therein resides the essence of his quest for legitimacy in the world order, a quest which still eludes us, and which, if I am not altogether wrong, honesty requires that we acknowledge cannot any longer be successfully pursued in strictly Wilsonian terms. Wilson's vision of a world order was a religious vision: of the natural goodness of man prevailing through the Holy Ghost of Reason. The religious beliefs from which this vision came, while still widespread and deeply felt among individuals, are no longer seen to imply political belief as well. Wilson in that sense speaks to us with a diminishing, ever more distant voice. And yet a distinct one to which today we need to listen again.

He died, as recorded, in Washington in 1924, but of course he died in the public sense five years earlier in Pueblo, Colorado, when he suffered an incapacitating stroke. He was only once ever again to speak in public, on Armistice Day in 1923, a short while before the literal end. The Pueblo speech deserves to be reread. It is surely a premonition, an evocation almost, of death. A speech from the cross. A speech, to be sure, by a Presbyterian Saint Jerome, contesting texts to the very end, but a Passion withal. It is a premonition of his own death, and a prophecy, I suppose, of the death of the Western civilization that would not be saved. Excepting always that, while those who believed would be saved, the city would not be saved: the city would be lost to war and rumors of war.

The biblical cadence, the New Testament ecstasy in that extempore speech are as moving as anything in the language of the American presidency:

Again and again, my fellow citizens, mothers who lost their sons in France have come to me and taking my hand, have shed tears upon it not only, but they have added, "God bless you, Mr. President." Why, my fellow citizens, should they pray God to bless me? I advised the Congress of the United States to create the situation that led to the death of their sons. I ordered their sons overseas. I consented to their sons being put in the most difficult parts of the battle line, where death was certain, as in the impenetrable difficulties of the forest of Argonne. Why should they weep upon my hand and call down the blessings of God upon me? Because they believe that their boys died for something that vastly transcends any of the immediate and palpable objects of the war. They believe and they rightly believe that their sons saved the liberty of the world. They believe that wrapped up with the liberty of the world is the continuous protection of that liberty by the concerted powers of all civilized people. They believe that this sacrifice was made in order that other sons should not be called upon for a similar gift — the gift of life, the gift of all that died — and if we did not see this thing through, if we fulfilled the dearest present wish of Germany and now dissociated ourselves from those alongside whom we fought in the war, would not something of the halo go away from the gun over the mantelpiece or the sword? Would not the old uniform lose something of its significance? These men were crusaders. They were not going forth to prove the might of the United States. They were going forth to prove the might of justice and right, and all the world accepted them as crusaders, and their transcendent achievement has made all the world believe in America as it believes in no other nation organized in the modern world. There seems to me to stand between us and the rejection or qualification of this treaty the serried ranks of those boys in khaki, not only these boys who came home but those dear ghosts that still deploy upon the fields of France.

He tells of visiting a cemetery in France where French women tended American graves:

France was free and the world was free because America had come. I wish some men in public life who are now opposing the settlement for which these men died could visit such a spot as that. I wish that the thought that comes out of those graves could penetrate their consciousness. I wish that they could feel the moral obligation that rests upon us not to go back on those boys, but to see the thing through, to see it through to the end and make good their redemption of the world. For nothing less depends upon this decision, nothing less than the liberation and salvation of the world.

What is one to make of this? Was he right? We have almost given up asking such questions, much less answering. But this, surely, is clear. It was very late in the history of the West to put any large public question in such terms. Carl J. Friedrich and Charles Blitzer are correct, surely, that with the religious revival of the seventeenth century, and the wars of that century, "Once again, and for the last time, life was seen as meaningful in religious, even theological, terms. . . ." For the last time.

But was he right? In 1944, a quarter century after the Pueblo speech, when we seemed well into the grim future Wilson had foreseen, Gerald W. Johnson asked this question:

It is not a pleasant idea, for if he was right, the rest of us were wrong. . . . Dead men scattered from the Solomon Islands to Italy suggest that we may have been wrong. Fine ships by hundreds shattered and sunk suggest that we may have been wrong. Billions upon uncounted billions wrung from our toil; mourning in every city and town, in crowded tenements and lonely farmhouses, weeping women and prematurely old men . . . suggest that we may have been wrong.

And "those dear ghosts that still deploy upon the fields of France" — what do they suggest?

Events up until the time Johnson wrote, and in the three decades since, suggest at the very least that the United States remains as uncertain as ever about the terms on which the then President of the United States helped, first, to set in motion an extraordinary world dynamic of political independence accompanied by a rhetoric of personal freedom; and sought, secondly, to establish a world order which, by legitimating and channeling these forces, would sufficiently contain them. Events suggest further that having failed, or having insufficiently succeeded, in the second effort, the United States has commenced to recede in its commitment to the first. The events in this instance are better known than the argument to be made for them, for indeed the argument lies essentially in the acceptance of seemingly ineluctable events. If the Wilsonian thesis was too wordy, a shade too eager to persuade, its antithesis stands in something very like "dumb insolence" — a serious charge in British courts-martial, not least because it is so difficult to prove and impossible to bear. In a word, events increasingly persuade us to act as if Wilson were wrong.

Our susceptibility to such doubts goes far back. Wilson as President failed, did he not?: never good for a reputation. More importantly perhaps, for Americans, as in the course of the 1920s the person emerged from the President, it came to be seen that the person himself was not without failings. Johnson writes: "He was full of faults. They stuck out like spines upon a

cactus . . . he was arrogant . . . bullheaded . . . puritanical
. . . vengeful . . . icy . . . blistering." His racial attitudes were
certainly deplorable. At times he displayed a measure of
selfless devotion to political gain such as to qualify as a case
history in Puritan aberration. In this regard, his speeches just
before entering active politics as Democratic candidate for
senator from New Jersey in 1907 are of textbook quality.
Addressing the Southern Society at the Waldorf Astoria, he
feared that "America has fallen to the commonplace level of all
the other nations" because she had abandoned her egalitarian
ideals. "When she ceases to believe that all men shall have
equal opportunity she goes back upon the principle on which
the nation was founded." And how best to have equal opportunity? By not discriminating. Which is to say by not having a
graduated income tax. "There is only one sort of taxation that
is just, and that is taxation that does not discriminate." Or
redistribute income: "I know of only one legitimate object of
taxation, and that is to pay the expenses of the government."
("Woodrow Wilson Attacks Paternalism," went *The New York
Times* headline; "Government Can't Do Everything, He Tells
Southern Society.")

Familiar stuff. In office, of course, he became a guarded
advocate of graduated taxes, and devised more than a few new
ways of spending them. There are words for such behavior and
they are directed, with no special impact, to most public men.
The craft of President ordains a certain craftiness. But Wilson
had rather implied that he was not to be measured by such
standards. The greater the shock, then, when the doings at
Versailles began to leak out, as inevitably they were to do, and
it became unavoidably clear that in dealing with leaders of the
Allied Powers Wilson, in order to win the Covenant, had
accepted many more "lesser evils" — Hoover's term — than
were ever proposed in the way of reservations to the Treaty of
Versailles which the moderate senators had held out for and
with which it would have been ratified. In a word, he did for

Clemenceau what he would not do for Senators Frank B. Kellogg or Porter J. McCumber; he was willing to bend a principle for Lloyd George, but not for William Howard Taft or Elihu Root or Charles Evans Hughes.

Further and fatefully, a kind of corrupt Wilsonianism carried on as a dominant theme of American foreign policy for years after him. The Republicans who took over scarcely abandoned his ideals. To the contrary, the 1920s were nothing if not the era of American-inspired disarmament conferences and treaties renouncing war as an instrument of national policy. The problem, as with the Great Experiment itself, was that the men in power were willing to proclaim the ideals but not to enforce them. Or, some would say, to proclaim ideals that were unenforceable. It comes to much the same thing: irresponsibility. In what must surely be the best writing yet on this subject, Ernest W. Lefever has given the name of moralism to this kind of irresponsibility; it is, he says, the corruption of the foreign policy traditions of both "rational idealism" and "historical realism," of Tom Paine and Walt Whitman on the one hand, Burke and Madison on the other. Moralism evades both of these moral traditions. Morality is a synonym for responsibility. Moralism is a conscious or unconscious escape from accountability.

There is first of all in this mutant a fundamental hostility to authority. "The soft moralistic view tends to distrust the state, especially its coercive power, while Western ethical thought affirms the necessity of the state and insists on the responsible use of power." In another variant, it sets the most unavailing of all criteria for worth: "Soft moralism tends to associate virtue with weakness, just as it associates vice with power." Whence the lunging forward to do good and the reeling back when it is learned what will be required — "This strange combination," to continue Lefever, "of reform-intervention and security-isolation [which] turns foreign policy on its head." The first task of foreign policy, in what we would hope to be our ethical tradition, is peace and security. Moralism substitutes — for this — the modes and objectives of internal policy to the disadvantage, even denigration, of first things. When it fails, moralism will typically prefer no foreign policy to a necessary one.

The reform-intervention phase of this mind set became manic in the years just after the period in which Gerald Johnson wrote. From Lake Success onward to about the Bay of Pigs, it seemed at times almost to prevail (again with Republicans succeeding to and acquiescing in a kind of Democratic heresy). A necessary counterargument was made by men such as George Kennan, and before the era was over "Wilsonian idealism" had become synonymous with dangerous nonsense: the prattle of soft and privileged people in a hard and threatening world. Vietnam, with its own sequence of "reform-intervention" and "security-isolation," appeared all the more to confirm the folly of that world view. That the subsequent "neo-isolationist" argument came so often from precisely those who had earlier made the case for intervention seemingly settled the matter: a tendency of thought, a tone of voice, a tintinnabulation of the schoolyard bells that we had best as grownups put behind us.

But this was a corruption of Wilson. Surely we can accept this now, what with the naïveté of the Kellogg-Briand treaties behind us and the worst of the Cold War obsessions also. The essential Wilson remains, the Wilson whose singular contribution to the American national experience was a definition of patriotism appropriate to the age America was entering at the time of his presidency, which is to say patriotism defined first of all as the duty to defend and, where feasible, to advance democratic principles in the world at large. (In this he expanded the original — and singular — American definition of citizenship as a matter not of blood or soil or religious faith, but of adherence to political norms.) Always to defend them —

prudently if possible, but at the risk, if need be, of imprudence.

One suspects this came easily to Wilson in an intellectual sense: Scotch-Irish, his father a Presbyterian minister, his mother a Presbyterian minister's daughter, in whom, Richard Hofstadter wrote, the Calvinist spirit burned with a bright and imperishable flame. "Their son learned to look upon life as the progressive fulfillment of God's will and to see man as a 'distinct moral agent' in a universe of moral imperatives." His belief in his country was an extension, a secularization I suppose, of his belief in his God, a belief of concreteness and content virtually absent from the presidency since. (Jimmy Carter would be, of course, an exception. But just that: an exception.)

The American people in the aggregate, however, retain their religious beliefs and practices very much intact. But such conviction has all but evanesced among political elites in the United States much as it has done, for example, in Britain. And in the absence of religious conviction, it is not possible to establish an obligation of the Wilsonian kind to the state. Our elites accept the state rather as Margaret Fuller accepted the universe, and it might be said of them what Carlyle said of her: By gad, they had better. If, for Wilson, the properly directed state was an instrument of his Calvinist God, then obviously, for Wilson, patriotism, however physically demanding, posed no intellectual problems. But it does pose intellectual problems for the American and British political elites today: *it is, verily, a crisis of faith.*

There remains, however, in both countries — and very much in both countries — a strong ethical sense with respect to public matters, a sense of justice and procedure, a feeling for law, which is wholly serviceable as a belief system around which to organize a national life. What was missing then and is missing now is the dimension of duty. Again, it appears as a problem not so much of people in general as of elites. Hofstadter describes Wilson as "the preacher of a mission of world service to the most insular and provincial people among all the great powers." He could have added — and would have done, I think, had the point been raised — that Wilson succeeded to a considerable extent in this mission. The American people were with him on the Covenant, as were, overwhelmingly, the peoples with whom he was in touch abroad. If survey research tells us anything, it is that this conversion, warts and backsliding and all, is very much intact a half century later.

It may be noted in this connection that of all the institutions of American public life, the one which has never wavered in its Wilsonian commitment is the one perhaps most expressive of the popular ethos — the labor movement. Presidents have come and gone, and the labor movement has disagreed with most of them on these matters, and shows not the least distress at having done so. One does not know how long this will continue. It may be a generational phenomenon. But so long as it does continue (and they attend!) the American labor delegates to the International Labor Conference will insist, for example, that a free trade union is what Samuel Gompers and his associates thought to be a free trade union when they drafted the ILO Charter in Paris in 1919, and only that, and that no necessity or convenience of state has any power to make them pretend that a captive trade union is a free trade union. None. The case could generally be made that the mass of the American people has remained substantially loyal to the standard Wilson raised. It is the others who come and go.

This is the kind of thing Wilson knew. He was a learned man. He knew, for example, that you could trust Gompers, who for his part told an audience in Paris, doubtless also in dinner jackets, "You do not know how safe a thing freedom is." (An age when English was spoken.) Wilson knew that the most distinctive fact of the American polity was the degree to which it had informed the thought and action of ordinary citizens with a conception of patriotism that elsewhere, in democratic nations no less than autocratic ones, was rare to the point of being a preserve of privilege.

In his Southern Society speech of 1907 — reflecting the frame of mind in which he forsook the academy for politics — Wilson took patriotism for his topic, quoting Tennyson's lines:

> *A nation still, the rulers and the ruled;*
> *Some sense of duty, something of a faith,*
> *Some reverence for the laws ourselves have made,*
> *Some patient force to change them when we will,*
> *Some civic manhood firm against the crowd.*

"Patriotism, properly considered," he said, "is not a mere sentiment; it is a principle of action, or rather is a fine energy of character and of conscience operating beyond the narrow circle of self-interest." Then an unusual point, as if to emphasize how explicit he meant to be. "Every man should be careful to have an available surplus of energy over and above what he spends upon himself and his own interests, to spend for the advancement of his neighbors, of his people, of his nation." That the specter of statism hovers about such words need not be contested. It always will, when attachment to the state rather than mere submission is proposed. But the state as an extension of the moral force and responsibility of the individual is a different thing from the state as the mere monopoly of force. The Wilsonian state might properly claim its tithe in energy and resource (whether or not raised by graduated income taxes!).

This at least is not moralism. It does not discover virtue in weakness. It argues, rather, the unique and necessary virtue of strength, of men and women becoming all they are capable of being, beyond anything accorded them as possible in the past. For, said Wilson, it was in America that the ordinary citizen was first "put in the way" of such "statesmanlike thinking."

I like to recall that passage of de Tocqueville's in which he marvels with eloquent praise at the variety of information and excellence of discretion which our polity did not hesitate to demand of its people, its common people. It is in this, rather than in anything we have invented by way of governmental forms, that we have become distinguished among the nations, by what we expect of ourselves and of each other.

Is it a sustainable vision? Hard to say. The history of this century is that of men and women enduring the most awful trials in pursuit of visions every bit as secular, differing only in their willingness to submerge the individual in the mass. Wilson argues the elevation of the individual, the differentiation of each. It may be more than we can do: but this very thought, so much a product of the events that followed Wilson, is the essential case for trying. And the context for any such effort remains exactly that which Wilson first perceived: the worldwide struggle between free societies and those not free.

Wilson conceived of patriotism not as an instrument of the state, but as an expression and extension of the moral capacities of the individual, specifically of men seeking freedom in its many manifestations. He saw that in the age then commencing, such a patriotism would be meaningful only as it manifested itself in a world setting, engaging its energies in a world struggle. Democracy in one country was not enough, simply because it would not last. In twentieth-century America Wilsonianism has been disparaged for enthusiasm, much as High Church Anglicans disapproved of the Methodists of eighteenth-century England. And yet the Methodists, had they been ordained, almost surely would have kept the English people in the church, and possibly also their bishops. Instead the people wandered away into nothingness. Does not the

American faith in democracy face something of this dilemma, and are we not adopting much the same course at the silent behest of men who know too much to believe anything in particular and opt instead for accommodations of reasonableness and urbanity that drain our world position of moral purpose?

It may be that no other leadership is coming our way and we will have to make do. But before becoming too accepting, or admiring, of the course events are taking, we still have time, surely, to consider where such a course is likely to lead. Granted, we may end up alive: no small virtue in a policy, explicit or implied. But we shall also very likely end up lonely, which is no small disadvantage.

It comes to this: the Wilsonian world view is already half achieved. Most people of the world live in independent states demarcated along lines of hoped-for ethnic legitimacy. This very achievement makes for intense difficulties with the remaining internal ethnic divisions. Nevertheless the principle of self-determination has not only succeeded at the level of a norm but has also largely been implemented.

The quality of the incumbent regimes is another matter. Few measure up to Wilson's hopes. Numerically there are not many more democracies now than in 1919 (although of the two additions to this short list, India and Japan are scarcely insubstantial). Even so, most of the other regimes dare not speak of themselves except in terms of Wilsonian ideals. In other words, *these ideals — seen widely as American ideals — still establish the internal right to govern,* just as, equally, Wilsonian ideals establish the national right to exist.

Does this not impose a duty? Wilson would have thought it did. Not many do today. Very well, then, does it not at the very least make a certain claim on our calculations — namely, that it is not a circumstance likely to go away, and like it or not, it is going to influence, even dictate, a great many things we shall find ourselves doing, even as it does already? The reason for this is quite external to the political eschatology of Wilsonianism. It resides, rather, in a political reality for which he had no little distaste: that of a multi-ethnic population. We are a nation of nations and inextricably involved in the fate of other peoples the world over.

This was already wholly clear at the time Wilson governed, although he does not give the impression of having understood just what forces his principles of self-determination of nations had set off within his own nation. Indeed, he saw perhaps too many Azerbaijanis in Paris (one could wish he had got to know Ho Chi Minh, who was then busy about the conference) and perhaps too few Irish in Washington. The loss of Irish support damaged the prospect of the Covenant — and scarcely improved the peace treaty, if self-determination was what it was supposed to be about. Less noticed at the time, the first armed rebellion (the Ghadr rebellion) against British rule in India had been planned in Stockton, California, among immigrant Sikhs in the early years of the war, and after aborting in India itself, was prosecuted by the American government when the United States entered the war.

But offsetting these losses was the support of all those Central European nationalities whose homelands gained independence through the treaty. For instance, a declaration favoring the formation of the Republic of Czechoslovakia, was issued in Pittsburgh during those months. This was a foretaste of the pressures to which American foreign policy would be subject in the years of world power status to come. The reality has exceeded any expectations and will in all probability go on doing so, for while the matter has not received much attention, the United States is quietly but rapidly resuming its role as a nation of first- and second-generation immigrants, almost the only one of its kind in the world, incomparably the largest, and for the first time in our history or any other, a nation drawn from the entire world. The Immigration Act of 1965 drastically altered the shape of American immigration and increased its size. (I should not be surprised if one third of the population increase of the United States today consists of first-generation immigrants or their children.) Our immigrants in wholly unprecedented proportions come from Asia, South America, and the Caribbean. (In fiscal year 1973 the ten top visa-issuing posts were Manila, Monterrey, Seoul, Tijuana, Santo Domingo, Mexico City, Naples, Guadalajara, Toronto, Kingston. I would expect Bombay to make this top ten list before long. By the end of the century there should be a million Asian Indians in the United States — unless, that is, the Secretary General of the United Nations is successful with his recent proposal that a worldwide system of emigration taxes be established in order, somehow, to benefit the underdeveloped nations.) The Vietnamese immigration came suddenly, and with dramatic effect.

In short, by the end of the century, given present trends, the United States will be a multi-ethnic nation the like of which even we have never imagined. This means at least one thing. There will be no struggle for personal liberty (or national independence or national survival) anywhere in Europe, in Asia, in Africa, in Latin America which will not affect American politics. In that circumstance, I would argue that there is only one course likely to make the internal strains of consequent conflicts endurable, and that is for the United States deliberately and consistently to bring its influence to bear on behalf of those regimes which promise the largest degree of personal and national liberty. We shall have to do so with prudence, with care. We are granted no license to go looking for trouble, no right to meddle. We shall have to continue to put up with obnoxious things about which there is nothing we can do; and often we may have to restrain ourselves where there are things we can do. Yet we must play the hand dealt us: we stand for liberty, for the expansion of liberty. Anything less risks the contraction of liberty: our own included.

It is not likely to be a formally welcomed role. The political elites of most of the world are poisonously anti-American, and will remain so while the spell of Marxism and the British universities — what Orwell cited as the "right Left people" — persists. This circumstance is well known and much noted. Our own intellectuals are becoming demoralized, even victimized, by it (although I should think such influence will much diminish over the next thirty years or so). Less well known is the parallel circumstance that the peoples of the world remain extraordinarily faithful to Wilsonian ideals, no longer much if at all associated with him, but still widely associated with the United States and giving every sign of persisting. Among these peoples, I count the American people: not as an act of piety or wishfulness but rather, and assertively, as a fact repeatedly established by voting behavior and opinion research. Wilson's photographs are nowhere to be seen, but in the working-class homes of Pittsburgh, in the barrios of Bogotá, in the mud villages of South India, portraits of John F. Kennedy will be found next to the Sacred Heart of Jesus, or Bolívar, or, as I have once seen, Gandhi, for Kennedy too was in the Wilson tradition. It is not the only tradition of American foreign policy, and that it can be an aberrant one no one any longer questions. But that we lose it at the risk of the ethical integrity of the nation ought not to be questioned either.

2.
How Much Does Freedom Matter?

A T SOME POINT in the early hours (presumedly) of the week of April 20, 1975, the first slogan of the new era of peace appeared on the walls of an eating club in Cambridge, Massachusetts. "The War," it proclaimed in the neo-Togliatti style of the region, black on red brick, "Is Not Over."

And yet it was, and its aftermath commenced to engage us. Promptly, there has arisen a debate over the reliability of American commitments, variously described, to other nations. For the third quarter of the twentieth century was, in truth, characterized by all manner of American-initiated military alliances and a not less considerable profusion of alliances for economic and social progress. As these commitments have not always produced results either of security or of progress, the question easily arises, especially following the Vietnam experience, as to how valuable such commitments may be.

It is not, however, too soon to ask also: How willing is the United States any longer to make such commitments? Clearly, certain necessities impose themselves here. Supposedly the nation will remain resolute in that range of concerns that touch directly on security interests, or are thought to do so.

Widening and deepening the Rio Grande, perhaps. But what of the far larger sense of our role in the world that prompted an American President to declare, in his inaugural address: "Let every nation know, whether it wishes us well or ill, that we shall pay any price, bear any burden, meet any hardship, support any friend, oppose any foe to assure the survival and the success of liberty"?

Clearly, a statesman in any way sensible of what has gone on in the almost twenty years since would not be likely to make such a statement in public; but would any think in such ways? Would any seek to convey such an impression through a subtlety of language, a nuance of reference? How much does freedom matter to us? Not only our own, but that of others? Not only among nations, but within nations? Does democracy, other than American democracy, much matter to us anymore?

These were thoughts an American Ambassador to India unavoidably brought home after some time in the world's largest democracy, observing from a distance the ways of the world's second largest. Unavoidably, because to have lived in India as a representative of the United States is to have been surrounded and suffused with evidence of an extraordinary American commitment to that nation, made at the time of independence, and based almost wholly on the fact that India *was* a democracy. No strategic interest took us there. No economic interest. No interest of consanguinity or coreligiosity. No cultural ties; at most a flickering recollection that a German-born Oxford don, Max Müller, had established that our languages are somehow related.

There were, in truth, some serious connections, but few knew about them. Consider the Ghadr rebellion mentioned above. But even there the influence went from us to them, rather than the other direction. No: in 1948 the most the Indians could claim to have done for us was to have occasioned Columbus's discovery, and to have provided the designation Brahmin for the elders of Boston. And yet, unhesitantly — I believe the term is warranted — we undertook to provide India economic support in very large amounts, and military support also, *because it was a democracy.*

It was impossible for anyone living there in the final years of the Vietnam agony not to see that our relation to India was in ways the reverse of the Vietnam coin. We provided some economic assistance to South Vietnam, a prosperous enough area, and enormous military aid, including our own forces. To India, a military power, we supplied relatively small amounts of military aid, but vast amounts of economic assistance. The same men did both, and for much the same reasons. How, then, if the Vietnam commitment was so terribly wrong, could the Indian commitment have been right?

A man sits in Delhi with the temperature 115 degrees at noon and thinks of such matters, especially if he had desired to see the first involvement ended, having for a long time thought it mistaken and worse, and yet wished to see the second involvement continued and strengthened. It did not take much insight to see that both were ending, nor any especial sensibility to know that things would thereafter be different.

One was kept busy in India, but more at *un*doing things than otherwise. One legacy of our earlier involvement was a vast rupee debt owed to the United States by India, mostly for food shipments during the 1950s and 1960s. The greater part of it written off: the largest debt settlement in history. The Indians noticed, and took the point, I like to think, that the United States wanted a relationship of equals, which could never obtain where one party owned a third of the currency of the other.

Another legacy of the earlier era — American suspicion and disapproval of nonalignment — was at least modified. The Secretary of State came to New Delhi, and in a formal address said, "The United States accepts nonalignment." But again, while the Indians noticed, the Americans did not. Had it not been for Murray Marder of the *Washington Post,* Americans might not even have learned of it, for the press corps accompanying the Secretary was not much interested. Congress, certainly, was interested not at all. It only wanted India to go away. In 1974 a veteran congressman, formerly an economics professor from Maryland, amended an appropriation for the World Bank to provide that the American representative shall automatically vote against any loan to India. (We voted against, but did not lobby against, and so the loans go through. But still . . .) In that year a young businessman from Texas, in his second term in Congress, got a $50 million limitation on aid to India. A reform Democrat from Manhattan and an unreconstructed Republican from Waterloo, Iowa, joined to lead a floor debate in the House of Representatives to prohibit any aid at all. It was not until 1977 that the Indians — who had terminated the American aid program during the Vietnam War — agreed to a token resumption. But it was no more than this. By the end of the decade there were fewer than a dozen American businessmen in the whole of India. We had quite vanished: much like the moguls, much like the British. But for such different reasons.

An American Ambassador was saddened by this, especially one who believed that the initial conception of American policy was correct. Indian democracy did represent in Asia an identifiable and credible alternative to Chinese totalitarianism. I could accept with no difficulty that we had exaggerated our ability to influence the outcome of this competition, but wondered at the increasing assertions, echoing the demands for military disengagement, that we should avoid peaceable entanglements too.

The essential fact of India at the present is that the Hindu nation is free of foreign rulers for the first time in a thousand years. It is free of Western rulers for the first time in centuries. And yet it is in some essentials a Western culture. The British failed to Christianize the subcontinent (even as their predecessors had failed to bring about a mass conversion to Islam), but did bring about a secular conversion without equal in history. They left behind them a unified, contiguous nation occupying almost the whole of the subcontinent and governing itself as an English-speaking parliamentary democracy. (The Muslim areas broke off, of course. English may yet be replaced by Hindi, but it is still the normal language of Parliament and a common speech of the capital.) Equally as a result of this invasion of ideas and of men, India was to become a secular nation and a socialist one, its economic doctrines modeled on the British collectivist tradition, of which Professor Samuel Beer has written, just as its political doctrines flow from the British liberal tradition. Now all this is something astounding. Not only to have changed political forms, but to have changed economic forms as well, and to have changed language in the process. To find anything comparable in human experience, one must go back to the Christian conversion of Europe, with the emergence — a much slower process — of monarchy, feudalism, and Latin.

Such an event could scarce but attract some attention, and American policy makers were hugely interested at first, and at some level have remained so, recognizing that the United States has a stake in the success of the second most populous nation on earth, and the largest democracy. Every President since Franklin Roosevelt has said as much, and pursued foreign policies based on principles which clearly imply such a stake. At first certain kinds of commitment seemed naturally to flow from this interest. A huge American presence formed in India, a veritable demi-raj, devoted not to governance but to development. But it lasted only a brief time, from the mid-fifties to the mid-sixties. After that, our presence began to decline, and then almost disappear. Leaving India, I commented that our relations were cordial enough, but they were so thin as scarcely to exist.

How can this have happened? A nation which poured blood and treasure into the defense of mere independence in Southeast Asia, arguing a "domino theory" in which the most important end event would be the collapse of independence and democracy in India, came in the process to care very little whether either survived where India is concerned.

There is no time for niceties in this matter, and no need. There are three reasons why this happened. The first is that India did not support our efforts — as we saw them — to protect its independence, which is to say India opposed our role in the Vietnam War. The second is that India does not appear to be succeeding with respect to its influence in the world generally. When it first became the world's largest democracy, it seemed an ornament to that calling. Increasingly of late, it seems something less. While a political success (it remains independent, it remains a democracy), India has scarcely been an economic success.

A third reason flows from the preceding two. This is the failure of nerve of the interconnected elites which shaped postwar American foreign policy around the matching themes of the military containment of Communist expansion and the economic development of the non-Communist world — a failure of nerve, preceded by a failure of specific undertakings.

These have all, of course, been relative failures in the context of a generally successful policy. The Communist borders are about where they were in 1948, the major exception being Southeast Asia and Afghanistan; the economies of the non-Communist world range from the spectacularly successful to the merely marginally so, with but few instances of stagnation or actual decline, and the latter, in truth, more likely to involve nations such as Burma, where there has been little American influence, rather than India, where there has been considerable.

The fact that one could make a fairly positive case for our performance in recent decades is nothing alongside the fact that the will to do so has so much faltered. There has been a failure of nerve among those whose will is, or was, indispensable to a successful assertion of this kind, an assertion which in the past produced a mandate to do pretty much whatever seemed best in pursuit of what was evidently on balance a successful and honorable policy. The elites who made that policy either no longer think it successful or no longer think it honorable, or in any event no longer think it can be successfully defended. They have been effectively silenced. They have not been displaced, however. In the main, the elites who could shape American foreign policy, and did so in the decades after World War II, are still in place. But they are mostly immobilized. And so if one asks, "How much does freedom matter to the United States today?" those in a position to answer for the most part do not do so. Clearly this could constitute an accommodation to totalitarianism without precedent in our history.

I wish here to make a distinction between necessity and choice in dealing with the totalitarian world. Nuclear destruction is the great danger facing mankind, and will remain so certainly through our time. This has necessitated the compromises and accommodations — and they have come from both directions, for nothing was possible until the totalitarian powers came to share our view of the primacy of danger — which we knew as détente. My concern is not with this newest realm of necessity, but rather with the area of choice. We have for a long while been quietly moving away from a posture in the world in which we chose freedom, and saw ourselves as its natural ally and defender. But this was at first a barely perceptible process of disengagement. More recently, there has been a sudden and definitive shift. It has been rather like a great sailing ship coming about. The boom, hauled and tugged, moves slowly, resistingly at first, when with an abandoned sweep it hurtles across the keel line. The ship lurches, settles, and then, as if there had never been another direction, moves forward on the opposite tack. Those who were tugging knew what to expect, even if they may have doubted for a moment their ultimate success. Those who ducked are still on deck. The ship moves on, oblivious of its past, an affair henceforth of logs and courts of enquiry.

How has this happened? The answer, obvious if painful, is that in a contest of arms, we lost. We were not defeated, but we withdrew in a situation where not to win was to lose. In the long history of the Republic, this had never before happened to us. Moreover, we need not have lost in the sense that we did not have to fight. We chose to. The "we" in this sense refers in the first instance to the network of interconnected elites, supported by a not uninformed but essentially permissive public opinion, which accorded the greatest leeway to these elites to choose how an agreed-upon foreign policy should be pursued.

One risks vagueness to use the term *elites* without a detailed accounting, and yet in this case — those fifteen to twenty years of American life — there was a singular concreteness to the notion that this particular aspect of national policy was the province of an identifiable group of persons who knew one another, largely agreed with one another, presided over a variety of informal and not so informal procedures of coopting new members, and exercised the mandate they had been accorded by informed public opinion and major power centers to conduct foreign policy. In those years there was much talk of "the Establishment," and for such purposes, there surely was one. As was only proper, New York was its capital, law and finance were its primary occupations. But there was the closest connection and cooperation with the great universities of the land, and with the media. These channels kept it in touch with other centers of power in the nation, and for all the disputation, a substantially bipartisan consensus foreign policy was pursued. As the term *elite* or *Establishment* imparts a conservative cast, it needs to be emphasized that this elite was in most respects liberal, and in nothing more so than its concern for liberal values abroad, its concern preeminently for freedom as it understood freedom.

At the grave risk of being misunderstood and coming to wish

I had not tried, I shall try nonetheless to make a point here which appears to be essential to an understanding of where we are now, and where we are likely to be heading. Writing at the time, William Pfaff described Vietnam as "American liberalism's war." Not all liberals by any means: as early as 1962, David Riesman and Nathan Glazer had started a "Committee of Correspondence" to raise questions as to what was going on, while Benjamin V. Cohen was speaking in private of "the Top Secret War." But *most* liberals. Now is this really a dark and threatening misdeed, much to be concealed? Or is it rather an historical fact the acknowledgment of which is indispensable to a compassionate understanding of what happened and a sufficient reconciliation with it all? Decent men undertook this cause, and decent men and women supported it.

Anthony Lewis puts it that "the early American decisions on Indochina can be regarded as blundering efforts to do good," and that about says it.

It is perhaps common in the world for individuals (and nations?) to suffer for their noble qualities more than for their ignoble ones. For nobility is an occasion for pride, the most treacherous of sentiments. Pride led us into that morass in near-Faustian defiance of the Second Law of War as laid down by Montgomery of Alamein: "Never send troops to the mainland of Asia." (The First Law being "Never march on Moscow.") Pride made it impossible to accept that it was not going to succeed, a fact that was abundantly clear by, say, 1966. And so a group that had never known defeat entered a long dark tunnel, at the end of which no light appeared, and in the course of which the group itself all but gave up its position.

This too was an act of pride or, if you will, of honor. Elites have lost wars before without losing their nerve, generally by blaming others, or somehow eliding the fact of failure. There are exceptions. Some who had more than their share in the decision go about saying that they were only carrying out orders. Others, equally in evidence at the time, have succumbed to a form of childhood amnesia, to use Freud's term a repression brought about by the "psychic forces of loathing, shame, and moral and aesthetic ideal demands." The adult dare not know what the child thought and did. But these *are* exceptions. In general, the American foreign policy establishment has not done this. It chose not to because, as I believe, it was and is superior in honesty and in intelligence to most such congeries of talent and position that have exercised their brief or prolonged authority in the affairs of the world.

But this does not account wholly for the silence. Another event intervened. In the face of mounting failure of policy abroad, support for it collapsed at home. Not a total collapse; not for a very long time at least. Rather, it was a most selective event, and it occurred where it was least expected. The foreign policy elites, thinking themselves perhaps a shade more liberal, more advanced in their views than possibly they were, were more than alert to attack from the right. At times they seemed almost to long for it, as if it would have a confirming effect on the liberalism of those being attacked. And in truth, something of this sort occurred in the course of the Korean War. But not this time. In the case of Vietnam, opposition appeared instead on the left, and it appeared in precisely those institutions and settings in which the policy being attacked had originally been conceived. Most important, it appeared in the universities, where, along with much principled and reasoned opposition, there occurred a minority response that was almost a caricature — fashioned with infantile cunning to be a devastating, homegrown caricature — of just that totalitarian mentality against which the United States found itself arrayed abroad. Before the decade was out, the Viet Cong flag would fly from the Washington headquarters of the Peace Corps.

It is not necessary to the argument being made here that one agree or disagree with the harsh charges made against American leaders during this period. Someone such as I, who does not agree, is forced nonetheless to grant that a great many men one had thought of as good acted in ways unmistakably bad; that men one thought of as sane acted in ways that were not sane. In particular, and unforgivably, the American government, after a time, commenced to lie and to conceal. This deceit was especially devastating in the relations of the foreign policy elite to its own institutions, and the cadres that had been conducting foreign policy for so long, and had for so long successfully defended themselves from outside attack, now found themselves attacked from the inside, and proved defenseless. "Defending liberty" came to be redefined as "killing babies." In time not only the morality of the actions was called into question, but the legality as well. To talk today of keeping commitments necessarily raises the question of who made what commitments and how. And with what right? And by whose leave? And with whose knowledge? To repeat, one may see these events in quite different ways — as a merely incremental extension of previously extended presidential powers, or as wholesale subversion of the Constitution — and still agree that it was the charges coming where they did and from whom they did that had the greatest unsettling effect.

William Schneider, in a remarkably informative analysis of survey data in *Foreign Policy,* Winter 1974–1975, notes that in the aftermath of the 1960s, the well-educated classes of the nation have become singularly ideological in their views of foreign policy, and that among the college educated, an extraordinary cleavage in ideological opinion has opened between young and old. He writes: "Working class Americans have tended to see the entire generational conflict of the last decade as a war between the upper middle class and its children — and they were right." The consensus among the college educated, which supported postwar foreign policy, has "disintegrated," he continues:

The fallout from the Vietnam war among liberals has taken the form of anti-militarism — opposition to defense spending and pressure for military disengagement — while the effect on their partners in the great antiwar coalition, the poor and the poorly educated, has been more fundamental — mistrust of leaders on such issues as aid and hostility toward all international involvement.

Now of course this coalition was not all-inclusive. The American labor movement's leaders, in part perhaps because they have not encountered such generational conflict, have not wavered in their support of the libertarian commitment implicit in our postwar policy. Were President Kennedy to return, they — many of them — would wish him to sound that very trumpet once again. But few others would. The American Catholic hierarchy, for example, once so militant in such matters, is silent now. To use a medical analogy, it seems very much a case of sympathetic silence, for those to whom they looked, the core elite, are most silent of all.

And this may be the most devastating loss. For to strip our past of glory is no irretrievable loss, but to deny it a measure of honor is devastating.

A generation or two hence, historians will perhaps tell us what President Kennedy was talking about; but if those who were part of that history decline now to defend what is defensible about it, then our time will know no such defense. As Christians believe in the immortality of the soul, so social scientists profess the "circulation of elites," and there is no need to despair of new circles moving into one another's orbits and recreating a network of influence and opinion which can give stability and coherence to American foreign policy. But one cannot conceive that any consensus likely to emerge in the future would have anything like the past commitment to freedom abroad. What there will be instead is freedom *from* American involvement.

In any event, we no longer find that much freedom in the world. What? Thirty-five countries? And is it not the case that there has been a change in our understanding of what it is we represent to the world? We commence to see the liberty of which President Kennedy spoke — too readily, perhaps, but with conviction — as a social arrangement which may obtain in the United States and a few such nations, but which has no necessary relevance to any other place. It may command our loyalty, as Christianity once did for most of us; but in no wise are we warranted in proselytizing and propagandizing, for who can be sure what is best?

Fair enough. But it is useful to be clear that when the heirs of a fighting creed commence to talk in such manner, there has been a change. For the better, some will say. Others will say otherwise. But when crusades come to an end, a change has occurred.

Solely as an exercise, let us suppose that India were to become involved in a military contest, open or indirect, with its great neighbor to the east. When this happened in 1962, the Indians came instantly to us, asking for help, and just as instantly help was provided. In a farewell address on leaving India in 1963, Ambassador John Kenneth Galbraith took note of America's unbending determination to continue that military support, speculating that the Chinese had invaded India (a point itself since disputed) because the Indian economy was proving too successful, and that Chinese Communism stood to suffer by comparison. What in such circumstances would the United States do today? Nothing. Or next to nothing. Somewhere in *that* range of options.

We would have to do some talking to ourselves. Many voices, perhaps a majority of those likely to be heard, would explain that no one could clearly state where the interests of the people of India lay. The present regime, it would be said, is corrupt and inefficient. What, it would be asked, does democracy mean to a starving man? The masses, it would be said, are ruled by an upper-caste clique, an exploitive class of landowning and capitalist families, with here and there the token untouchable.

This clique, it would be said, even speaks a foreign language, so it is cut off from the people of India. The ruling party, it would be pondered, has never once attained a majority of the popular vote in a nationwide election, and this despite widespread corruption, based on levies exacted from capitalist interests, a fact attested to by sources of unimpeachably anti-Communist sentiment. In consequence of exploitation and corruption, the masses of India live lives of indescribable suffering and unrelieved despair. It is little wonder, it would be hinted, that they secretly identify with those they know come from a society where, whatever else may be, every family is guaranteed food and clothing, shelter, medical care, and education.

Others would speak more pragmatically. They would point out that we fought in Vietnam, as we thought, to preserve the freedom of such as India, and got precious little support for doing so. Indeed, got little but abuse. Where we have been involved in the defense of other free societies, such as that of Israel, India has hardly been with us. We have helped with economic aid, more than to any other nation; we have been available for advice and assistance concerning matters which on the record we know something about. Growing food, for example. But India of late has been scornful of American involvement in any of these areas. All it has managed to do is preserve a democracy. Again, all this is speculative, and yet again, we are not without data. A survey, "American Public Opinion and U. S. Foreign Policy 1975," sponsored by the Chicago Council on Foreign Relations, found that only 16 percent of a "public" and 17 percent of a "leader" sample would favor U.S. military involvement "if Communist China attacked India." A full 70 percent of leaders would oppose any such involvement. (Only 39 percent of the public would fight for Western Europe.)

It is the second of the two possible responses to Indian difficulties which seems to me the more serious, for it is the more honest. It speaks for the post-Vietnam mind, and for its conscience also. There are things we no longer feel can be justifiably done in defense of freedom in the world, and things no longer worth doing. We no longer much care for those nations, whatever the nature of their regimes, which do not think much of us and cannot do much to us. There is a true loss here, for most of the new nations started out with a genuine commitment to just those principles President Kennedy said we would do anything to defend. Edward Shils in his *Center and Periphery* (1975) writes of those splendid beginnings:

There are no new states in Asia or Africa, whether monarchies or republics, in which the elites who demanded independence did not, at the moment just prior to their success, believe that self-government and democratic government were identical . . . something like liberal democracy was generally thought to be prerequisite for the new order of things.

I believe the legacy of those brave beginnings persists, and that it is still the best hope we have that the world at large will not enter that dark totalitarian night we in the older democracies so very much feared at the time the new nations made their appearance. Nonetheless, the new nations made their appearance. Yet the new nations, most of them, have been none too careful of preserving liberal democracy where it existed, much less creating it where it did not. And they have been surpassingly indifferent to the fact that we have managed to preserve ours; indeed have all too readily adopted the autotherapeutic rhetoric that in America liberty is oppression, and freedom, confinement. There are leaders of that new world who know better than this but say so anyway. History is not likely to be kind with them, for in diminishing the reputation of the American democracy, it is likely that they will have more than a little imperiled their own. They might well be measured by the warning of President Kennedy's inaugural: ". . . we pledge," he said, "our word that one form of colonial control shall not have passed away merely to be replaced by a far more iron tyranny." He said we shall not expect them always to be supporting us. "But we shall always hope to find them strongly supporting their own freedom. . . ."

Well, we have not so found them. And they may yet find themselves — I would expect probably will find themselves — in a world in which the United States will respond with surpassing inattention to the demise of Western political institutions in non-Western nations. We could *all* end up courting the favor of the totalitarians.

To wish otherwise, as surely I would do, and probably most of us would do, is scarcely to affect events. Harry C. McPherson, Jr., has written of the void of leadership across the widest spectrum of activity. This appears as a failure of individuals, but in truth, it is whole cohorts which do not respond. For institutions have collapsed along with confidence — or diminished where not collapsed; all in a torment of conscience that will not be appeased. One thinks back to Henry James's description of Nathaniel Hawthorne's world:

No State, in the European sense of the word, and indeed barely a specific national name. . . . No sovereign, no court, no personal loyalty, no aristocracy, no church, no clergy, nor army, no diplomatic service . . . no great Universities nor public schools — no Oxford, nor Eton, nor Harrow . . . no political society, no sporting class — no Epsom nor Ascot.

Leaving aside James's excessive partiality for things English, it is a fact that institutions formed slowly in America, and it is a further fact that such authority as they exercised has been grievously reduced in recent years. Or properly so, if one chooses that gloss. Either way, there is less than there was, and as we recall Robert Nisbet's formulation, "Freedom lives in the interstices of authority," we sense the larger movement of which I have been discussing one aspect. James today could compile a similar list, puzzling only to those who could not see — as recently as the presidency of John F. Kennedy — a sovereign, a court, personal loyalty, a diplomatic service, great universities, a political society, a sporting class. A society, in other words, in which something as abstract as freedom could be regarded as a concrete object of foreign policy.

James instructs us further as to why in the end it doesn't seem to have come off. We are hopelessly a culture of conscience, and usually of bad conscience, and never more so than when pointing to our sins of affluence and arrogance. This, James said, was so much the result of "the importance of the individual in the American world." And with that American individual, the American conscience.

An Englishman, a Frenchman — a Frenchman above all — judges quickly, easily, from his own social standpoint, and makes an end of it. He has not that rather chilly and isolated sense of moral responsibility which is apt to visit a New Englander in such processes. . . . American intellectual standards are vague, and Hawthorne's countrymen are apt to hold the scales with a rather uncertain hand and a somewhat agitated conscience.

What it comes to is that life is tragic for those who are impelled by conscience to pursue objectives which can be attained only through means which conscience find abhorrent. Whereupon that conscience turns on itself, and a fearsome thing it is when loose. Rather like the artillery of the Duke of Urbino, whose sad but instructive history it may be useful to recall. In the Holy Year 1500, Cesare Borgia, at the end of the Pope's forces, was intent on laying siege to Camerino, and persuaded the pious and learned duke to lend him his artillery and other forces, the better he might smite the foes of righteousness. And so Borgia marched off, but then turned and laid siege to Urbino instead. The duke fled to exile.

A sad history indeed, and yet one from which the wrong lesson can be learned. Borgia was dead at thirty-two. The duke returned to his library. The very conscience that makes us hate what we have done will very likely before long have us hating what we are *not* doing. Freedom concerns us, and will continue to do. But in a world of which we no longer think of ourselves as the natural leader.

3.
Presenting the
American Case

IN THE PERIOD AHEAD, there will be much talk about the decline of American influence in the world. This will give pleasure to many and instruction to some, and is perhaps to be welcomed on that score. A case could be made for holding rather closely the knowledge that this decline has been going on for quite a long while, and that it commenced for reasons having nothing to do with the events or the political leaders of the third quarter of the twentieth century. American prestige in the world reached its height in 1919 with the founding of the League of Nations and the extraordinary position of Woodrow Wilson, who for a moment seemed to embody, and in that sense to unify, the hopes of the peoples of the "civilized" world. The moment did not last long, owing in part to a failure of men and institutions in the United States itself. We were not prepared to make the commitment that would have made possible some practical consequences of this extraordinary, if unfocused and fleeting, consensus. It is a sorrowful enough memory, and there is no use to dwell upon it overmuch, but it is useful at this time for at least some persons to be clear about what influence means for a nation: it means other nations wish to be like you.

The United States had had such influence for a long while — most of the nineteenth century. In that period anyone starting up a new government in the Western world was quite likely to model it on that of the United States. This influence was shared, to be sure, with the British and French, whose own institutions could be seen as closely related. But America's size and economic power, along with its newness, steadily eclipsed the constitutional example of the two older nations. In the first chapter of *The American Commonwealth* James Bryce put it that the "institutions of the United States are deemed by inhabitants and admitted by strangers to be a matter of more general interest than those of the not less famous nations of the Old World . . . for they are believed to disclose and display the type of institutions towards which, as by a law of fate, the rest of civilized mankind are forced to move, some with swifter, other with slower, but all with unresting feet."

The seemingly decisive American entry into World War I on behalf of the Allies further confirmed the American ascendancy. New nations and new governments, actual or hopeful, not only wished to be like the United States; some wished to be associated with it as well. Wilson at Paris enthusiastically took up the cause of the Armenians, who, unluckily for them, never succeeded in getting the association they hoped for. When it was agreed that the world itself needed a new government, the American President had the very thing, a world order modeled directly on the American federal system — constitution, court, legislative, executive, and all.

Now *that* is influence! Americans, however — and this is not so very unusual, either for individuals or nations — did not seem especially aware of this influence. Or, if they were aware of it, they were not notably zealous to preserve it. At one level, we actively sought to shed it. Certainly it was far reduced a quarter century later when of a sudden we found ourselves again concerned with such matters, and commenced the fretful assessment that has rather characterized us since. This could not be reassuring, and has not been. For the United States in 1945 had a curiously unbalanced mix of power, of which the ideological component was even then recessive. Hans J. Morgenthau, in *Politics among Nations,* describes political power in the context of international relations as deriving from three sources: "the expectation of benefits, the fear of disadvantages, the respect or love for men or institutions." It is probably rare for a great power to possess these advantages in a wholly symmetrical manner, and there was certainly a significant imbalance in the American position of a generation ago. We could evoke the expectation of benefits — history will surely attest to that. We had given evidence of the disadvantages of being on the opposite side from us in a major conflict. But we did not evoke that much "respect or love," either for "men or institutions."

How so? Two elements appear significant. In the first place, we were too successful; it was unnatural. There, in 1945, was a world substantially in ruins, or, in the case of colonial nations, still in fetters. Only the Western Hemisphere escaped, and we stood astride it. All was humiliation save for us. How could we not be detested? The few exceptions are instructive. Britain emerged from the war with enough self-respect, France without enough. Their postwar relations with the United States seemed controlled by this beginning circumstance. Germany and Japan, defeated, found it easiest to be emulative. The process by which oversuccessful nations are combined against by other nations and reduced in circumstance is nothing new. To all appearances, some such thing began almost the moment the American colossus made its appearance, a process much abetted by the genuine American desire to see other nations rise again.

If one element of the American difficulty arose from having too little competition, another arose from having too much. For much of the world was then engaged, for several generations had been engaged, and has continued to be engaged, in an ideological struggle between totalitarian and democratic socialism. The American liberal example attracted few followers. Those who were attracted have not necessarily been the worse for it, but their experience has produced little emulation, suggesting that history has simply not been with us in this time.

The first Communist revolution — totalitarian socialism — came with the end of World War I. After a phase of expansion, Communism was consolidated as "socialism in one country" for a period that lasted a generation. With the end of World War II, expansion resumed with great success, only to cease for the moment in 1948. By that time — less noticed, somehow, but not less emphatic — the rise of democratic socialism had commenced. The scores of new nations that came into being the world over modeled themselves not on the United States, nor yet on the Soviet Union, but on various paradigms of democratic socialism that had been formulated in Western Europe earlier in the century and had to some degree been put into practice there. The most conspicuous example was that of Britain under the Labour Party, an example certainly not lost on the forty-one new nations formed from the British Empire after 1947. This trend has been so marked, I have argued, that if the first event is to be termed the Russian Revolution, the British Revolution seems a fair designation for the second. In each instance, a nation was first influenced by an ideology, whereupon the ideology was influenced by the nation. A distinctive compound emerged, to be adapted in some settings, transmuted in others, but always with this genealogy in its past.

In the "Russian" and "British" competition, the United States was ever a poor third. This was not merely a matter of other models of government being more attractive: *both* these other models had acquired specifically anti-American biases so strong that to be attracted to them was to grow averse to us.

For Communists, we were capitalists; nor could Communists forget that after their revolution had begun, Woodrow Wilson sent American troops to try to put it down. For socialists, we were, in the old sense of the word, liberals. Charles Francis Adams, as minister in London, was perhaps not wrong when he wrote in 1865, "The progress of the Liberal cause, not in England alone, but all over the world, is, in a measure, in our hands." Well, the liberal cause was not the socialist cause, certainly not as time went by, and this opposition, however muted at first and however civil, was never lost from view and in time grew less civil. Henry Pelling, in his study *America and the British Left,* traces the century-long transformation of the American image from admiration in the nineteenth century to something near detestation — certainly fear — in the twentieth. On the British Left, America came to be singled out as a place where the worst was likely to happen: *not* a good kind of country to be. Pelling notes that to such British observers, "the New Deal itself, it seemed, might be a first step on the road to the creation of a Fascist state." Little wonder that when American economic and military power declined relatively, the time should have come when American influence as a whole would be seen to have precipitously declined.

This history, if it be accepted as such, does somewhat suggest how the United States might respond to this declining position. At the very least it suggests the nature of the decline. It must be understood, for example, that while we have spent a generation mobilized or actually at war on the borders of the Communist world, during that time the socialist world, a different world, has been changing in ways little to our advantage. It must be understood, too (a point made by Zbigniew Brzezinski), that the Soviet Union is increasingly the beneficiary of confrontation between the United States and the new nations, just as the new nations had benefits from confrontation between the Soviets and us. Perhaps first of all it must be understood that ideas matter in world affairs, and that competence in dealing with ideas is likely to become more, not less, important. Hence Max Weber:

Interests (material and ideal), not ideas, dominate directly the actions of men. Yet the "images of the world" created by these ideas have very often served as switches determining the tracks on which the dynamism of interests kept actions moving.

If we had had, for example, a better sense of our ideological disadvantage in the world, we might have better understood what we were getting into in Southeast Asia.

Such reflections, if sound, would be warranted at almost any time, but they would appear to have a special relevance to this moment when so many indices tell us that the long postwar era is coming to a close. Political commentary has more than its share of this coming and going of eras, the half-life of any one of which suggests that *episodes* might be the better term. Yet the signs this time are persuasive.

And so new kinds of relations begin to assume a saliency that in some cases is long overdue: economic policy toward the Communist nations; military policy toward the new nations; outer space and the seabed: all these enter the domain of international politics. The problem of war continues, while the specter of famine and pestilence, long essentially absent from the West, reappears as an aspect of domestic no less than international politics. For an incontrovertible aspect of the international system that Mr. Wilson helped to found is that *the claims one society may now routinely make on another are of a kind once virtually reserved to communities within national societies.* A further aspect of the emerging international system is that it begins to reflect the *bias for equality over liberty* that is more and more in evidence in the world — making it, in that measure, a world more and more distant from the one Wilson would have wished for. This must be seen as a matter of balance. The liberal tradition can be utterly indifferent to equality and see it as quite opposed to liberty, but this is a nineteenth-century heresy more than anything else. Correspondingly, the socialist tradition has room aplenty for liberty. (The question may be asked whether Communism is in this sense a nineteenth-century socialist heresy.) But as liberty is the first principle of liberalism, equality is the prime test of socialism, the first object of collectivist politics, as Samuel Beer has used the term.

In domestic politics, collectivism asserts a high level of obligation not so much between individuals as between groups — particularly groups defined by economic function and status: the rich, the poor; the middle class, the workers; the dock laborers, the intellectual workers. Collectivism is not so far from the medieval concept of estate, with its notion of entitlement. *What is easily, and routinely, left out in the modern and secular version is the corresponding notion of obligation.* Certainly this is so in the international version of collectivism. In the present world, nothing contrasts more sharply than the fierce individualism and assertion of absolute rights of sovereignty over their own resources of those very states that are making collectivist claims on the resources of others.

So it might better be said that *the language of world politics is becoming collectivist.* The main claims of collectivism are for the redistribution of wealth, for equality; hence the preponderance of these claims will now be made upon the United States. They will be made primarily by governments — now the majority of governments — that having proclaimed egalitarian collectivist ideals within their own societies and, finding it difficult or impossible to achieve these ideals within the constraints of their own domestic politics, turn to world politics for relief. They hope to gain resources to import; if not, they can export blame. This means there is going to be a lot of blame around, for the world is now made up largely of regimes that have made promises (usually decent and understandable promises) on which they have not been able to deliver and on which they are not likely to be able to deliver in the politically relevant future.

Consider India, the first of the new nations to engage in serious socialist planning, proclaiming collectivist goals. What have been the results? Padma Desai and Jagdish Bhagwati, in a paper presented to the 1974 meeting of the American Economic Association, report: ". . . Growing studies of income distribution in the country suggest strongly that the bottom deciles have not improved their consumption levels since planning began and may, in fact, have become worse off." Consider what will have to happen in India for this to change much. It has been noted that in India the growth rate of per-capita income from 1958 to 1973, or roughly since planning began, was a respectable 1.7 percent. This is better than the historic growth rate of Europe in the nineteenth century. Yet at this rate it would take India 120 years to reach the $1,300 divide that in the international statistics of 1973 separated the developed from the underdeveloped nations.

And this is the hard reality. The world is now almost wholly given over to nations whose governments are committed to social equality and economic growth. But few have much of the former, and even a good deal of the latter produces only slow changes. In this setting, the temptation of governments is to direct attention to inequalities between nations that ascribe national ills to international causes. This argument invariably goes to the matter of economic inequalities, never to inequalities in political and civil liberties. As Theodore A. Sumberg notes, *"Freedom and economic growth used to be allies."* But somewhere in the postwar period the connection was lost — a change all but unremarked. No national leader engaged in this rhetoric need have any serious concern that his own regime might be found wanting by similar international comparisons addressed to inequalities of liberty.

It is the sad but inescapable fact that almost everywhere save in Europe, and a few English-speaking outposts, democratic socialism has become steadily less democratic in the quarter century since regimes of this order began to be founded in such profusion. We cannot know whether this is because socialism produced demands on government which made democracy impossible; or because that socialism was never nearly so democratic as we thought, and always was marred by Marxist-Leninist authoritarian tendencies; or, as is increasingly proclaimed, that democracy is a fetish of Western intellectualism and has no place in non-Western societies. What we do know is that the world is now mostly made up of Communist and socialist nations (a distinction persists, and an important one), none of which looks to American democracy as an example of anything desirable. Our economy is envied, but the response is not to try to emulate it so much as to try to destroy it. In the 1970s the Non-Aligned nations have consistently supported international action which has had the effect or would have the effect of slowing American growth. This has been so even when the action involved, as with OPEC price increases, has been devastating to the developing economies as well.

To write of this phenomenon with ill temper or with ridicule is unworthy. For all the despots and boodlers of the Third World, the main voices are still those of men and women with an honest commitment to social justice who can make sense of their own world only by ascribing an abiding malevolence to ours.

Especially in the new nations, the received political culture of European socialism just doesn't provide alternative explanations to problems that must be explained. (Latin America, with a different tradition, has nonetheless found a compatible and reinforcing language.) Thus, at a meeting of the Non-Aligned Bureau in Havana in 1975, the Indian minister of external affairs, Y. B. Chavan, found the world economic situation "on the verge of a crisis of global proportions" and did not hesitate to see the cause for this in the political economy of the developed nations:

This global phenomenon has been caused mainly by the policies of the developed countries, by their mass production, technology, by their prodigal consumption standards, by their growth mania, by their diversion of resources towards a meaningless arms race and by the rapid depletion of the world's non-renewable raw materials. In the result we have more and more missiles, hair dryers and tape recorders, and less and less foodgrains, fertilizers and essential goods.

. . . If the present situation were to continue unchanged, we shall see the rich nations getting richer and the poor nations poorer, while the earth's non-renewable resources disappear.

The fact that liberty seems to be disappearing even faster seemed not to matter. Seemingly for all, the ready answer is available: economic inequality has made freedom impossible. Very simply, at this time, it appears to be a sufficient answer to the question.

Moreover, it has been for some time, which is to say that the rise of collectivist doctrine in Britain and elsewhere ineluctably diminished the independent claim that liberty could make on social arrangements. It is useful to recall that to the liberal nineteenth century, freedom was the *key* to social harmony, including international harmony. Hans Morgenthau records, in his *Politics among Nations*, that adherents of free trade, such as Cobden and Proudhon, "were convinced that the removal of trade barriers was the only condition for the establishment of permanent harmony among nations, and might even lead to the disappearance of international politics altogether." Cobden was more than convinced. "Free trade," he pronounced, "is the international law of the Almighty."

This confidence did not survive the twentieth century, certainly not in Britain. In 1942, the National Executive

Committee of the Labour Party issued a report, "The Old World and the New Society," most likely written by Harold Laski, which made this transition explicit. The war was basically attributed to an "unplanned economic order [which] went into a frenzy of unreasoning nationalism." The capitalist class in Germany and Italy destroyed democracy to protect its privileges. Similar interests elsewhere acted similarly.

It was fear for privileges which, in the epoch of "appeasement," led so many of the corresponding classes in Britain, France and the United States to sympathize with the habits and the purposes of the Fascist and Nazi dictators. . . . They preferred to break the League of Nations rather than risk the overthrow of the forces of privilege in Germany and Italy. . . . All the major evils of the "appeasement period" are directly traceable to the unregulated operation of our economic system.

The report continued: "We have learned from the war that the anarchy of private competition must give way to ordered planning under national control." The nation must own and operate the essential instruments of production. Wartime controls in industry and agriculture must be retained. This would enable "the reorganization of our export trade to proceed in an orderly and balanced way." In commodities, for example, there would be an end to "reckless speculation" — and so through a familiar prescription for economic controls, *but now linked to an international as well as national order.*

Thirty-three years later, in 1975, a Commonwealth Conference convened in Kingston, Jamaica. The Jamaican Prime Minister, Michael Manley, set the tone for the meeting. Since the era of political colonialism was almost at an end, he declared, the time was at hand for the Commonwealth to turn its concerns to "the wide disparities in wealth now existing between different sections of mankind." He noted one recent response to the unregulated operation of the world economic system: "The third world has been driven by its poverty and the inexorable working of the free trade system to the discovery of the producer association. The Organization of Petroleum [Exporting] Countries has changed fundamental equations of economic power as decisively as did the Industrial Revolution." What the Almighty will think of this is not certain, but what is fairly clear is that the inequality of economic conditions between different nations has become politicized — in the sense that in the community of nations it is a situation which is seen as appropriate for collective political action.

Two further matters seem equally clear. First, the present situation is not going to change very much very fast. *Some* large changes have occurred: the rise of Japan and the decline of Britain. But in the main historic relationships persist, changing only slowly. It has been pointed out that the ratio of per-capita income in America to that in the Soviet Union is today only ever so slightly lower than it was before the Russian Revolution. If the Soviets have not closed the gap in more than six decades of intense competitiveness, with a continent to work with, what may be expected for the often artificial, frequently resource-poor new nations of the world?

In sum, it should be clear that the United States faces a world of Communist and socialist regimes — at various times thirty or so nations in the world might be otherwise — in which the language of politics persistently rejects any argument that might make American arrangements appear attractive or even legitimate. *Ideas, just now, are mostly against us.* How, then, is the American case to be presented?

A first point, not that obvious, is that the American case must *be* presented. It no longer speaks for itself, as it may have done in 1945. Others no longer speak for it, as was the case perhaps in 1918. *From now on, our competence with ideas and the vigor with which we present and examine them will have consequences for us of a higher order than we are familiar with.*

Here again it is essential to distinguish the socialist from the Communist impact on the world scene. American foreign policy could ignore "rhetoric" so long as it was Communist, on the repeatedly demonstrated grounds that such rhetoric was not in itself much of a threat. It won no elections. Communism everywhere "came out of a barrel of a gun." (Which only seemed to enhance the natural primacy of security politics.) But this was not, and is not, the case with the rhetoric and ideas of nationalist socialism. They have great persuasiveness in the widest range of economic and political settings. To ignore them or to deal with them amateurishly is to make matters, in the present situation, worse for ourselves and not better for anyone else, save the elites who manipulate this rhetoric for narrow purposes.

Our task is to be compassionate and yet reasoning. It should be seen as a task, an undertaking. It should be seen as something we have not done before. It should not be seen as something we are not likely to do well.

We do not wholly believe our own case. There is the nub of it. The influence of "American" political ideas in the world reached its high point in 1919, and has declined in America also. It is scarcely elegant to chop up a century into ideological epochs before any one ideology has fully run its course, and yet there is a certain Hegelian structure to the libertarian, totalitarian, collectivist sequence, and in that sequence "American" ideas grow steadily more remote. In the meantime, subsequent waves of doctrine have broken on these shores also, and have had their impact. Thus the Russian Revolution had an enormous, and after a point quite visible, impact on American intellectual life. There was a time in the 1930s, as Robert Warshow wrote, when "virtually all intellectual vitality was derived in one way or another from the Communist party." A huge proportion of American intellectuals were within the party orbit; those outside were likely to be in opposition and devoted much of themselves to maintaining that opposition. In its Stalinist form, this doctrine was not only implacably opposed to "American" ideas, it was also viciously illiberal. Lying became a routine tactic, and deceit a normal device; so that when this influence began to move into the universities, as it did after World War II, resistance to it was often disorganized and uncomprehending, save for that of former Communists and others of the Left who had been close enough to the phenomenon to recognize it.

It would not be accurate to say that the wave of collectivist influence came after the Communist, as it did in the world at large. In reality, it came first. The American encounter with both socialism and Communism has been greatly influenced by immigration, so much so as to be in some ways as much an ethnic as an ideological phenomenon. Immigrants brought their doctrines with them, or were waiting when doctrine, as it were, followed on the next ship. But socialism was a doctrine not only of continental Europe and suchlike regions of emigration, but of Britain also. Indeed the most prestigious and influential of all socialist movements — the least Marxist, by far the most liberal, and the most brainy — was British socialism, especially Fabian Socialism. More than a doctrine, it was a culture, such that by the early years of the twentieth century, when America was still very much a colony in such matters, merely to be cultured meant to be influenced by socialist doctrine. At a time when still relatively few persons had "read an American book" or in any event "seen an American play," which American, if he saw plays at all, had not seen one by Bernard Shaw?

With time — a Fabian mode! — this influence grew and spread. American arrangements changed under the influence. It might not be too much to say they were transformed. The time came in post–World War II America when avowedly Communist ideas had become once again sectarian, at most a marginal influence on the culture with almost none on politics. But socialist ideas had by then gained the widest currency, although rarely with socialist labels. Americans were becoming British indeed, willing to change anything but the appearance of things — a sensible arrangement, but not one that makes for intellectual clarity. Expenditure in the public sector, largely for the provision of social services and myriad forms of redistribution, rose to a third of the GNP. But somehow the point was lost as successive national administrations denied they were engaged in any such social transformation. Educated youth began to partake of that curiously dichotomous view of American life to be encountered among the upper-class Left throughout the world. We are seen as a society of wanton consumption which is somehow denied the unpropertied.

Postwar American diplomacy has failed to see that the presentation of the American case is a task that requires professional competence, especially as addressed to the new nations. Mere empathy is not enough. The ideas and ideologies of these societies must be understood *as they are experienced,* as well as propounded. Without exception, socialism in the third world is a variant of state capitalism. (Desai and Bhagwati observed that socialism in India has resulted in a *rentier* economy in which the key class lives off rents obtained from the ubiquitous government license.) The first imperative most governments face is not to redistribute wealth, but to contain ethnic conflict, be it racial, tribal, religious, or whatever. The function of planning is to collect enough power at the center such that some kind of government is *possible.* American diplomats may not know this. Those they deal with do. It is possible to be realistic whilst retaining respect for ideals not attained.

It is possible also to be severely unimpressed with the accommodation the new nations have reached with the Soviet Union. The Non-Aligned were formed as a group at Bandung in 1955. There were twenty-four nations present, most of them democratic in the sense that the governments had been elected; all of them desiring to keep their distance from either of the "superpowers." In 1979 the "Movement of Non-Aligned Countries" met in Havana. One hundred five nations were present, of which Freedom House listed only eighteen as "free." The draft Final Declaration was distributed on stationery of the Cuban foreign ministry. Adopted without significant change, it was a document of servile conformity to Soviet views, and corresponding vilification of American imperialism, colonialism, militarism. ("Détente," however, was found to have "benefits.") The malevolent association of South Africa with Israel — "the racist regimes of South Africa and Israel" — was pressed in strict accordance with Soviet doctrine, and the ultimate accusation was made against the Jews. Zionism was declared to be a crime against humanity.*

This document was drafted and adopted in the third year of the Carter administration, one of whose principal claims was that by its understanding and sympathetic attitudes unprecedented levels of understanding and cooperation had been reached with the new nations. This was autotherapeutic fantasy. At the risk of caricature, the new nations had learned that they could say anything about the United States to the representatives of the Carter administration and the representatives of the Carter administration would agree. Accordingly, they did. Or, rather, they went along with those who wished to.

I have learned to my cost that this argument for presenting the American case is a difficult argument to make. It will be read as a proposal for confrontation and a sure formula for making matters worse. I would reply that things could hardly be much worse so far as the United States is concerned, and that they aren't that much better for the Non-Aligned. A great and honorable tradition, that of democratic socialism, is being lost. I acknowledge those who contend that the tradition never

*"205. The heads of State or Government reaffirmed that racism including Zionism, racial discrimination and especially *apartheid* constituted crimes against humanity and represented violations of the UN Charter and of the Universal Declaration of Human Rights."

really took hold in the new nations. One man, one vote, one election, as the saying goes in Turtle Bay. Yet it seems to me that the returns are not yet finally in. Not while India, Sri Lanka, and others struggle on. Would it not be a massive betrayal to abandon hope and settle for the sovietization of the new nations? There was a decency in that socialist tradition which we ought not to forget; nor should we allow those whose tradition it was to forget it. That we can welcome such regimes is no small part of the American case.

We must learn socialism as we once learned Communism. There is, after all, a respectable record of our having found ways to comprehend, and eventually to interact with, Marxist-Leninist leaders. We have not much engaged the new nations at the level of ideology. Over and above any sense that we might not come off very well, there was, in American foreign policy circles, a kind of redskin disdain for such paleface maundering. *Drip* was the term with which one of the great men of postwar American foreign policy would dismiss the crazy talk, as he saw it, which in the end would lead to such things as a tenfold increase in the price of oil. There was also, possibly, a certain misreading of the "end of ideology" thesis. As Seymour Martin Lipset has now noted:*

What we were referring to was a judgment that the passionate attachments of an integrated revolutionary set of doctrines to the anti-system struggles of working class movements — and the consequent coherent counterrevolutionary doctrines of some of their opponents — were declining, that they were, to repeat C. Wright Mills' term, "a legacy from Victorian Marxism." They would not reemerge in advanced industrial or "post industrial societies," although they would continue to exist in the least developed nations.

Well, of course, they have indeed continued, and have grown more intense, in language at the very least. To meet the

*"The End of Ideology and the Ideology of the Intellectuals," in *Culture and its Creators,* ed. Joseph Ben David and Terry Clark, University of Chicago Press, 1977.

challenge so presented, ideological politics are going to have to be elevated somewhat. The United States government now has more than its share of intelligence and energy within its bounds, and more is yet available. But such talent will not be directed to this range of matters unless it is known that the issues are seen to be important. It needs also to be understood within the larger society, and notably within the circles concerned with foreign policy, that to deal with these matters is no longer to court the easy approbation that may once have come from going along with whatever seemed the sentiment of the hour. Not only outside but within the United States, persons charged with this responsibility will encounter suspicion and hostility from just those quarters where they might wish their actions to be most clearly understood and even valued.

One hesitates to prescribe, and yet we are not altogether without experience in coping with such situations. It is an honored maxim of folk medicine that cures are found where maladies arise. Something similar holds in politics. The American response to Communism in the world, and within America itself, was enormously informed, even fashioned, by persons who had been near to or even involved with that doctrine. In the present not so very different situation, it is on the Democratic Left that we are most likely to find both informed and unintimidated advocates of a vigorous American role in world affairs, and equally unashamed partisans of American performance.

In the clamor of recent years, with so many newer voices and shriller ones raised in protest of one form or another, the social democrats of America have had difficulty being heard. But they are with us now as they were with us before, closely involved with the labor movement, committed to long perspectives in politics, and able somehow to live without overmuch illusion. If the essential statement to be made about presenting the American case is that those elements in American society which might most be expected to do this are today the least disposed to do so, and the least able, then the next most important statement is that in the present circumstances the most effective presentation of the American case is likely to come from quarters least associated with the celebration of liberal capitalism. It is not that the labor movement and the social democrats like what we have, so much as that they are aware of the alternatives, and acculturated, if the term may be used, to the realm of ideology in which the American case must be presented. In time a foreign service might be trained to this task, but it will be difficult. Its recruits will come from universities where, in the main, the American case is not believed. They will, in the main, be the offspring of a demoralized business class where the American case is not thought to be important. In any event it will be a long task. For the moment we should look to the defenders we have. As in point of fact we are not likely to do this, we must accordingly not expect to be well defended.

4.
Pacem in Terris

THE GREAT QUESTION, always, of political philosophy concerns the nature of the individual and the claims which the state may make on the individual. Both the drafters of the American Constitution and the writers of the papal encyclical *Pacem in Terris,* issued during the reign of John XXIII, insisted that the individual was divine and that the claims the state may make upon him are strictly limited and also conditional on the behavior of the state itself. To assert this may be nothing exceptional; but to conclude it, as the issue of a detailed and coherent account of the nature of man and of his world, sets these men apart from most men at all times and, most particularly, most men in these times.

It is for just this reason, is it not, that we find ourselves drawn to such coherent and comprehensive statements as we try to deal with issues of foreign policy in our time, issues which have assumed such a cosmic quality. The reason for this is known to everyone, and quite clearly stated in John XXIII's *Pacem in Terris* itself:

Men are becoming more and more convinced that disputes which arise between states should not be resolved by recourse to arms, but rather by negotiations.

It is true that on historical grounds this conviction is based chiefly on the terrible destructive force of modern arms; and it is nourished by the horror aroused in the mind by the very thought of the cruel destruction and the immense suffering which the use of those armaments would bring to the human family. . . .

In the atomic era, the encyclical concluded, war could never be just and ought to be unthinkable.

For some while American statesmen saw this. Building on their efforts, Richard Nixon and Henry Kissinger engaged our great nuclear adversary, the Soviet Union, in a dialogue from which the compelling and mutually shared conviction emerged that unless the nuclear arms race is ended mankind is doomed. And so they set about to end it, commencing the process we know as détente.

Before many years had passed, the high hopes with which détente began were much diminished. The Strategic Arms Limitations talks did not seem to limit the growth in the number of strategic weapons. The troubling thought emerged that as a device arms treaties might even tend to produce an increase in arms, a kind of legalized arms race. It is not at all uncommon for "systems" to behave in such perverse ways. Similarly, détente seemed not at all to lessen political tensions between the "superpowers." Although commitment to détente persisted under new Presidents, an understanding of it, especially of its political aspects, continues to elude us.

At least so far as political competition is concerned, there is no need for such uncertainty. The essential fact of détente is that it is not a condition, but a process enabling us to shift the balance of force toward either peace or war accordingly as we successfully manage the process or fail to do so. The process arises from the necessity to deal with two nominally incompatible imperatives. The first is the technological imperative, which commands that we cooperate, as with a partner; the other is the ideological imperative, which commands that we compete, as with an adversary.

A fleeting acquaintance with sociobiology — with the argument of Edward O. Wilson, for instance — suggests that this combination is not at all unnatural; indeed, that all manner of species manage something of the sort. But it is troubling to men because of our poor efforts to get things straight in our minds, which for most of us comes down to trying to be consistent. Détente (by whatever term) demands inconsistency — inconsistency of the highest order of constancy. Clearly it is going to make demands on us of an unusual order, and yet of an order not accessible to analysis, even of a certain clarity.

The technological imperative is easy enough to grasp: a generation is coming of age in America which has known it since birth. So, equally, is the ideological imperative to those who will grasp it. *Détente* is a word we use to describe an approach to nations who are not friends, whose governments are based on principles different from ours, whom we are not sure we can trust, and who have great military power which they have shown an inclination to use to the detriment of freedom. This is something we have understood in the past — the essential antagonism of the Communist system to ours — and most of us in truth still do understand it. Our problem has to do with continuing to understand that this is not an everyday fact, but rather a salient, central fact, one from which an imperative arises every bit as compelling as that which arises from the facts of nuclear armament.

Why is this difficult?

It has not helped that we picked the wrong word to describe the present process. *Détente* is a French word which means, first, relaxation of tension, as with muscles. Now, such wholesale relaxation is exactly what will not happen under détente. (Again, whatever the term.) To the contrary, political détente can at most lead to a redistribution of tension from the technological sector to the ideological one, such that there will be a pronounced increase in the latter.

It is probably not a good thing to rely heavily on mechanistic analogues for human behavior, but in this instance it seems justified. The Communist system contains a certain amount of energy capable of doing work. Any lessened expenditure on military technology will lead to an increased expenditure on what the Communists will see as the equally inviting, equally productive area of ideological conflict. The relaxation of tensions in the one sector will lead more or less automatically to more intense conflict in the other. That is what détente means. The question, to repeat, is why do we find this difficult to grasp?

It helps to note that the Soviets have had no such difficulty. It is fairly clear that ideological conflict has been stepped up on their side, or at the very least expanded to new areas. With the fall of Southeast Asia, the perimeter of pressure in that region is much expanded, with results already evident. Where necessary, military force is used. Since 1965 the Soviets have stationed Cuban troops in Africa, even as they are consolidating their military facilities in the southern Arabian peninsula and expanding in the Himalayas. It is fair to assume they mean to expand their influence in Africa, and manifest that they are already partially successful, their main problem being opposition from another Communist power.

Blocked at one point, they shift to another. The United Nations offers nearly limitless opportunities in this respect. When the General Assembly in 1975 declared that "Zionism is a form of racism . . .," this was seen as an Arab initiative. But was it? The Ukraine, for one, was a sponsor of the resolution which directly served an announced Soviet cause. In 1971, *Pravda* published — and indeed *The New York Times* reported it on February 19, 1971 — a two-part article, "Anti-Sovietism Is the Profession of the Zionists," accusing Jews of all manner of plots against Communism, much as Hitler had accused them of plots in support of it. A campaign was begun which explicitly and heavily stressed the Nazi-Zionist theme.

This was all one campaign, serving the Soviet need to deal with what is one day going to be its central political problem — or may already be — that of internal ethnic conflict, and also serving its general aims in the Middle East. It is a daily occurrence in Turtle Bay, as elsewhere in the world.

Now there is nothing devious in this. The Soviet leaders have repeatedly stated that détente does not mean an end to ideological competition. They have not perhaps stressed that it means an increase, but surely that is something for us to perceive, not for them to proclaim.

Once again, why do we have such difficulty? I will suggest three clusters of influence, ranging from the temporary to the persisting.

The first, and temporary, condition arises from what I have elsewhere called a failure of nerve within the American elites that controlled and directed foreign policy in the postwar period. Nineteen sixty-three, the year *Pacem in Terris* appeared, was crucial in this regard: it was the year the commitment to Vietnam became, if not irreversible, then at all events one which was never reversed until failure was both inevitable and visible.

Now this sort of thing happens. Nations lose wars, and there are almost always consequences that are not so much political in nature as social. This is to say, a class, or even a caste, is defeated in the process. Something of this sort has happened. The Vietnam war was quintessentially an elite decision, made by a confident, essentially coherent, and, to that point, undefeated foreign policy establishment.

Then it was defeated.

The results were curiously unnerving. There was an immense effort to transfer blame. (One recalls the spring of 1970, when the tensions between supporters and opponents of the war led to broad hints in high places that the continuation of the doomed enterprise in Asia was a scheme to use the "hard hats" — that is, the working class — to bring about neo-fascism. Or something.)

Most significantly, the elites involved found themselves assaulted from within. Not to put too fine a point on it, their children would not fight in their war. Before it was over, the Reserve Officers Training Corps building at Harvard had been converted to a day care center — worse, a singularly derelict day care center, as if fecundity itself had been discredited, and shame was everywhere. Saul Bellow was quick to see it. His Mr. Sammler described a New York that would not defend itself.

Time heals such hurt. What it means for the moment, however, is that in the area of ideological encounter our responses are much slowed. Where we had been quick to sense danger — even, sometimes, quick to perceive opportunity — we are now slow to do so. Events have to penetrate much deeper into the political and bureaucratic system in order to evoke a response. There has been a decline in authority. Students of public administration delight to tell the story of a congressional hearing during World War II in which the then war production chief, a Detroit executive, was asked why he thought a certain proposal he had made would work, to which the executive replied that the General Motors Corporation paid him two hundred thousand dollars a year to know when something would work, and when it would not. That kind of authority is gone. Hence, in this temporary sense, the Soviets have an advantage and détente has difficulties.

An intermediate cluster of influences which retard our responses to Communist aggression may be simply stated as the superior capacity of Marxist argument to induce guilt. Observe that this is stated as a relative relationship. Liberal democracy makes great claims on nonliberal societies, and has done so for some time. There is probably not now in the whole of the world a totalitarian state which does not have a constitution guaranteeing individual liberties. On the other hand, it is a rare liberal society which does not contain a Marxist or neo-Marxist movement dedicated to its demise on grounds that it is — illiberal! Nor is there any liberal society which is not torn by doubts on this score.

It is said that if a Communist regime were to take over in the Sahara there would in time be a shortage of sand, and we shall doubtless in time have tested that hypothesis, but we can be fairly confident that to the very end there would be those in the West convinced that the sand had gone to build swimming pools for the rich. In the West. The *Communist Manifesto* is heavy with such accusation, interpolated between Marx's and Engels's insistent analysis of the creative dynamic of the doctrine. It is for a master such as John Dollard to delineate the role of guilt in liberal society. It is what makes us most humane as well, if, at times, a bit absurd. But none can doubt that it is a weapon used against us by our adversaries.

More specifically, it is a weapon which our adversaries contrive to have us use against ourselves. This technique was much in evidence at the United Nations when, on the thirtieth anniversary of the UN and in a moment of relative peace in the world, the United States introduced a resolution calling for a general amnesty for political prisoners. Now, if there is one thing Communism has brought to human experience, it is the phenomenon of political prisoners on a societal scale. Not just individuals but masses. The Soviets know their interests in such matters. TASS immediately denounced the American proposal as an "unsavory stratagem" to distract attention — truly — from the anti-Zionist resolution passed two days earlier.

The first American press accounts written in New York took a different line, to wit, that the resolution had been introduced in *retaliation* for the anti-Zionist resolution. (It was not.) But the general effect of such accounts, in this country and others, was to distract attention from the measure we had proposed to the question of what motives we had in doing so, a classic mechanism for inducing guilt. Some American commentators all but apologized for what we had done.

One need not go on.

No forgiveness; no redemption. John XXIII took the name of a disgraced antipope, and resumed the Johannine tradition. Not so the guilt-ridden American.

This guilt is most difficult to handle just now in our relations with the postcolonial nations. We begin with the assumption of exploitation, a burden of guilt (the final burden of colonialism) which we evidently assumed when we took on "the leadership of the free world," as the phrase once went. This is not to say that there was no exploitation. There was the humiliation of peoples the world over. The point here has to do only with the impact of these events on the American conscience, generations later and vast distances from events which Americans were scarcely aware of and only in the most peripheral way involved in at the time.

But more recently — and I would venture more importantly — there has been the more complex phenomenon of the steady falling away from politically liberal norms and the gradual establishment of leftist totalitarian regimes in the formerly democratic postcolonial states. This has been a great disappointment to the West, and the disappointment is now almost final. Speaking somewhat beyond the evidence, I would suggest that our emergent reaction is one of questioning where we went wrong, where we failed. Did we, for example, give enough aid? Hence, the more demanding the claims made upon us by the new nations, the more support such claims gather, from some at least.

I would not wish to be seen as dismissing all of this response — even that part of it which seems to me uncalled for and unhelpful — and contrasting it to a decent and constructive concern to help others. I am prepared, however, to ask whether some part of it is not based on fear — the fear, again, among Western elites — that comes of seeing the vast multitudes of the world nominally turned against us. The fact of the matter is that most of the new nations have opted for the regimes we now see in those areas not from egalitarian urges, but from the very opposite. In most such nations a postindependence generation has come to power, and within that generation an elite which finds in leftist, statist doctrine an excuse for gathering all power to itself, an excuse which cannot be found in democratic doctrine. Ergo. There is no nation so poor it cannot afford free speech, but there are few governments which will put up with the bother of it.

There is an element of guilt in our relations with many of the newly leftist nations in the world which is not to be accounted for by older concerns. Part of it may be accounted for by the continuing success of Marxist doctrine in including guilt in the West, part by a separate but related sublimation of aggression. Neither of these phenomena is likely to fade rapidly; but on the other hand, if we observe that the Soviet Union commanded unreasoning, irrational sympathies in the West only for about two generations, we may reasonably guess that our present difficulties in dealing openly with the newer nations will not last much longer than that.

The third cluster of influences is the long-term ideological drift away from liberal democracy, the influence of which, as argued above, crested at the end of the First World War. In a lecture given at the University of Detroit, just weeks before the appearance of *Pacem in Terris,* Leo Strauss, the foremost political philosopher of his time in America, spoke more generally of the failure of what he called the Modern Project. This was a world system that grew out of the political philosophies of the sixteenth and seventeenth centuries and which in, say, 1914, seemed well on the way to triumph. The West, at this time, was certain of its purpose, a "purpose in which all men could be united." It had a clear vision of its future "as the future of mankind." It was not less certain of its power. At that time, Strauss observes, this country, Britain, and Germany, if united, could have had their way, without force, in any region of the world.

All went well, or well enough, for a bit thereafter, until Communism, which had been seen as a parallel movement to the Modern Project — part of it really, "a somewhat impatient, wild, wayward twin" — revealed itself, as Strauss puts it, to "even the meanest capacities" as something else, as Stalinism and post-Stalinism. Fierce despotism was once again a major force in the world; and finally, to cite from Strauss, "the only restraint in which the West can put some confidence is the tyrant's fear of the West's immense military power."

For the rest he saw decline. Specifically, the purpose of a universal society — "a society consisting of equal nations, each consisting of free and equal men and women, with all these nations to be fully developed as regards their power of production, thanks to science" — that purpose is no longer sustainable. In its stead, political society in the foreseeable future reverts to what it almost always has been, what Strauss called "particular" society, a "society with frontiers, a closed society, concerned with self-improvement."

One must accept this as a long-term condition, but also see in it the essence of what might be our long-term security. For a "particular society" is a society that can be defended — and, I think, will be.

It comes to that. *Out of the decline of the West there will, I sense, emerge a rise in spirits.* We have shortened our lines. We are under attack. There is nothing in the least in the culture that suggests we will not in the end defend ourselves successfully.

We shall do so because we have in our armamentarium the incomparable weapon of liberty. We are of the party of liberty: all of us. And as the lights go out in the rest of the world, they shine all the brighter here. This requires discipline of

ourselves — by government and about government. But that is
not beyond us. How did we get to a bicentennial without
knowing something of such matters? In the United Nations
today, half the nations have had a violent internal change of
government within the past eleven years.

What it requires most of all is truth-telling — to one another
and to the rest of the world. Those who would concede some
authority to *Pacem in Terris* are not merely advised in this
matter, we are commanded: "The first among the rules
governing the relations between states is that of truth."

Already we hear voices from the other world asking for
truth . . . from us . . . about them. Most particularly and most
poignantly, we hear individual voices from the Soviet Union
which ask no more than that which *Pacem in Terris* commands:
that as between governments and their respective peoples "it is
not fear which should reign but love. . . ."

This is our strength: that we can speak such truths and that
the nations with which we are leagued can speak them. Those
who cannot must perforce hear us with ever mounting concern,
a concern which they attempt to allay by measures which only
enhance it.

Surely we must see this. Just as we must see the persistent
attempt to dissuade us from speaking out for what it is, a
concession of their weakness and our strength.

In 1975 when the United States introduced the resolution in
the General Assembly calling for amnesty for political prisoners, a German newspaperwoman called, by previous appointment, on the American Ambassador to the United Nations. As
the two sat down the journalist remarked, "Before beginning,
let me just tell you that already the news of what the United
States has proposed is being whispered from cell to cell in East
German prisons. You would think such news would never
reach such places, but it does and it is what keeps prisoners
alive." How did she know? "I know," she replied. "I spent four
years in one of those jails."

The amnesty resolution failed. Not even the West Europeans supported it. An American columnist, convinced his country was incapable of doing anything decent, had predicted with something like glee that our initiative would be met with "a deadly silence." Looking back, this would seem to have been the case. But was it? Or was it that we have still not learned to hear the whispers?

Sursum corda.

5.
The Advent of Party in International Politics

THE TWENTIETH CENTURY began with great expectations for the development of international society along the lines of the Western democracy. There was great emphasis on law and the peaceful settlement of international disputes, associated with The Hague. (Bryan, as Wilson's Secretary of State, negotiated thirty arbitration treaties, all but two of which were approved by the Senate.) There was much talk of disarmament treaties and, of course, of a society of nations. Most of these proposals were, in fact, adopted; few fulfilled their expectations. The international court had as well not existed. Arms limitation treaties seem to increase arms. The United Nations would not be much noticed save for issues where it has a jurisdiction inherited from the League mandate system. (The mandate, the quintessential legal situation of an adult assuming temporary responsibility for the affairs of a minor. As, for example, Palestine!) By contrast, unheralded and perhaps unwelcome, a major parliamentary institution does seem to be evolving. Nations seem to be forming parties.

It is common to hear the world described in images suggesting that it has grown smaller: a global village; spaceship earth. A succession of sages discover that we are become interdependent. (Among these were Marx and Engels, who use the term in the *Communist Manifesto*.) Less common but nonetheless recurrent is the observation that while the world may be growing smaller, there is also a sense in which it is becoming more complex, inasmuch as the number of nation-states which are recognized members of the international community has grown very considerably in only half a century. Forty-one states started the League of Nations, with a handful of defeated powers temporarily excluded. Fifty-one states started the United Nations, again with a handful of powers temporarily in limbo. By 1979 membership of the UN had reached 150 and seating is to be provided for 165.

In response to all this, it is now being said that Orwell's forecast for 1984 must not only be revised, but reversed. The world is not, after all, to evolve by a relentless logic of aggregation into three vast sovereignties locked in desultory but permanent conflict. Rather, it is proposed that something closer to regression is taking place, that we are lapsing into the timeless mode of tribal fragmentation and strife. Not hegemony but anarchy is to be our fate, or at all events our near future.

Rhythms of this kind are not unknown. In the nineteenth century political units, in the main, became larger. In the twentieth they have become smaller. But fragmentation has not led, or at least has not yet led, to unmanageable chaos. Is the many-state system that has replaced the old empires different from the system the empires replaced?

Let me suggest that this may indeed be the case: that a new kind of world political order is emerging. This world order is made up of an increasing number of distinct sovereignties, but these multiple sovereignties are learning to manage their affairs in a fairly coherent and instrumental fashion through the formation of what by analogy may be called world political parties.

The term *political party* emerges, as the *Encyclopedia of the Social Sciences* records, in the nineteenth century with the development of representative institutions and the expansion of the suffrage in Europe and the United States. And yet, the *Encyclopedia* continues, there is still a "scarcity of viable party theory." Instead one finds, as in much of political science, degrees of advocacy represented as analysis. A tradition associated with the continent sees parties as an instrument of their membership, often that of an incipiently revolutionary mass. An Anglo-Saxon tradition sees parties as an institution devised or evolved for the public good, and in that sense primarily responsive to the electorate as a whole. In America the Founders' distrust of "faction" persists, and analysis concentrates on why parties and party members behave as they do, the assumption usually being that some powerful motive — gain — must be adduced to account for the aberration.

Not much to go on. But Harvey Mansfield, Jr., has offered a perspective which helps considerably. In his reading of Burke's advocacy of party — a heretical stance at the time, and in Mansfield's judgment a prophetic one — party would give stability and longevity to ideals and standards of public conduct which might well reside in great men but, great men being no less mortal than others, could not in that way long endure. It was all very well for the great peers of his age to be "above party," much as Madison and Hamilton wished Americans to be. But what would remain after the first yellow fever epidemic or, for that matter, the first idiot heir?

In sum, party evolves out of the sheer organizational needs of large political systems, and from the sense that ideals and objectives should be given a stable institutional setting. Thus they constitute a kind of routinization of charisma, a phenomenon with which Max Weber has made us familiar. And there is Emerson: "An institution is the lengthened shadow of one man." Either way: first the great leader or leaders of the movement; then the party to carry on the tradition, sometimes faithfully, but never to the satisfaction of all.

Not all this applies to the history of international relations in the twentieth century, but enough of it does to make for a suggestive parallel. Party arises with the advent of representative institutions and the expansion of the suffrage: precisely what this century has brought into the international sphere. To be sure, neither the League of Nations nor the United Nations evolved out of representative impulses. Both amounted to arrangements by which a handful of nations momentarily ascendant in world affairs attempted to arrange those affairs so that their ascendancy would persist. We may recall Theodore Roosevelt's address to the Nobel Committee of May 5, 1910, which is frequently cited in discourses on the origins of the League: "Finally, it would be a master stroke if those great powers bent on peace would form a league of peace, not only to keep the peace among themselves, but to prevent, by force if necessary, its being broken by others." Ruhl J. Bartlett has reminded us of the preemptive nature of so much of this enterprise in his study of the League to Enforce Peace. To *enforce* peace.

But shortly after the Treaty of Versailles, what might at least be seen as tendencies toward party appeared. This was most pronounced where economic issues were involved. The International Labor Organization, after all, was designed on party principles: it was comprised of a workers' party, a business party, and a government party. (That government would be a party showed more insight than perhaps was recognized at the time.) Within the League of Nations itself, the advent of Hitler's Germany produced a movement of "have-not" nations — mostly losers under Versailles — protesting the inequities of the international economic order and demanding a new one presumedly to be led by Germany. (This development never went very far, as the League managed to expel the dictatorships, recognizing at least that they would never abide by the Covenant.)

With the end of World War II, a formal peace settlement

proved impossible, but an international system was reconstituted, including the various representative bodies of the United Nations, all of which experienced a rapidly expanding membership. Immediately two blocs of nations, Eastern and Western, Communist and anti-Communist (or whatever) took form. These differed on fundamental political issues and commenced to vote as blocs against each other in various international settings, including the parliamentary settings of the United Nations. The formation of these two blocs led in turn to the formation of a third, the Non-Aligned nations, which proclaimed a distinct identity, and program, as regards the other two.

In short order most nation-states were to be found in one group or another. Gradually they began to conduct themselves in the manner of political parties. (One might emphasize the gradual nature of this development, and note that this too parallels the experience of national representative bodies. The British have produced the maxim that the function of the opposition is to oppose, but it was only very late in the nineteenth century that the opposition in Westminster began automatically to vote against whatever it was the government proposed, and to do so as a disciplined bloc.)

In time the organization of the three competing blocs grew more complex, especially that of the Communists and the Non-Aligned. Conferences were convened, complete with party secretariats and party manifestos. Regional subdivisions such as the Organization of African Unity appeared, while at the United Nations specific caucuses developed, notably the Group of 77 (now many more than one hundred) which functions in a manner not dissimilar to the parliamentary Labour party in Westminster — that is, as a legislative subdivision of a larger party organization.*

---

*Bernard Lewis sees four blocs at the United Nations: Western, Soviet, Arab, and Non-Aligned. There are at least three, and there are likely to be more as time passes. My argument here is simply that there are now groups of nations that behave in some respects *like* political parties.

There are many nations today. There will be yet more. This is the discrete contribution of ethnicity to the present world order. It is the demand for ethnic distinctness and separateness that has brought about the breakup of the great empires, all save that of the Soviet Union, and which promises to go further and break up many of the newer entities formed from the old empires. (With the Russian empire presumedly to come.) There is nothing inevitable about this prospect — certainly the African states have so far successfully avoided such fragmentation. But still, there is little reason to suppose that the most dynamic political force of this era has yet spent itself. And the more the world comes apart in this respect, the more it will be forced to come together again in various party groupings.

The advent of party often takes political systems by surprise, perhaps, especially, planned political systems. Certainly that has been the American experience. For all the genius of the framers of the American Constitution, they did not foresee, indeed strove with all their unexampled ingenuity to prevent, the emergence of "faction." And yet faction there was almost from the outset, and most would agree that faction has had much to do with the stability of the American political system, or at least of its capacity to endure.

May not something similar be true of the advent of party on the international scene? The world in the near term had to turn out some way, and this way is scarcely the least promising. An international society developing institutions analogous to those which appear to serve national societies reasonably well provides some ground for reassurance.

So far as the United States is concerned, at the very least this analysis suggests a conceptual framework in which we might better come to grips with a number of problems which at times seem to baffle us. At the United Nations and other international agencies, for example, we persist in the manner of Whig magnates determined to be "above party" and are both bewildered by and frequently out of sorts with the majority of nations who insist on acting otherwise. Let me give three examples of how this obtuseness operates to our disadvantage.

On July 26, 1973, the United States vetoed a proposed Indian resolution in the Security Council which was strongly condemnatory of Israel for its continued occupation of the territories seized in the 1967 war. The resolution was unbalanced in the extreme. Security Council Resolution 242, the basic Middle East agreement, which called for Arab recognition of the state of Israel and for secure borders for Israel, was quite ignored. In this sense the Indian resolution fundamentally revised Resolution 242, and the United States was altogether right to veto it. Yet the United States did so alone, with no support from any other nation. The United States was seen to be isolated, yet adamant. In the Egyptian version of the event, the American veto led directly to the judgment in Cairo that there was no alternative to war. The Yom Kippur War followed. Henry Kissinger, as Secretary of State, allowed that the veto of the Indian resolution was a major influence in the Egyptian decision to attack. The world has not been the same since. It has been considerably worse for the United States.

Now what business had India in sponsoring such a resolution? None, save party business. India was acting not in its own interest but for the Non-Aligned, putting its still considerable prestige forward on behalf of a party view about a region which from a perspective of New Delhi could surely be described as a faraway place of which they knew little. I was at the precise moment United States Ambassador to India, negotiating a settlement of the vast rupee debt we had accumulated there in return for the grain shipments of the 1960s. We owned, by rough count, the equivalent of two thirds of the Indian currency.

The Indian government was obsessed with this situation and understandably wanted an end to it. So did we. In these circumstances it was entirely without the powers of American diplomacy to get the Indians to stop their troublemaking in

New York. The Indian permanent representative was not a very high-ranking civil servant, and the Indian government made nothing at home of what it was doing in Turtle Bay. Yet no such American effort was undertaken. Washington never asked. In New Delhi we were barely aware that anything was happening. American policy was blind to the essential reality. It did not see India acting as an instrument of party politics within a world order and on a world scale. There was no conceptual framework which enabled American policy-makers to make any sense of the Indian behavior. And so they ignored it, at what we must judge to be considerable cost to the West.

A second example. In 1974, Congress, at the behest of the AFL-CIO, began withholding its contributions to the International Labor Organization and faced an automatic suspension of membership. Our withdrawal would have been (and would be, for the issue is not yet settled) an extraordinary event. We helped found the ILO. We joined it when we joined no other League organization. It is an institution unique in its association with Americans — with Gompers, with Wilson, with Roosevelt, and above all with free trade unionism. And yet by 1974 the American labor movement wanted out. And what was their complaint? Not that free trade unions were no longer in a majority in Geneva as they once had been. What the representatives of the American labor movement had come to judge intolerable was that on critical votes, where they were prepared to be defeated, they found themselves not defeated but annihilated. It is one thing to lose in an international forum with thirty free countries at your side. It is another thing to go down in the company only of New Zealand, Costa Rica, and (not always) Israel. Not least — as in the case of the Indian resolution in the Security Council — such lopsided votes signal the antidemocratic and nondemocratic nations alike that the West really doesn't stand by its professed principles. It signals decline. In the end, the United States withdrew from the ILO, which it need not have done had our government seen its role there as forming a Western bloc.

A third instance. On November 10, 1975, the General Assembly of the United Nations adopted a resolution declaring Zionism to be a form of racism. The United States had fought hard against this measure, declaring it to be an obscenity, declaring it to be a threat to peace in the region and to the world organization itself. The resolution nonetheless passed, with 72 votes in a membership of 143. Even so, to cite but one region, a majority of non-Muslim African states voted with us. The anti-Israel bloc got fewer votes that day than in any similar encounter in a decade. Despite this, the whispers immediately began: If we hadn't fought, we wouldn't have lost. A year went by. The same sequence commenced once more, with resolutions somewhat less dramatic but every bit as poisonous as those of 1975. This time the United States was "reasonable." And this time the vote against Israel, instead of being two to one, was five to one. On the same day, a not less vicious anti-Western resolution dealing with South Africa was adopted 110–8.

The *Wall Street Journal,* at least, noted the event:

. . . the United States must vigorously defend its position in the UN or be submerged by bombast. America is still likely to come out on the losing end of votes, given the makeup of the UN, but it is essential not to accept defeat without making a serious effort to defend one's values and beliefs. Is it really so surprising that the more the UN majority is convinced the U.S. lacks the will to fight back, the harder it will press its attacks?*

*I touched upon these contrasting outcomes in my book *A Dangerous Place* (1978). In a review in *Washington Post Book World,* Charles Yost, who of course was one of my predecessors at the UN, makes the point that even though the 1976 vote was technically more of a defeat than 1975, because we made no fuss about it, no one paid any attention and it had less harmful effect. This defines a clear difference of opinion. Yost is a career diplomat of the highest achieve-

American response to situations of this kind has alternated between equally unsatisfactory extremes. At one moment we will declare the system to be at fault, and suggest that any arrangement that could produce such outcomes is hopelessly flawed and the outcomes are meaningless. The next moment we will be found declaring that there must be something profoundly flawed about the United States if the world can be so united in opposition to us or our interests. In each case nonsense. Nonsense of the same order that produces such concepts as the Third World, a notion that countries not being like the nations of the Soviet bloc or the American bloc must be like one another. The fallacy of negative definition. As a group these nations have nothing more in common than do nations generally. But they have organized, and this organization *creates* common interests. The African nations in particular seemed to have learned this art.

Ought we not respond accordingly, organizing a Western block in multilateral settings and bargaining with the others? The Soviets do this. The international network of Communist parties gives them a resource — what intelligence agencies call an asset — in most of the Non-Aligned nations which can be deployed with or against the government in power. In Africa and increasingly in the Middle East, they have the Cuban armed forces, which they can deploy with or against a government in power. Terrorism is an increasingly institutionalized force which the Soviets seem to deploy also. All in all this makes for a good deal of influence in countries with little history of stability and, in effect, the death penalty for losing.

Thus in 1978 and 1979 the United Nations Committee on Decolonization voted progressively more condemnatory resolu-

---

ment. And yet I think him wrong about this matter. I think what he really means is that few in the United States (apart from the *Wall Street Journal*) paid any attention, and accordingly the State Department had no great grief. But what of the rest of the world? A few days after Yost's comment appeared a *New York Times* story by Kathleen Teltsch was headlined: "P.L.O. Makes New Gains at U.N." (December 25, 1978).

tions on the United States relationship with Puerto Rico. In each instance about half the members of the committee voted for the Cuban resolution and the others abstained. (With China not participating.) In each instance those who abstained explained that to go against the Cubans was to risk retaliation. Which is normal to politics. What is not normal is the disinclination of the United States to devise countermeasures. As a result we have the spectacle of the 1979 meeting of the Non-Aligned heads of state in Havana, with two thirds of the nations of the world subscribing to an endless succession of pro-Soviet, anti-Western pronouncements of a distastefully virulent order.

This is absurd. If the distant Soviets, with their creaky government and depleted doctrine, did not actually enjoy such influence, it would be difficult indeed to devise a political scenario by which they would acquire it, and after the Chinese schism, hold onto it. It is hard not to credit an explanation (of conduct in the United Nations) offered by Bernard Lewis, in the course of a review of my book *A Dangerous Place* (*Commentary*, March 1979).

There is in the Euphrates area where Syria and Iraq meet, near the Turkish frontier, a little-known Kurdish sect called the Yazidis, an aberrant offshoot separated from Islam at an early date. They are described by their neighbors as devil worshippers. This is a slander. The Yazidis are in fact dualists, surviving holders of a religious belief, once widespread in the Middle East, that there is not one but two eternal spirits, one of good, the other of evil, contending for the domination of the universe. Since the good spirit is by definition good and will remain so, the Yazidis devote most of their worship to propitiating the spirit of evil. Given their assumptions, this makes good sense. It is, thus, unfair to call their beliefs devil worship; they might more appropriately be described as theological nonalignment.

Similar considerations affect the policies of many countries at the United Nations. To attract or offend the Soviet Union can be dangerous; to differ from the Arabs, costly and perhaps also hazardous. To attack the United States and its policies, on the other hand, brings no penalties. On the contrary, in addition to gratifying the Soviet bloc and its allies, attacking the United States wins acclaim and respect from large segments of American opinion, including many policy-makers, and, above all, the media. In these circumstances, the choice is not difficult, and it is not surprising that before very long the United States found itself in a permanent minority, where the best it could hope for was abstentions by its more devoted and loyal friends.

In the end, however, the Soviets can provide neither investment nor trade in any significant amount, and these limits become more evident. (By the close of the 1970s the Soviet economy languished, and the society also. Mortality, presumedly from alcoholism, was *declining,* and the state had ceased to publish vital statistics.) There are those who think that trade and investment do not influence or ought not to influence foreign policy, but few such persons are heads of state. In 1979 an editorial from the *Daily News* of Nigeria spoke with a certain candor on this subject.

The situation in Africa at the present time is such that the Soviet Union is losing out to the Americans, not so much because African countries detest socialism, as because the Soviet Union is unwilling to, or incapable of, providing more economic than military aid.

Sudan and Egypt are already sold on the Western way of life. Somalia's problem was a little different, but it boiled down to the same issue of incompatibility of purposes. Ethiopia is still basking in the first phase of military brotherhood, and may yet ask the Russians and Cubans to leave. Mozambique and Angola are already flirting with the West (that's what "non-alignment" usually means). Guinea has decided to mend its fences with France. And Zimbabwe and Namibia are unlikely to go a different course.

It is a truly ironic situation, for what it means is that all Americans have to do is fold their hands and wait for the honeymoon to end before stepping in for the picking. The Americans are, of course, well aware of this, and their protests against Russian incursions into Africa are designed precisely to accelerate the process of disaffection and disillusionment.

In a quite profound sense, what it does mean is that African nations, often against their own inclination, are being denied all meaningful options in terms of the economic arrangements they have to make for themselves. But it also means that we need not get too starry-eyed about the possible gains to be had from the Russians, at least in terms of our concern for economic development. They would have to modify their policies first.

They won't. After sixty years of revolution, theirs is still an economy of scarcity. Ours is not. Certainly that of the other democracies is not. An elemental setting for the politics, as Madison would say, of faction. And precisely that "intercourse of nations" which makes for the competition of ideas which is our great strength and which ought also to be our purpose.

6.
The Politics of
Human Rights

There's an ideological struggle that has been in progress for decades between the Communist nations on the one hand and the democratic nations on the other. Mr. Brezhnev and his predecessors have never refrained from expressing their view when they disagreed with some aspect of social or political life in the free world. And I think we have a right to speak out openly when we have a concern about human rights wherever those abuses occur.

—JIMMY CARTER
March 25, 1977

IT IS AS SIMPLE as that. What needs to be explained is not why the United States raised this standard, but why it took so long. Anthony Lewis observed of the President in a 1977 *New York Times* column: "He is giving not just Americans but people in the West generally a sense that their values are being asserted again, after years of silence in the face of tyranny and brutality." But again, what needs to be explained is how those "years of silence" came about, and what they signify. For there *were* reasons, and deep ones, and they could reassert themselves far more readily than many might suppose.

Human rights as an issue in foreign policy was by no means

central to Jimmy Carter's campaign for the presidency. It was raised in the Democratic platform drafting committee, and at the Democratic convention, but in each instance the Carter representatives were at best neutral, giving the impression of not having heard very much of the matter before and not having any particular views.

This is understandable enough, for by 1976 those "years of silence" had done their work. As a tactical or strategic concern of foreign policy, human rights had disappeared so completely from the councils of the West that a newcomer to the field might well never have heard the issue even discussed. Given our celebrated penchant for promptly forgetting even the most recent history, it may serve to record just how nearly total this blackout on human rights had become.

As I have noted, on November 12, 1975, as Permanent Representative at the United Nations, I introduced to the Third Committee of the General Assembly a United States proposal for a worldwide amnesty for political prisoners. The General Assembly, our delegation argued, had already that year taken two important steps in such a direction. A resolution had been adopted calling for unconditional amnesty for all political prisoners in South Africa. The United States had supported that resolution. Further, a resolution had been adopted calling for amnesty for all political prisoners in Chile. The United States had supported that resolution as well. But, we now asked, was there any reason to stop there? There were then 142 members of the UN. Were we not all bound by the same standards that bound Chile and South Africa?

There were grounds for a concern with universality in this matter which struck us with special force. Did not the selective morality of the United Nations in matters of human rights threaten the integrity not merely of the United Nations but of human rights themselves? Indeed at the United Nations at that time, and since, the language of human rights was routinely turned against precisely those nations where human rights are respected and upheld. Most of the nations that sponsored the resolutions calling for the release of political prisoners in South Africa and Chile were notoriously guilty of the same offense.

It might be supposed that the totalitarian nations and their allies would have gone to great lengths to abort this American initiative. They did not. There was no need. The democratic nations did it for them.

There is a "Western" caucus of sorts at the UN. Somnolent in most matters, it was roused to decisive action by the threat which the American resolution presented to the peace of the General Assembly. A meeting was called. We were asked to explain ourselves. We said we were worried about the perversion of the language of human rights and its transformation into a weapon against democracy. We also said that we thought it a good idea for the democratic world to regain the ideological initiative after the setback we had just suffered over the resolution declaring Zionism to be a form of racism. This explanation was greeted with a cold dismay that edged onto anger. It was quickly agreed that if the resolution were somehow to pick up sponsors and to pass, the caucus would immediately insist on a formal undertaking to define the term *political prisoner*. I asked: Would this be carried out along the lines of the recently completed exercise to define "aggression"? Yes. But that, I said, had taken from 1951 to 1974, nearly a quarter century. Yes. But our resolution called for amnesty, a voluntary act of governments. Inasmuch as no one would be telling governments who their political prisoners were, no formal definition was necessary. The response remained unyielding. The other democracies would not join in sponsoring our resolution. There the matter ended.

Two points essential to an understanding of the issue of human rights and its political meaning are to be seen in this episode. The first is that the issue of human rights is nothing new to international politics in this age. To the contrary, *as*

defined by the totalitarian nations, the issue of human rights
has long been at the center of international politics. In fact,
from the time the Soviets commenced to be so hugely armed
that their "peace" campaigns lost credibility, and Khrushchev
opted for Russian involvement in "liberation" struggles, the
issue of human rights has been acquiring greater and greater
salience. Which is to say that in human rights terms the
Western democracies have been attacked without letup. The
second point is that the Western democracies, having allowed
themselves to be placed on the defensive, finally ceased almost
wholly to resist. In the language of diplomatic instructions,
this passivity was known as "damage limitation." In truth, it
was something very like capitulation, a species of what
Jean-François Revel has called "Finlandization from within."

If anything is to come of American initiatives in human
rights, these points will have to be far better understood. It
needs to be understood, for example, that it was a British
Labour government which was primarily behind the move in
the Western caucus to disown the United States amnesty
proposal. Earlier Labour governments would not in all probability have acted in this way. It was said of Ernest Bevin,
Britain's first postwar Foreign Secretary, that he regarded
Communism as a dissident faction of the Transport and
General Workers Union — the point being that such familiarity bred contempt. By the mid-seventies, a different kind of
familiarity was at work. The Labour party in October 1976, for
example, could invite the likes of Boris Ponomarev — head of
the international department of the Soviet Communist party
and a notable figure in the Stalin purges of the 1930s — to
London on a "fraternal" visit and arrange to have him received
by the Prime Minister and the Foreign Secretary of a Labour
government.

What was true of Britain was true of the West in general.
Democratic regimes and values were under totalitarian assault in every region of the world, and resistance was every-

where weakening. The great exception was Israel where Dr. Johnson's adage that the prospect of hanging wonderfully concentrates the mind still seemed to apply. In the West, by contrast, the preferred contrivance for dealing with the prospect of hanging was denial. A stunning instance of just such denial was the Western response to the 1975 resolution of the UN General Assembly equating Zionism with racism. In this case, denial took the form of a refusal to recognize the extent to which Soviet inspiration lay behind the resolution.

A long-established propaganda technique of the Soviet government has been to identify those it would destroy with Nazism, especially with the racial doctrines of the Nazis. Following World War II, for example, pan-Turkish, -Iranian, and -Islamic movements appeared in the southern regions of the Soviet Union. They were promptly accused of Nazi connections and branded as *racist*. Jews escaped this treatment until the Six-Day War of 1967. That event, however, aroused sufficient pro-Israel, pro-Jewish sentiment within the Soviet Union to evoke the by now almost bureaucratic response. In October 1976 Bernard Lewis wrote in *Foreign Affairs*: "The results were immediately visible in a vehement campaign of abuse, particularly in the attempt to equate the Israelis with the Nazis as aggressors, invaders, occupiers, racists, oppressors, and murderers." Within a short period of time, and coincidentally with the introduction of *racist* into currency as a general term of abuse, Soviet propagandists began to equate Zionism per se with racism. In a statement released to the press on March 4, 1970, a "group of Soviet citizens of Jewish nationality" — making use of the facilities of the Soviet foreign ministry — attacked "the aggression of the Israeli ruling circles," and said that "Zionism has always expressed the chauvinistic views and *racist* [my emphasis] ravings of the Jewish bourgeoisie." This may well be the first official Soviet reference to Zionism as racism in the fashionable connotation of the term.

Steadily and predictably, these charges moved into international forums. In 1973 Israel was excluded from the regional
bodies of UNESCO. In 1974 the International Labor Conference adopted a "Resolution Concerning the Policy of Discrimination, Racism, and Violation of Trade Union Freedoms and
Rights Practiced by the Israeli Authorities in Palestine and
Other Occupied Arab Territories." The charge of racism was
now pressed.

In February 1976 the United Nations Commission on
Human Rights found Israel guilty of "war crimes" in the
occupied Arab territories. The counts read as if they could have
come from the Nuremberg verdicts:

— annexation of parts of the occupied territories,

— destruction and demolition,

— confiscation and expropriation,

— evacuation, deportation, expulsion, displacement and
transfer of inhabitants,

— pillaging of archaeological and cultural property,

— interference with religious freedoms and affront to humanity.

In April 1976, in the Security Council, a representative of the
Palestine Liberation Organization spoke of the "Pretoria–Tel
Aviv Axis," making an explicit reference to the "axis" between
Nazi Germany and Fascist Italy in the 1930s. In May, in the
same body, the Soviet Union accused Israel of "racial genocide"
in putting down unrest on the occupied West Bank of the
Jordan River. The same month, in a General Assembly
committee, a PLO document likened Israeli measures to Nazi
atrocities during World War II: "The sealing of a part of the
City of Nablus is a violation of the basic human rights . . .
reminiscent of the ghettos and concentration camps erected by
the Hitlerites. . . ."

That the purpose of all this was to delegitimize Israel in the
interest of its Arab enemies was of course obvious to everyone.
What should have been equally obvious was that the assault

on Israel — the most exposed of the democracies — served a more generalized effort to deprive the democratic nations of their legitimacy as democracies. Salami tactics, as the Communists used to say — first one small unit of the democratic world, then the next. For in true Orwellian fashion, the free societies in the world were under attack precisely and paradoxically for *not* being free. *They were attacked for violating human rights.* The charge could range from genocide to unemployment, but it always followed the Orwellian principle: Hit the democracies in the one area where they have the strongest case to make against the dictatorships.

Representatives of the Soviet Union and other Communist countries are not especially adept at this. But in a diplomatic maneuver which foreshadowed the military strategy of using Cuban troops as surrogates, they could sit back and allow most of the talking to be done by spokesmen from the Third World, some of whom were very good indeed at the Orwellian game. Of course, just as the Arabs had their own good reasons for attacking Israel, quite apart from any benefit to the Soviet Union, so these Third World regimes had their own good reasons for attacking democracy. With a handful of exceptions, the fourscore new nations which have come into the world in the last twenty-five years or so began their existence as constitutional democracies. By now the vast majority have succumbed to dictators and strongmen of one kind or another for whom the opportunity to attack any countries which *have* remained faithful to their constitutional vows is — to put it mildly — compelling.

Western policy has never seen the new nations in this light. For one thing, there was the tremendous investment of hope in what we saw as the small seedlings of our various great oaks and a corresponding reluctance to think, much less speak, ill of them. Then there was the trauma of Vietnam, which perhaps made it seem even more necessary that we should be approved by nations so very like the one we were despoiling. In consequence we were as disturbed by these onslaughts from the Third World as we were when the Russians came up with the Cuban army as an extension of the same school of diplomacy.

Then, suddenly, something changed. It would be hard to establish just why, but a useful axiom is that of Michael Polanyi: People change their minds. They wake up one day to find they no longer think as they did. Something like this happened in the case of human rights. The Democratic national platform in 1976 suddenly proposed that human rights be a central element of foreign policy. The Democratic administration that followed did just that. To the extent that some of this had begun at the United Nations under the preceding Republican administration, the issue had become one of constructive competition between the parties to seem to do best what the public demanded.

The problem is to sustain the initiative of the mid-1970s. The Carter administration had no more than begun when the difficulties appeared. It is one thing to raise issues of human rights against weak allies. It is another to raise them with strong adversaries. Most importantly, no one has found a way to address the new nations (and some of the old nations of Latin America) on this issue. To raise the subject is to give offense; to keep silent is to become an accomplice. There is a good deal of what psychologists call cognitive dissonance. How can nations, freed from the shackles of oppression by foreign masters, turn and oppress their own? The answer is that it is not hard to do, and indeed is done every day. But it is not a satisfactory answer: few willingly assent to the unhappy truth. The more then is this an area of policy to be codified. We need to know in advance how we will behave. Our behavior needs to be principled, and to be seen as such.

The cost of *not thinking* this subject through was to be seen in the seismic events of the summer of 1979 when an intense division arose within the American public over the role of the

Palestine Liberation Organization. From the time it came to office the Carter administration was careless to the point of willfulness in its use of the symbols and code words of the totalitarians. The process of "semantic infiltration" was never more on display. Thus the Secretary of State would refer to the multiracial, pro-Western government of Bishop Muzorewa in Zimbabwe as "the Salisbury group," while describing the Soviet armed groups based in neighboring Zambia and Mozambique as the "Patriotic Front" or the "liberation forces" and professed neutrality as between them. The notion that these symbols (and comparable ones from other regions) could be transferred to the Middle East did or did not occur to administration officials. I would not wish to speculate. But when, on July 31, 1979, President Carter was quoted on the front page of *The New York Times* as having "likened the Palestinian cause to the civil rights movement in the United States," it was foretold that twenty-two days later the same front page should report, "Civil Rights Leader Backs Cause of P.L.O. after Meeting at U.N." He who says A says B.

Four principles come to mind on which to construct a base.

First principle: *International law and treaty obligations are wholly supportive of human rights initiatives.* That for so long a period we appear to have forgotten this gave an inestimable advantage to the totalitarians. The Soviet reaction to the signs that our memories are stirring has been angry. But this "surprising adverse reaction to our stand on human rights," as the President characterized it, will get worse, not better — they would be fools to respond in any other way. The more then should we know and understand that the law is on our side.

The United Nations Charter imposes two obligations on members. The first, which is well known, is to be law-abiding in their relations with other nations: not to attack them, not to subvert them, and so on. But there is a second obligation, which very simply is to be law-abiding in the treatment of one's own citizens. The United Nations Charter requires that members govern themselves on liberal principles, as these principles have evolved and are understood in the Western democracies.

Article 1 enjoins them to promote through the UN "respect for human rights and for fundamental freedoms for all without distinction as to race, sex, language, or religion."

These words mean just what any of us in the Western democracies would assume they mean.

The Russians knew what they were signing. We do well to remember that they began World War II as allies of Nazi Germany, partners in the conquest and partition of Poland. They had a true pro-Nazi past to overcome. In the early days of the United Nations they sought to do this by taking the lead in asserting that members had to be — liberal states! In the first year of the new organization, the question arose as to whether Spain should be admitted to membership. Absolutely not, said Andrei Gromyko in the Security Council: to the contrary, punitive measures should be taken against Spain. Then in December 1946, on the initiative of Poland, the General Assembly adopted a resolution directed to Spain providing that:

. . . if within a reasonable time there is not established a government which derives its authority from the consent of the governed, committed to respect freedom of speech, religion, and assembly, and to the prompt holding of an election in which the Spanish people, free from force and intimidation and regardless of party, may express their will, the Security Council consider the adequate measures to be taken in order to remedy the situation.

Poland and all the Communist members voted in the affirmative. Spain was not admitted until 1955.

Today there is not one member of the United Nations in three which can meet the standard of the Polish resolution. And yet it is those very nations which go about attacking members who do maintain those standards. There is a term for this: *the big lie.*

The second principle: *Human rights must be a political component of American foreign policy, not a humanitarian program.* It is entirely correct to say (as was repeatedly said during all those "years of silence" in Washington) that quiet diplomacy is much the more effective way to obtain near-term concessions from totalitarian regimes with respect to particular individuals who seek our help. But the large result of proceeding in this fashion is that the democracies accommodate to the dictators. Concepts of human rights should be as integral to American foreign policy as is Marxism-Leninism to Soviet or Chinese or Yugoslav operations and planning. Yet it seems clear that this is not what the career officers in the State Department who make up the permanent government wish to see, and the signs already suggest that the Secretary of State is not resisting the permanent government.

At Law Day ceremonies in the spring of 1977, Cyrus R. Vance delivered his first public address since becoming Secretary of State, and chose for his subject "Human Rights and Foreign Policy." "Our human rights policy," he said, "must be understood in order to be effective." He would "set forth the substance of that policy, and the results we hope to achieve."

This effort was surely in order, for the policy was still singularly unformed. The President's single sentence in his inaugural address — "Because we are free we can never be indifferent to the fate of freedom elsewhere" — had led to press speculation, then queries, then to a sequence of presidential acts — for example, a letter to Andrei Sakharov, a meeting with the Soviet dissident Vladimir Bukovsky, and partial statements such as those in an address at the United Nations on March 17, 1977 — but still nothing that could be described as a policy. The impression was that of a President responding at successively higher levels of commitment to successively greater levels of approval, but with no very clear notions of where it would all come out. There is nothing much the matter with this in a democracy. But there comes a time when the agents of policy must be told what to do. This is a Secretary of State's task, and Vance undertook to perform it.

The result, it must be stated, boded disaster. The Secretary's speech missed the whole point. For the entire thrust of his speech was to assert that human rights is not a political issue but rather a humanitarian one, a special kind of international social work. After rousing the rage of the Muscovite and the scorn of Latin American grandees, after stirring the timorousness of European allies and inducing something between anxiety and fear in smaller capitals around the world, it turned out that all we really intended was to be of help to individuals.

The Ford administration established a "Coordinator for Human Rights and Humanitarian Affairs" in the office of the Secretary of State. The coordinator had three deputies: "Refugee and Migration Affairs," "Prisoners of War and Missing-in-Action," and "Human Rights." To reflect the greater salience which these issues are now to have, the Carter administration asked Congress to make the coordinator an Assistant Secretary and this was done. However, in the past, when this kind of change has been made, it has in fact signaled that the Secretary of State was no longer that much interested in the issue involved, and was turning it over to the bureaucracy. Thus, only a few years ago, coordinators or special assistants for environmental affairs and population matters were to be found in the Secretary's office. But with the fading of those issues, they were turned over to the office of the Deputy Assistant Secretary for Environmental and Population Affairs, reporting to the Assistant Secretary for Oceans and International Environmental and Scientific Affairs. Secretary Vance may not have intended to relegate human rights to the destiny of departmental routine, but in organizational terms, this is what was done.*

---

*There is a difference between acting in accord with established principles and reducing a matter to routine. The Monroe Doctrine, for all its variants, was an example of the former; United States immigration policy, of the latter.

Rounding out the pattern of a depoliticized conception of human rights, the Secretary in his speech announced: "We are expanding the program of the Agency for International Development for 'New Initiatives in Human Rights' as a complement to present efforts to get the benefits of our aid to those most in need abroad." He added that the Department's Bureau of Educational and Cultural Affairs would also be involved. He declared our efforts would "range from quiet diplomacy . . . through public pronouncements, to withholding of assistance." We would meet at Belgrade to review the Helsinki accords and "to work for progress there on important human issues: family reunification, binational marriages. . . ." He mentioned that "many [*sic*] nations of the world are organized on authoritarian rather than democratic principles." He did not mention totalitarian governments.

One could soon detect this disposition even in the President's words. Only weeks after the Secretary of State's speech, expressing surprise at the "adverse reaction in the Soviet Union to our stand on human rights," President Carter said: "We have never singled them out. I think I have been quite reticent in trying to publicly condemn the Soviets. I have never said anything except complimentary things about Mr. Brezhnev, for instance." But the Soviets are *necessarily* singled out by any serious human rights offensive — and they know it. They are singled out by the force of their arms: they are the most powerful opponents of liberty on earth today. They are singled out by the force of their ideology which, since the destruction of Nazism and the eclipse of fascism as a school of political thought (Franco's Spain having been its last bastion), remains the only major political doctrine that challenges human rights *in principle*. When the authoritarian regimes of the Right violate human rights nowadays, they never do so in the name of a variant political creed but rather in the name of national security. They must torture, they say, to uproot leftist guerrillas and terrorists; or they must keep political prisoners to protect themselves against armed subversion from without and within. Unlike the Soviets and their ideological progeny in other countries ruled by Marxist-Leninist regimes, these right-wing regimes do not deride liberty as a "bourgeois" illusion. They commit abominations in practice; the Communist countries commit abominations on principle. Anyone who cares about human rights will know what type of abomination is the more destructive of those rights.

According to a presidential aide quoted in mid-1977 by *The New York Times,* the President's human rights initiative, among other things, has alarmed the Soviet leadership. The Soviets had "viewed the United States under the Ford and Nixon administrations . . . as running a kind of defensive, rear guard foreign policy of retreat. . . . Mr. Carter and his advisers feel the Soviet leaders have been dismayed by the thought that their concept of the decline of the West might no longer be valid."* If the human rights initiative of the mid-1970s is sustained, the Soviets will have cause to be dismayed.

This will not be easily done. The forces that made for a "defensive, rear guard foreign policy of retreat" in the administrations of Presidents Nixon and Ford were soon enough in evidence under that of President Carter. They are institutional: they have to do with the way we think. Consider the Carter address at Notre Dame, also given in the spring of 1977, the first comprehensive statement of the foreign policy of the new administration. The President began by reaffirming "America's commitment to human rights as a fundamental tenet of

---

*June 26, 1977. The *Times* may not have known it, but it was onto a government secret here of possibly more interest than the Pentagon Papers. In the first half of the 1970s the Democratic opposition generally attacked the foreign policy of the Nixon-Kissinger-Ford era as aggressive, risk-taking, and sometimes mindlessly anti-Communist. In truth, within the Republican administration itself, and at least within the more sophisticated circles of the Democratic opposition, it was understood that, to the contrary, what was going on was precisely a "kind of defensive, rear guard foreign policy of retreat. . . ." Moreover, it was understood that the Russians understood it this way.

our foreign policy." But when he went on to explain what this commitment required of us, he suddenly changed the subject: "Abraham Lincoln said that our nation could not exist half-slave and half-free. We know that a peaceful world cannot long exist one-third rich and two-thirds hungry."

This is a most startling and extraordinary transition. The first sentence reminds us, truly, that the world today *is* half-slave and half-free. Out of four and a quarter billion persons, something approaching a billion and a half live in totalitarian Marxist states. Freedom House lists a full 40 percent of the world's population in 1978 as "Not Free." We have come to think of this opposition as the East-West conflict. But then, having thus reminded us of it, the President immediately directed our concern away from this conflict to quite a different matter, that of relations between the industrial North and the developing South. He even called on the Soviets, as part of the former group, to join in "common aid efforts" to help the latter (although the Soviets accept no responsibility whatever for the plight of the developing world: in their unwavering view it is altogether our responsibility).

The implication seemed clear: we were to divert our attention from the central political struggle of our time — that between liberal democracy and totalitarian Communism — and focus instead on something else. We can do this, said the President, because we were now "free" of the "inordinate fear of Communism" which led us at times to abandon our values for the values of the totalitarians. But was our fear of Communism "inordinate"? And is there nothing to fear from Communism today? Did the President mean to suggest that the military and ideological competition we face from the Soviet Union has declined? If so, why have the Soviets engaged in the massive military buildup which his administration would soon enough acknowledge? And why do they continue and even intensify their ideological offensive against the West?

Whatever his answer to these questions, the President did

state explicitly that it was our "inordinate fear of Communism" which led us to the "intellectual and moral poverty" of the war in Vietnam. This causal connection can also be challenged. Some of us said at the time that the enterprise was doomed, because it was misconceived and mismanaged. Are we to say now — in this, echoing what our enemies say of us — that it was also wrong or immoral to wish to resist the advance of totalitarianism? President Carter did just that: in July 1979 he declared that the war in Vietnam had been "immoral." This is certainly a legitimate view, and one which many hold. But it is not enough in itself. Those who hold it, especially a President, must have an obligation to state just what they think would have been *moral* behavior on the part of Kennedy and McNamara, Rusk, and the Bundys in 1962 and 1963, when the war commenced in earnest.

Further, those who assert that the challenge of the time ahead is that of North-South relations are, or ought to be, under an obligation to attest that they are not acting from a private agenda which seeks to distract attention from the realities of Soviet behavior. It was an official of the Carter administration who ascribed to predecessors a "foreign policy of retreat." It was for the same officials, if you will, to establish that theirs was different.

Whence to the third principle: *Human rights has nothing to do with our innocence or guilt as a civilization. It has to do with our survival.* President Carter staffed the Department of State and the Department of Defense with curiously opposite groups of persons who attracted each other in a not wholly reassuring way. Put plainly, the leading foreign policy and defense policy officials of his administration made their reputations running the war in Vietnam. The second echelon of officials made *its* reputation by opposing that war. There is something troubling in this cross-generational relationship. The top echelon seemed to seek absolution from their juniors for what the President himself called the "moral and intellectual poverty" of their ideas in the past.

Of the new Secretary of State, Hedrick Smith, of the *New York Times,* reported:

With the hindsight of history, Secretary of State Cyrus R. Vance, who as Deputy Secretary of Defense played a major role in the American buildup in Vietnam, has publicly said that he now feels that "it was a mistake to intervene in Vietnam." And those who know him well say that the Vietnam war is the single most important experience in shaping this current outlook.

One did not ask of the Secretary that he not be influenced by that experience; only that he be thoughtful about it. (At the University of Georgia Law School, where he spoke on Law Day in 1977, he shared the platform with Dean Rusk, a Secretary of State who evidently came to office preoccupied with "the loss of China," the opposite experience.) The Vietnam War was at minimum a mistake because we could not successfully halt a totalitarian advance there — not at costs acceptable to a liberal society. But it did not end the expansion of totalitarianism, nor yet the need to resist. If anything, it added enormously to the importance of ideological resistance, and this precisely is the role of "Human Rights in Foreign Policy."

Guilt as a political weapon is but little understood. Still, it should be evident that it is used quite effectively within the United States and against the United States. Some years back Nathan Glazer observed that the political rhetoric of our age was capable of depicting a prosperous and tolerant and reasonably creative society such as our own as utterly detestable, and could persuade many of those best off in this society that this is exactly the case. In 1977 an Associate Justice of the Supreme Court declared in an opinion handed down from that bench that it were better never to be born than to be born an American and go to "second-rate" schools.

In foreign policy guilt asserts that we are no better, possibly worse, than other nations, and that in particular we have no business asserting our standards as somehow superior to those of others. At a more sophisticated level, a worldly, ex-ambassadorial, Council-on-Foreign-Relations posture will have it that Americans simply must stop being such moralizers.

There is no way to deal with this position save to raise it to the level of awareness, and to repudiate it. Human rights is a weapon in the struggle for the survival of our nation — a nation partly right and partly wrong, as it ever has been and doubtless ever will be. That we have a right and a duty to survive ought to be obvious. That it is not obvious to our political culture is a measure of how savagely our guilt is turned against us.

Guilt can paralyze our relations with the developing world — and this leads to the fourth principle of a sound human rights policy. *The new nations must be made to understand that our commitment to them depends on their ceasing to be agents of the totalitarian attack on democracy.*

Only a handful of these nations are Soviet satellites. But a Marxist might well say that time and again they *objectively* support the Soviet cause. The concept of objective political behavior is, of course, a favorite debating device of Marxists. Thus, Lucio Lombardo Radice, a leading member of the Central Committee of the Italian Communist party, explained in an interview in *Encounter* in 1977 that Stalin in the 1930s realized the dangers of Nazism and ceased attacking Western Social Democrats. "In the situation existing at the time, Stalin was, objectively speaking, supporting the struggle for freedom, democracy, and peace." The time has come to explain to the representatives of a great many nations for which on other grounds we have a good deal of sympathy that, "objectively speaking," they are supporting anti-Semitism, totalitarianism, and war.

An example was on display in 1977 at the International Labor Conference in Geneva. The American labor movement is one of the few groups to have sensed early on the drift of world events and Soviet tactics. In 1974, after the International Labor Organization passed a resolution denouncing Israel for racism, the labor movement, supported by our business representatives, asked that the United States give notice that we would withdraw if such intrusions of antidemocratic politics into the proceedings of ILO did not stop.

The ILO charter requires a two-year notice of intent to withdraw, and this was given in the fall of 1975. The letter made clear that the United States did not want to withdraw. We, after all, had helped to found the ILO. We had joined it when we never joined any other of the League organizations. We have provided the great share of its funds, and it was we who helped turn its attention to the problems of developing nations which now almost exclusively concern it. All we asked was that it stay out of international politics of the kind associated with foul-mouthed excoriations of Israel. This position was characterized by *Trud,* the Soviet labor paper, as a demand by "reactionary circles, and primarily the U.S. delegation . . . to exclude . . . political questions connected with the people's struggle against imperialism, neo-colonialism, and racism."

We got our answer early in the Conference. "Using a procedural device," *The New York Times* reported, "the Communist and Third World countries blocked action on an American-inspired proposal that the assembly's rules be amended to screen out politically motivated resolutions." With a handful of exceptions, the Third World sided with the Communist world against the democratic world.

Thereupon, the Secretary of Labor, Ray Marshall, told a press conference that the United States would now likely leave the International Labor Organization and subsequently we did. It was wrenching to those who have cared much about that organization which once seemed to hold such promise. But why did it happen? Because the Third World *objectively* chose to back Communism against democracy. *They* know this. And they will make a distinct judgment about which way the world is headed depending on whether we make clear to them that we know it. (In point of fact the United States departure seems finally to have impressed our arguments on the ILO, and following the 1979 conference there was talk of our returning, which we have since done.)

Jean-François Revel puts the case at the most extreme in his book, *The Totalitarian Temptation*. He describes a world struggle between a truly revolutionary democratic model of society (to give Secretary Vance his due, he did quote Archibald MacLeish: "The cause of human liberty is now the one great revolutionary cause") and a "Marxist-Leninist-Maoist model, with all its little brothers," implementing a brand of totalitarian socialism which Revel calls "unofficial Stalinism." These, Revel writes, are the real reactionaries, but in his view they are winning, because more and more the world finds such regimes to be more attractive: "Therefore . . . the new American revolution, or the new world revolution that started in America, will probably fail — not because of the United States but because the world steadily rejects democracy."

This is the "worst case," and there are those who are resigned to it and appear already to have made their peace with it. Thus, George Kennan in his book *The Cloud of Danger: Current Realities of American Foreign Policy* asserts that democracy is a North Atlantic phenomenon, and in no way a "natural form of rule for people outside those narrow perimeters." It were folly and worse, he maintains, to go about correcting and improving "the political habits of large parts of the world's population."

This is an arguable point. Does it not display a certain disdain for what is after all a well-documented and seemingly persistent human aspiration, namely, the desire to be free? But my point is a different one. I believe that Mr. Kennan underestimates the impact *on the democracies* of the totalitarian attack. (In 1977 more than half a dozen *British* universities banned Jewish spokesmen from their campuses on the ground that Zionism is a form of racism). Most of the world is not free, and what we can do about that is problematic. But surely we can do something — surely we should do everything — to preserve that part of the world which *is* free. The point, Revel's point, in putting the case at its worst is not to become resigned to the present state of affairs but to elicit countermeasures that will prevent the worst case from coming true. And it is here that the issue of human rights becomes essential.

For the moment our first task is our own defense. An implacable, forceful, and unfailing counterattack — "castigating mercilessly the prevailing mendacity," as Walter Laqueur puts it — whenever the issue of human rights and the nature of our respective societies is raised by adversaries could yet save the democratic world from "Finlandization from within." Human rights is the single greatest weapon we have for the ideological defense of liberty. It would be calamitous if we allowed ourselves to be robbed of it by fear and guilt, inside government or out.

TWO

In 1965, in the first issue of The Public Interest, I wrote of "The Professionalization of Reform," the emergence of a group — class if you will — of persons who lay claim to a special competence and status with respect to the management of social problems. I was on the whole sanguine about this development. Some years and much mischief later Samuel H. Beer, in the 1977 Presidential Address of the American Political Science Association, spoke of the "dual revolution" of the 1960s: "the technocratic takeover" and "the romantic revolt." There appears to be something of a cycle with respect to romanticism. But the professionalism, or so I have thought, is something new. Beer described it in terms which anyone much involved with government will recognize:

In the sixties a new professionalism emerged in the public service. Founded on the expertise produced especially by the enormous advances in the natural and social sciences during the postwar years, it gave to technically and scientifically trained people in government a growing influence on the initiation and formation of public policy. The new professionalism displayed its influence most strikingly in the fields of defense and space policy. But in the diverse fields of domestic

policy — health, housing, urban renewal, highways, welfare, educa-
tion, poverty, environment — the new programs of the sixties and after
drew heavily upon specialized and technical knowledge in and around
the federal bureaucracy for conception and execution.

Even before the development was fully described, Robert Nisbet
rose to deplore it. In a 1975 article entitled "Knowledge
Dethroned" he stated that the public had become quite disen-
chanted with all this technocracy, that if the social scientists in
particular were not universally regarded as "a combination
ne'er-do-well and enemy of both nature and the human commu-
nity," then at least their claims to special knowledge about
social problems were no longer credible. Nisbet ascribed this to
"the behavior of men of knowledge during the last quarter
century and in the whole structure of what came to be called, so
pretentiously, the knowledge of industry." He continued: "An
alien spirit of pride, even arrogance, seized the learned disci-
plines," and their members came forth to "assume the role of
priests in the new church of knowledge." But nothing, or
nothing much, worked.

Joseph Epstein, editor of The American Scholar, *was much*
taken by Nisbet's article and asked a number of social scientists
to contribute to a symposium entitled: "Social Science: The
Public Disenchantment." We were asked to comment on Nisbet's
general point, and further to ask what effect this diminution of
prestige — which Epstein seemed to accept — would have on the
social sciences and on social policy. The replies were predictably
spirited. Harold Orlans, for one, would have nothing to do with
the notion that "the spirit of pride" was "alien" to social science.
It has been there from the beginning, he stated, citing Ecclesi-
astes, rooted in "its founders' search for immutable, infallible
truths about mutable, fallible men."

Our current pretenders to the throne of science were preceded by
enlightenment rationalists, Marxists, racists, geographic determinists,

eugenicists, evolutionists, technocrats, sociometricians, mouse psychologists, national characterologists, and countless breeds of behaviorists. Extravagant, simplistic, ponderous, or monistic explanations are the mark of many influential intellectuals (the influence of ideas has, in any event, little to do with their validity, as the history of astrology, Catholicism, monarchy, or communism shows).

I took a diagonal view. It seemed to me there had been a good amount of manifestly good work done in the 1960s, the effect of which had been precisely to dispose of that presumption of special knowledge and arcane competence, and that this was an achievement of considerable consequence for social policy as well as social science.

I had hoped for some response to this proposition. There was none. And so I repeat here some of what I wrote, for it serves as an introduction to several essays written since.

Briefly, in the course of the 1960s a series of empirical studies all but demolished the expectations that significant social change of the kind the United States was seeking to bring about could be brought about through the means then in vogue and, to some extent, still in vogue. This is not to say nothing worked in that period. On the contrary, the Civil Rights Act of 1965 and the Voting Rights Act of 1964 were monumental successes. But other forms of intervention — the Safe Streets Act, shall we say — were not successful, and it was foreseen that they would not be. No large social theories were involved here: indeed none was attempted. Rather, there was a maturing of two methodological techniques — survey research and computer analysis — which persons of genius had developed a generation earlier. By the 1960s — although talents of the first order were sometimes involved — mere competence could produce findings unattainable, even by a genius, a generation earlier.

For some time I have been searching for a term by which to describe this event — for indeed it had the compactness and uniformity of just that. . . . I wonder if the term Reformation *will not serve. . . . For too long, as Lionel Trilling had foreseen and feared, the tenets of progressive government had been exempt from serious external or*

internal pressure. They had become overassertive and underexamined.
Things were promised that could not be delivered. . . .

   *Along came a group of relatively young and profoundly serious
scholars . . . who challenged all this, and called for a return to
essentials. I am attracted to the image of the Reformation not least by
the fact that, with few exceptions, none of the reformers was of heretical
disposition. Almost all had been and wished to remain faithful
members of the Church. If there are some outside today, let me bear
witness that they were driven out — by their intellectual and moral
inferiors. . . . To my recollection, the "event" commences with the
appearance in 1964 of Andrew Greeley's and Peter Rossi's* The
Education of American Catholics. *The authors had set out to determine the effect of parochial education on religious practice. Contrary to
the assumption of six generations of bishops, they found hardly any.
That year Martin Anderson showed that urban renewal reduces the
housing supply rather than increasing it, as had been assumed for a
generation by housing experts, if not the poor. In 1965 I published a set
of statistical correlations that showed that general economic conditions
had once had a tight relationship to social structure, but that this
relation had disappeared. I predicted that much social disorder was
probably in store. . . . In 1966 James Coleman published his report*
Equality of Educational Opportunity, *which found virtually no
correlation between educational effort and educational results. . . . The
single rehabilitation program that the President's Commission on Law
Enforcement and Administration of Justice could cite as a clear
success, on reexamination turned out to be a clear failure. Jencks, et al.,
in 1973, reached even more bearish conclusions concerning other sorts
of social intervention. . . .*

   *Most of these findings were received with hostility or confusion,
which was only natural. The public remained generally unaware of
what was going on. But in the tougher reaches of the profession —
observe the open prejudice of that description! — the case was quickly-
made that something had happened and things were not as they had
been. . . .*

   *It was feared, and widely charged, that this new research had
conservative political motives. This was calumny, but representative of
this period. On the other hand, there is a sense in which this research
did air certain concerns more common to conservatives than liberals.*

The lively sense that liberals have of the possibility of progress is matched by a conservative sense of the possibility of decline. Both concerns need attending.

The three essays presented here deal with institutions of government which aren't working as well as they might, and in some cases as well as they did. I would like to think there is a basis, however modest, in social science for the arguments presented. Thus the notion that organizations in conflict tend to become like one another is not perhaps cosmic in its implication. Yet it helps explain the paralysis that so soon overcame the Carter administration. It helps. Nothing more.

Resentment against the research findings of the 1960s continues, and has commenced to distort public decisions. As an example, in 1979 a young scholar was first appointed Acting Commissioner of Education and then of a sudden dismissed from the post. It was discovered (sic) that he had been one of Christopher C. Jencks's associates in the preparation of the study Inequality. *As it happens, this group was much on the "left," and for all their findings that income seemed randomly distributed in the United States they managed to propose "socialism" as a solution. (With what irony we do not know.) But the findings were unacceptable. This most illiberal of actions originated among the putatively most liberal elements in the administration. The Vice President's office gave the order.*

Official Washington was silent. Some no doubt thought they were protecting options for social progress by suppressing evidence. I was a member of the task force which drew up the War on Poverty for Lyndon B. Johnson in 1963–1964. I have seen a steady dropping away in the belief that significant social progress can be made, and the spread of the understanding that the prudent public person will not get too much involved.

Did something such overcome the liberal optimism of nineteenth-century Britain? G. K. Chesterton has a striking commentary on Sargent's portrait of Arthur James Balfour:

It is the portrait of a philosopher and a statesman — a sad philosopher and a sad statesman. In its presence we feel the sober truths about the English governing class, its wide and ruinous scepticism, its remaining pillars of responsibility and reason. . . . The tones of the picture are grave with grey and silver, as of the end of a day not wholly either of failure or victory, a day that leaves men fairly honourable and wholly disillusioned. . . .

We haven't exactly a governing class. But we are wholly capable of a "wide and ruinous scepticism."

7.
The Iron Law
of Emulation

An Imperial Presidency Leads to an Imperial Legislature Leads to an Imperial Judiciary

THE QUESTION OF SIZE and of effectiveness in American government is beginning to take on aspects of constitutional as against merely political debate. For the better part of a century now, those who have objected to the size of government, especially the national government, have typically been objecting to the nature of the new functions the government was seeking to carry out. Of late, however, we encounter the argument that government growth has not added to the effectiveness of government, but may even have impeded it. Thus, before Jimmy Carter finished his first year in office, the nation was awash with wonder that the presidency had attempted so much and seemingly achieved so little. At first, political explanations were put forward for this, principally that the President's difficulties were of his own making. But then, with increasing frequency, commentators began asking whether the more important explanation could be found in the way our government at present works, or does not work. It is a matter that deserves inquiry.

Further, to the degree that we are dealing with a question of constitutional dimension, it deserves inquiry carried forward in the spirit of the framers of the Constitution, which was very much a scientific spirit.

To state once more, the establishment of the American government in the latter part of the eighteenth century took its foremost distinctions from the belief of those involved that they were acting upon scientific principles. Hamilton noted, in the ninth *Federalist* paper, that previous republics had had such stormy histories that republicanism had admittedly fallen somewhat into disrepute. This tendency could be overcome thanks to progress in political science:

The science of politics, however, like most other sciences, has received great improvement. The efficacy of various principles is now well understood, which were either not known at all, or imperfectly known to the ancients.

He went on to cite, as examples of "new discoveries," the various constitutional institutions with which we are now familiar: separation of powers, the system of checks and balances, popular representation in the legislature, the independent judiciary, and so on.

Whatever the impression, American government has maintained this early disposition. American political science has for the most part been a pragmatic discipline while American political scientists have not always been impractical men. The sixth president of the American Political Science Association became the twenty-eighth President of the United States.

It is in order, then, to expect that there should now be forthcoming a considerable effort to diagnose what so many consider to be the sickness of government in our time, a sickness associated with grossness, with the proposition that government is too big and doesn't work.

Within the federal government, developments now several generations old have caused the executive branch to become greatly enlarged, and, apparently in consequence, to function with greater difficulty. These developments have more recently appeared in the legislative branch, which commences to have similar difficulties. And these are now beginning to appear within the judiciary as well.

In the effort to understand this process, a good place to begin is with the familiar notion that by creating three branches and a system of checks and balances which enabled each to impede the functioning of the others, the framers of the Constitution built conflict into the American system. They thought it was inevitable, and on the whole desirable. If there was a disposition, it was for more conflict, not less.

This was a bold idea then and it remains a bold idea today. Most governing systems assume an inherent and ever more manifest harmony of interests and compatibility of behavior. Marxists, for example, presumably still await the withering away of a conflict-free Soviet state. As we look at the experience of the two systems of government, those who devised the American one surely emerge as men who knew more about what the world is really like. Or, alternatively, who were more honest about it.

In that same spirit of realism, James Q. Wilson — the political scientist of our generation who has most usefully studied bureaucracy in its various adversarial modes — holds that organizations come to resemble the organizations they are in conflict with. If one football team begins using offensive and defensive squads, its opponents will soon be doing so too. The German sociologist Georg Simmel pointed out in the early years of the century that organizations in conflict may *wish* their opponents to resemble them, even, surprisingly, in the degree of their power. Elaborating on Simmel, Lewis Coser writes:

If . . . there exists a rough balance of power, as in pluralistic, multi-group societies, the more strongly organized adversary may actually prefer that the weaker not fight with "unconventional weapons" (corresponding to a different organizational structure), but use weapons similar to his own, making it possible to fight according to comparable rules.

This insight clarifies many otherwise inexplicable phenomena, as in labor relations, where after a certain point big employers clearly preferred to deal with big unions; or, conversely, where Samuel Gompers, seeking to organize American workers, encouraged employers to organize as well.

The applicability of this theory — which might be called the Iron Law of Emulation — to American government is clear. We may put it thus: Whenever any branch of the government acquires a new technique which enhances its power in relations to the other branches, that technique will soon be adopted by those other branches as well.

Consider the Bureau of the Budget (now called the Office of Management and Budget), which was established in 1921. The Bureau of the Budget gave the President an enormous advantage over the Congress. In this all-important function of government, the President had a unified, centralized command as against a dispersed and often internally divided congressional force. Congress sustained defeat after defeat as successive Presidents raised federal expenditures to ever new heights. Interestingly, it was only when the time came that Congress for once wished to spend more money than the President — which is to say during the impoundment controversy with President Nixon in 1973–1974 — that Congress created a Congressional Budget Office of its own, and achieved a roughly equivalent competence in the techniques of fiscal management and disputation.

It might have been supposed that the executive would have resisted this, but the evidence (confirming Simmel) is otherwise. The executive seems almost to have welcomed the appearance at the other end of Pennsylvania Avenue of an organization similar to its own with which to conduct the annual Battle of the Budget. We can assume that at OMB it is much more agreeable to be dealing with officials at the CBO who not only know what the GNP deflator for the last fiscal year is, but who care.

This migration of technique from the executive to the legislative has been going on from the beginning of the twentieth century. Further thought would likely produce a more respectable taxonomy, but present purposes will be served by a list that begins with buildings and ends with attitudes.

In 1902 President Theodore Roosevelt built the West Wing of the White House, where the Oval Office is located. Of a sudden the President was an executive. He no longer worked in his living room, but had an office building in the manner of the business leaders of the age. (Here one observes the federal government as a whole adopting the techniques of the business world with which it was then increasingly in conflict.) The very next year the House of Representatives voted itself an office building, and the year after that the Senate did also.

As is well known, each branch continues to build more office buildings for itself, each of which fills up (such are the demands of the conflict with the other branches) until over-crowding requires yet another building. In 1978 and again in 1979 there were efforts in the Senate to stop work on a third office building, but nothing availed. This was not the first such conflict. Originally a senator's office was his desk on the Senate floor. These desks proved inadequate, and in the 1830s three-inch-high mahogany writing boxes were added to the desks. Daniel Webster refused to have his desk altered on the grounds that if his predecessor could have done without the additional space, so could he. His desk, now assigned the senior senator from New Hampshire, remains topless, or boxless as you will. But since 1909, when the first Senate Office Building opened, the expansion of space has been relentless. In the debates of 1978–1979 it was pointed out that the alternative to a third building was to continue renting the equivalent amount of space for staff already on the Senate payroll.

The man who has traveled abroad has an advantage in certain kinds of argument over one who has not. President and Congress stayed home until 1905, when President Theodore Roosevelt went to Panama. Next, President Taft went there also. Then President Wilson went to Paris. A generation later, Presidents spent an important segment of their time traveling in other countries. In 1954, Congress began to provide easily accessible funds for its own travel abroad. Today presidential and congressional groups crisscross each other in the farthest reaches of the planet. The practice seems even to have begun of Presidents' arranging to meet congressmen abroad, possibly because of difficulty in getting their schedules together in Washington.

The presidency acquired an investigative organization, the FBI (technically in 1908, but reaching its present status in 1924, with the appointment of J. Edgar Hoover as director), which was a formidable if not always straightforward weapon. There is now discussion in the Senate of establishing an investigatory arm for such purposes as screening presidential appointees, a function heretofore performed by the FBI.

Access to foreign intelligence is a key element in getting one's way in disputes over foreign policy. In 1947, the presidency obtained the Central Intelligence Agency, and for a period was uncontested master of the intelligence "secrets." Congress retaliated not by establishing an intelligence service of its own, but by creating, in 1976, the Senate Select Committee on Intelligence, with complete access to CIA information. The House, in 1977, established a similar committee.

In 1962, the presidency acquired the Office of Science and Technology, having previously, in 1957, established the President's Science Advisory Committee. In 1974, Congress acquired the Office of Technology Assessment with an Advisory Council that serves essentially the same function that PSAC once did.

Economic "expertise" is, of course, another characteristic technique of modern organization. In 1946, the presidency obtained the Council of Economic Advisers, a powerful institution not really matched by the Joint Economic Committee established by the 1974 legislation. Still, the staff of that committee does give Congress its own experts with which to dispute those of the President.

This pattern — of the executive branch acquiring a new technique, followed one, two, or three decades later by an equivalent action on the part of the Congress — is now well set; and it has come to involve the Congress in a great many executive functions. Thus in 1963, the presidency acquired the Special Representative for Trade Negotiations. In 1973, the Senate Finance Committee established a Subcommittee on International Trade, whose members are official advisers to the President's trade negotiators. In part, this mixing of functions may be seen as an attempt by one branch to prevail in conflict by coopting the other, which it invites into the decision-making process so that the final decision will be supported. But in even larger part it is an instance of the Iron Law of Emulation.

A more subtle process involves the emulation by one branch of another in order to eliminate any appearance of disparate levels of legitimacy. In 1941, the executive branch established the Committee on Fair Employment Practices. In 1975, members of the House established a Fair Employment Practices Committee (with an interesting mix of representatives and staff members). A Senate bar on employment discrimination was adopted in 1977.

For members of the executive, ethical standards, including financial disclosure, were promulgated by President Johnson in 1965. The House created a Committee on Official Conduct in

1967. In 1976, the Commission on the Operation of the Senate, chaired by Senator Harold Hughes, advocated the adoption of explicit standards. The task was completed by a committee chaired by Senator Gaylord Nelson, and resulted in the Senate's adoption of such a code in 1977.

The bureaucratized and differentiated structure of the executive and, increasingly, the legislative branches has not yet appeared in the judiciary. But there are signs that the judiciary is beginning to take on *functions* which are invariably associated with bureaucratization and differentiation. This is the rise of what Abram Chayes, in a May 1976 *Harvard Law Review* article, has called "public law litigation." Traditionally, adjudication has been understood to be a process for resolving among private parties disputes which have not been privately settled. But Professor Chayes holds that this traditional view cannot account for much of what is now actually happening in federal trial courts. Civil litigation increasingly involves determination of issues of public law, whether statutory or constitutional, and frequently terminates in an ongoing affirmative decree. The lawsuit does not merely clarify the meaning of the law, remitting the parties to private ordering of their affairs, but itself establishes a regime ordering the future interaction of the parties and of absent ones as well, subjecting them to continuing judicial oversight.

Chayes contends that such a role for the courts, pursued through decrees in class action suits, is unprecedented and raises serious concerns of legitimacy. He allows that the experience so far has been mixed. Reapportionment decrees, as an example, have in his view worked well, but it remains to be seen how successful federal judges will be at running mental institutions. He is, however, optimistic:

[D]espite its well rehearsed inadequacies, the judiciary may have some important institutional advantages for the tasks it is assuming:
First, and perhaps most important, is that the process is presided

over by a judge. His professional tradition insulates him from narrow political pressures, but, given the operation of the federal appointive power and the demands of contemporary law practice, he is likely to have some experience of the political process and acquaintance with a fairly broad range of public policy problems.

Second, the public law model permits ad hoc applications of broad national policy in situations of limited scope. The solution can be tailored to the needs of the particular situation and flexibly administered or modified as experience develops with the regime established in the particular case.

Third, the procedure permits a relatively high degree of participation by representatives of those who will be directly affected by the decision. . . .

Fourth, the court, although traditionally thought less competent than legislatures or administrative agencies in gathering and assessing information, may have unsuspected advantages in this regard. . . .

Fifth, the judicial process is an effective mechanism for registering and responding to grievances generated by the operation of public programs in a regulatory state. . . .

Sixth, the judiciary has the advantage of being non-bureaucratic. . . . It does not work through a rigid, multilayered hierarchy of numerous officials, but through a smallish, representative task force, assembled ad hoc, and easily dismantled when the problem is finally resolved. . . .

But if the federal courts are going to make law (a legislative function) and enforce law (an executive function) — which is what Chayes's term *the public law litigation model* implies — they are inevitably going to find themselves in conflict with the legislative and executive branches. In that conflict they will be just as inevitably led to adopt the techniques of the other two branches in order to prevail in the ensuing conflict; and, as Simmel would have it, they will be encouraged to do so. They will thus develop a "rigid multilayered hierarchy of numerous officials" of their own.

On this point I find Donald L. Horowitz, in his fine study,

The Courts and Social Policy (1977), rather more persuasive
than Chayes. After examining four cases of "public law
litigation," Horowitz concludes:

The four cases make plain the impotence of the courts to supervise the
implementation of their decrees, their impatience with protracted
litigation, and their limited ability to monitor the consequences of
their action. Called upon increasingly to perform administrative
functions because they are not burdened with administrative rigidi-
ties, the courts are also not blessed with administrative capabilities.

What experience suggests, however, is that if any organization
in need of administrative capabilities does not have them, it
will seek to acquire them.

Politics, as Maurice Cranston contended in his inaugural
lecture at the London School of Economics (1971), is an
argument about the future. Rarely, one would add, is any
person or party entirely correct. Usually predictions are
significantly wrong, and this is the problem the courts confront. Up until now, the primary task of the federal courts has
been to rule on the meaning of existing laws, the Constitution
foremost. The judges and justices can with some equanimity
rule on just what the Founding Fathers intended, for it is
extremely difficult to prove they are wrong, and, in any event,
they never *are* wrong until they themselves so decree. (Thus
the *Brown* [1954] decision declared *Plessy* v. *Ferguson* [1896] to
have been wrong. At this moment a considerable number of
scholars, notably Walter Berns in his *First Amendment and the
Future of American Democracy* [1977], hold that the Court's
interpretation of the "establishment clause" of the First
Amendment is simply wrong. But until the Court changes its
mind, the interpretation stands.)

But what about predictions of the future, where most of us
mostly are wrong and can be shown to be? What about

predictions of the therapeutic consequences of one form of psychiatric aid as against another? A court without an elaborate bureaucracy to fuzz the results and conceal its mistakes will soon be judged no court at all, but merely a panel of well-intentioned amateurs exposed to all the world as bumblers. The Court, accordingly, will get a bureaucracy.

In 1975, the architect of the Capitol was authorized by Congress "to prepare studies and develop a Master Plan for future developments within the United States Capitol Grounds, for the future enlargement of such grounds. . . ." Phase II of the architect's report appeared in August 1977. Note these passages concerning the Supreme Court:

The Office of the Marshal and the Administrative Assistant to the Chief Justice have outlined the Court's current and future space needs based on trends in employment and the Court's load. Since 1970 there has been a steady increase in support positions. To maintain the high quality of judicial consideration of an increasing case load, additional law clerks, secretarial, and messenger positions were added to the staffs of the Justices' Chambers. This has also led to the creation of a Legal Office staffed by career professionals. Of similar importance has been the appearance of career professionals in various offices of the Court to meet the challenges that have been experienced throughout the federal and state Judiciaries.

In predictable response, the executive has been getting itself judges. In August 1972, the title Hearing Examiner within the executive branch was changed to Administrative Law Judge. Indeed, there are now 1,071 administrative law officers in the executive branch who are formally designated Administrative Law Judge, twice the number of federal district and appellate judges. Twenty-nine agencies of the executive branch now have such judges; the Social Security Administration alone has 660. In the meantime, there are another 100 examiners, attorneys, and appeal board members within the executive branch who seem to have appropriated the title of Administrative Judge, though this is not a "proper" civil service category.

Once again, a more elaborate taxonomy will perhaps be developed some day, but the general pattern seems distinct. We don't yet think of this as a generalized pattern, but we behave as if the pattern had become general. Thus in the 1930s the congressional party (as it were) directed its strongest attack against the growth of the executive under the New Deal. A generation or so later, the presidential party in the person of Gerald Ford attacked the "Billion Dollar Congress." In that same election year, the successful candidate, Jimmy Carter, attacked both, with special emphasis on the "bloated, horrible bureaucracy."

In Senate hearings, Claiborne Pell of Rhode Island, a careful and perceptive committee chairman, observed that the Senate budget for fiscal year 1978 was to be greater than the budget of seventy-four countries. The Washington *Post Magazine* of April 23, 1978, featured on its cover a story entitled "The Senate: Snarled in Bureaucracy?" This story was perfectly recognizable as the same story that began to be written about the executive a generation or so earlier. The judiciary's time is at hand, as evidenced by the appearance of scholarly works — such as Nathan Glazer's 1975 paper "Towards an Imperial Judiciary." Such a judiciary will in due course be followed by investigatory journalism. (Indeed it has been, with the appearance in 1979 of *The Brethren: Inside the Supreme Court* by Bob Woodward and Scott Armstrong, a work without precedent in the history of the Court, and owing to Mr. Woodward's Watergate fame, a considerable if questionable success. In a devastating review, "The Justices and the Journalists," in *The New York Times Book Review*, Renata Adler suggests that the book could not have been written without the proliferation of clerks, which is to say, of staff.

There used to be one clerk per Justice; even in the late years of the Warren Court, when there were two, the relation was close. A clerk was, for a year, an apprentice, son, research assistant, ghost-writer, friend. . . . Whatever it was, it was a unique and fine relation. Now, with the mushrooming of clerkships (four to each Justice), there is a possibility that they have become a bureaucracy like any other — with confidences to violate. . . .

And indeed the book was one long "leak" from former clerks of information the public has no great need to know, but whose revelation might well affect the relationships of the Justices and hence a supreme institution of government.)

The most consequential result of all this is overwork. It may come as a surprise to the public to learn that persons in positions of authority in government are overworked, but almost all are. (Whatever, if anything, scientific management may have to say on the subject, I offer the impression that overwork begins at some point between a sixty- and seventy-hour work week made a year-round routine.) To be sure, persons who are overworked do not necessarily achieve a great deal. Overwork typically appears at a point where productivity begins to fall off. The whole of modern government is made up of men and women trying to jam ever greater resources into the ever tightening angle of an asymptotic production curve.

Overwork begins as a technique, a new way of achieving a goal, usually that of prevailing in conflict, but it soon becomes a condition in its own right, rather like bureaucracy itself. And as with most of the techniques we have discussed, overwork first appeared in the executive.

In general, the modern economy has brought about an inversion of effort as between managerial and production workers. What were known as "bankers' hours" certainly obtained in the government offices of the nineteenth century when there really wasn't that much for bankers or bureaucrats to do. Recall Trollope's portrait, in *The Three Clerks* (1874), of Mr. Fidus Neverbend, the premier workaholic in the civil service of his time:

Mr. Fidus Neverbend was an absolute dragon of honesty. . . .
A quarter of an hour spent over a newspaper was in his eyes a
downright robbery. If he saw a man so employed, he would divide out
the total of salary into hourly portions, and tell him to a fraction of
how much he was defrauding the public. If he ate a biscuit in the
middle of the day, he did so with his eyes firmly fixed on some
document, and he had never been known to be absent from his office
after ten or before four.

This compulsive wretch worked a full six-hour day!

Or consider the rather more inspiring figure of Henry L.
Stimson as Secretary of State during the administration of
President Hoover, a time of vast international crisis. Hoover
responded by spending ever more time on the job; Stimson
responded by horseback riding. In *On Active Service in Peace
and War*, Mr. Stimson and McGeorge Bundy write:

Mr. Hoover was a worker, capable of more intense and prolonged
intellectual effort than any other man Stimson ever met; his cure for
all his troubles as president was more and harder work. Stimson was
not made that way; his strength depended on regular rest, substantial
vacations, and constant physical exercise, nor did he accept as
suitable exercise Mr. Hoover's game of medicine ball — it seemed to
him as dull as weight lifting, and about as refreshing. More and more
after the middle of 1930, Stimson found himself oppressed by the
official atmosphere of Washington.

As with much else in the New Deal, then, overwork began
with Hoover, and was soon institutionalized. Government
became something of a trial of strength. Those in the Cabinet
and the White House not capable of sixteen-hour days were
driven from the field as inexorably as were the fainthearted
and weak-limbed in the tournaments of medieval courts.

Inevitably, overwork turned up in Congress. President
Roosevelt's Hundred Days are so designated because his first
Congress met March 9, 1933, and went home June 15, not to
return until the following January (for a "long" session that

lasted until June 18). In the 1930s, sessions began to lengthen. Then came war, and the first session of the 77th Congress (1941) met for 365 days. After the war, the duration of sessions dropped back, but in the 1960s it lengthened again. The first session of the 91st Congress (1969) ran 355 days. The Congress is now almost permanently in session.

The number of votes per session has increased more even than the number of days. In the first session of the 83rd Congress (1953), there were 80 votes in the Senate and 71 in the House. In the first session of the 95th Congress (1977), there were 636 and 706 respectively. A congressional study committee in 1977 found that for one third of their day, members of the House were supposed to be in at least two places at once, this being the result of multiple committee assignments.

Time, of course, is what is most in demand in an overworked institution. Energy is what is most lacking. "Energy in the executive," said Hamilton, "is a leading character in the definition of good government." Something not different is the case with the legislative. But energy is the first quality to disappear when the work load becomes too heavy. Energy and creativity.

Thus, in the sixteenth month of the Carter administration the *Wall Street Journal* reported "combat fatigue" had already set in: "A key White House aide talks of leaving. The general reason: loss of the exhilaration needed to endure seventy hour work weeks." Good men and women, who should be just about, in an earlier image, getting their second wind, were already used up. An absurd waste, but part of the system they were caught up in. To relieve the burden, President Carter proposed just the wrong remedy. In February 1978, he asked Congress to authorize one hundred "supergrade" and "executive level" employees for his immediate White House staff. This was surely startling in a chief executive who came to office not just formally pledged to cut the size of his office (as Presidents now routinely do) but seemingly determined to do so. Adding new

White House staff will, of course, require that those already there work even harder to keep up with one another.

By the time of the Carter administration the situation had become absurd. In 1979, in the midst of a major political crisis for the President, the press obtained a long memorandum sent to him by the chief of his domestic staff on dealing with the crisis. The advice was candid and detailed, and accordingly embarrassing, at least to the chief domestic adviser. Not really, the President's press secretary explained to the press, because the memorandum was not written by him, but rather by a member of *his* staff. Rumor in Washington had it that it had been leaked by a member of the staff of another chief of staff also in the White House. But it is enough that the staff now have staff.

The President suffers, and the presidency. In 1978, Arthur S. Link, the biographer of Wilson, gave the *Princeton Alumni Weekly* an interview comparing Wilson with Carter. He noted that Wilson "had a very warm working relationship with Congress." Asked why such a relation seemed to elude President Carter — and, one could have added, so many recent Presidents — Link replied:

The answer is complicated, but one main reason is the enormous White House staff, which has been a buffer between the President and Congress, and the people, too, and the heads of governmental departments. The President now has so many assistants of one kind and another that he spends his time running the staff, and the staff runs the country, or tries to. That was definitely not true in Wilson's time. . . .

A President with a staff of 400 has to spend most of his time dealing with that staff. You have to take the position that you are the leader. Truman put it very well: "The buck stops here." FDR had only two or three assistants in the White House before 1938.

The common assumption, Link continued, that it "has to be this way," is simply wrong: "If we had a Wilson in the White

House we'd see a dramatic change." This was not intended as personal criticism but was simply the observation of a wise and practiced historian concerning the effect institutions have on those who presided over them. Link concluded:

It's axiomatic today that the President has to have a battery of speechwriters. This began with FDR, and it's been assumed ever since that a President hasn't the time — or the capacity! — to write his own speeches. The whole office of the Presidency has become so bureaucratized and overstaffed that there isn't time for the President to perform the leadership role.

"There isn't time." This is the heart of it. After a point, reached sooner perhaps, than generally realized, increased assistance begins to defeat its purposes by consuming the very time and energy it was supposed to free up. The small group takes on a life of its own; it becomes an organization in its own right and commences to behave as organizations behave. Entropy mounts as more and more energy is consumed simply in producing outcomes within the organization itself.*

(More than just overwork is involved. The process can become pathologic, as Wilson himself foresaw. In *Constitution-*

---

*For a goodly part of 1979 my Senate staff devoted a fair proportion of its energies to negotiating with the staff of the Senate Ethics Committee over the question of whether I had used the word *I* more times per page in a proposed newsletter than the "Regulations Governing the Use of the Mailing Frank" permitted. A 1975 change to Section 3210(a)(5)(C) — *sic* — decreed that "Personally phrased references . . . shall not appear more than five times on a page." The essence of the argument was whether the term *we*, as in "we New Yorkers," implied the term *I*. A sample paragraph from the staff director of the Ethics Committee:

We . . . advised that the Committee has not yet ruled upon what is meant by "or other personal references," such as, "we," and "this office." It was suggested that until such time as we are able to obtain guidance from the Committee, that references which, arguably, might be construed as a personal reference, be avoided in situations where if counted, the total of all personal references on a given page would exceed five.

al Government in the United States [1908] he wrote: "Men of ordinary physique and discretion cannot be Presidents and live, if the strain be not somehow relieved. We shall be obliged always to be picking our chief magistrates from among wise and prudent athletes — a small class." Did Wilson himself break under the strain? No one knows, or will know.)

Overwork routinely leads to efforts to improve efficiency along lines of what is termed organizational rationalism. The first such effort in the executive, the Commission on Department Methods, headed by Assistant Secretary of the Treasury Charles Hallin Keep, was established in 1905. President Franklin D. Roosevelt established the more noted Committee on Administrative Management, headed by Louis Brownlow, in 1936. The first congressional committee of this sort was the Joint Committee on the Organization of Congress, established at the end of 1944 and chaired by Senator Robert LaFollette, Jr., of Wisconsin. Many of its recommendations became part of the landmark Legislative Reorganization Act of 1946. It was this law which established "professional" committee staff for the Congress, the congressional variant of the civil service, to be appointed "without regard to political affiliations and solely on the basis of fitness to perform the duties of the office."

The most recent, and notable, effort in the legislative branch was the Commission on the Operation of the Senate, established in 1975. The report *Toward a Modern Senate* was notable for a refreshingly candid statement of the nature of a senator's day — "long, fragmented and unpredictable. On the average, Senators put in an eleven hour day" — and a not less candid statement of the goal to help Congress organize to counter the expanding power of the presidency and the executive branch, "an expansion that recently threatened to upset the constitutional separation of powers. . . ." Predictably, the commission proposed that the Senate adopt more of the techniques of the executive.

Already the legislative branch had acquired one of the more important powers of the executive, the Congressional Veto, which was created by the Reorganization Act of 1932, and serves very much as does the executive veto provided in the Constitution. In 1975 alone, congressional veto provisions were incorporated into 58 laws.

As in the case of its acquiring judges of its own, the executive branch has responded to competition from the legislature by emulating legislative techniques. We could, for example, interpret the establishment, and now proliferation, of independent regulatory commissions — standing committees, as it were — as a legislative technique planted in the executive. This began, of course, with the Interstate Commerce Commission in 1887, an era of relative congressional ascendancy over the presidency.

Another, subtler, example may be found in the way Presidents now seem to negotiate with and mediate among their bureaucracies, much in the manner of House and Senate conferees working out their differences over a bill. Thus in the spring of 1978, after one full year of interdepartmental negotiation, President Carter announced his urban policy. It contained no initiatives of any consequence. It was rather an immensely complex agreement as to what new resources would be allocated to dozens of different, and already established, programs. Indeed, it was not a policy at all, for nothing of that order could have been achieved by negotiation.

The ultimate result of these parallel developments may be simply stated: stalemate. As each branch acquires more of the techniques of the others, especially as executive branch techniques migrate to the other two, each becomes more capable of thwarting the others' purposes, *and probably more disposed* to do so. For while there is surely a disposition to leave to others tasks for which one has no special capacity, this disposition disappears when everyone "knows" everything because everyone has his own information and experts — as is increasingly the case with each of the three branches of our government.

Is it not also likely that as the techniques of the three

branches become more alike, the branches will become more homogeneous? Or is that a tautology? The point is that the branches were intended to be distinctive and to attract distinctive personalities; and they have long done so. The judicial temperament is a real thing. Anyone who has been required to make choices for the judiciary comes to know it and respect it, even if he cannot too closely define it. The ability to manage is a distinctive gift which we associate with persons called executives, and is, we hope, to be found in the executive branch. The genius, the central, the all-informing, all-pervasive principle of the legislative branch, is that of representativeness. As each district, each state, is different, so each representative and senator is different and should be. None is like any other, and none is expected to be. If there is pressure on the individual, it is for him *not* to conform to his fellows. That is what is lost when bureaucratic routine and Weberian predictability take over from the principle of representativeness.

If a large (and unsupported) forecast may be permitted, it is that the long-run effect of competitive emulation will be to create government by submerged horizontal bureaucracies that link the three branches of government. They will speak their own language and stay in place while their constitutional masters come and go. (For some time, political scientists have recognized vertical bureaucratic ties that link state, local, and national government: the highway profession, for example, or social welfare.) Thus President Carter began by ordering each of his cabinet officers to *read* all regulations before signing and promulgating them. But this soon became impossible. The bureaucracy writes them and signs them, and, as the Washington *Star* bravely strives to establish, heaven help any outsider who tries to read them. They are probably comprehensible to the committee staff of the Congress, who draft the legislation which the regulations typically carry out. But I know it to be true in my case, and I cannot suppose I am alone, that most legislative language is incomprehensible. One depends on translators. One has the impression, little more, that judicial decrees are increasingly the work of staff. The end result of all this is surely predictable, almost, again, tautological: a mutation of democratic, elective government.

The question, then, is of a constitutional order. Americans, understandably, tend to think of constitutional change in terms of the amendment process. But this is not the only way change takes place. Certainly the federal judiciary has expanded its power relative to the Congress and the executive. Raoul Berger of the Harvard Law School has written that, along with Philip Kurland, he considers that "the usurpation by the judges of general governmental powers on the pretext that its authority derives from the Fourteenth Amendment" represents "the most immediate constitutional crisis of our present time." Should the tax revolt of the 1970s lead to a constitutional convention (which it well could, if three quarters of the state legislatures call for one), we may see an actual constitutional convulsion in our time. In any event, the American Constitution can evolve rather in the way the British Constitution is said to evolve, and indeed does. And the British experience ought to serve as a particular lesson to us just now.

I do not pretend to any special competence here, but I believe it is fair to say that in the course of the twentieth century the British have more or less abandoned the traditional functions of Parliament. I cannot imagine that at any point in the process the British electorate would have voted to do this; but successive incremental changes over three quarters of a century have brought it about as an accomplished fact. Every five years or so, as things now are, the British elect a body of persons (still called Parliament in accord with the British willingness to change anything but the appearance of things), which in turn elects a chief executive called Prime Minister.

This Prime Minister takes over the executive branch (called Whitehall) and governs with only the barest reference to Parliament for the next five years. (In 1978 a member of the cabinet of the British Labour government of that time described Parliament to me as being analogous to an American nominating convention.) Legislation takes the mode of the executive order under the American presidency. The bureaucracy drafts it, the Prime Minister sends it to Parliament, and with the rarest exception, the bills are enacted by the Prime Minister's majority, which exists by definition, else he would not be Prime Minister. On five occasions since 1945 a British Prime Minister lost his majority in an election. He was then replaced by another Prime Minister, who ruled in precisely the same manner. Parliament as such has no power to differ with the Prime Minister on any issue save the ultimate one of who should be Prime Minister.

In the Sieff Memorial Lecture at the Royal Institution in 1977, Roy Jenkins allowed that in theory Parliament is sovereign, but in practice:

What parliamentary sovereignty really means is party sovereignty: and a party that wins a bare majority of seats in the House of Commons enjoys the full fruits of sovereignty, even if it has won the votes of well under half the electorate. So long as its members obey the whip, such a party can force through whatever legislation it wishes, even on matters which in most other democracies would require an amendment to the constitution. Although the courts have begun to show more willingness to challenge the executive than they used to do, their ability to resist a determined government with a parliamentary majority at its back is severely limited.

Jenkins in fact suggests that the British at last get themselves some measure of judicial review to deal with the enormous and effectively unchallenged power of the civil service. In passing, he notes that the impotent Westminster Parliament "is notoriously overworked." Precisely: it has so little to do.

That the British, who think of themselves as caring very much about such matters and as attending to them, have let their institutions decline so is not a good omen.* But then we are in a far less etiolated condition. Our situation is not one of a single branch superseding the others. For some time we have had a pattern of one branch frustrating the efforts of the other, with moments of intensive cooperation coming at most every generation or so. We do not really have stalemate yet. But signs do appear.

Consider the question of the roving political elites, whose quest for power takes them first to one branch, then to another, bringing new techniques of conflict and *casus belli* with them. First the White House staff, then the congressional committee, then the judicial chambers. Their enthusiasms diminish as democracy catches up. They move on. But gigantism remains and entropy grows. This pattern needs to be identified more frequently, and very much to be resisted.

How might we respond? Here I would be adventurous. I would dare to think that the American polity is as capable now as it was at the outset of adopting wise modes of government because we think them wise. What James Q. Wilson writes is probably true. What Simmel wrote is probably true. Yet it is also true that a people that sees its self-interest in not doing what comes naturally can do otherwise. That may be more a wish than a rule, but who will know unless we try?

If the Iron Law of Emulation is to be broken, it must first be recognized. We require some consciousness-raising. The tendency to introduce new conflict techniques can be restrained by the knowledge that they will almost certainly be matched. Hence we need first to become more aware of the pattern of one branch adopting the techniques of the other, and to sense the futility of it all. Just this much might have real consequence.

---

*In 1979 the new Conservative government in Britain moved to establish a number of standing committees in the House of Commons which would have oversight responsibilities for departmental activities. This could prove an important assertion of parliamentary authority.

8.
Social Science
and the Courts

ROM THE TIME, at the beginning of the century, that American legal scholars and jurists began to speak of the "science of law" it was rather to be assumed that the courts would in time find themselves involved with the social sciences. This was perhaps more a matter of probability than of certainty, for it was at least possible that the "legal realists," or "progressive realists," as they are variously denominated, would have found the social science of that and subsequent periods insufficiently rigorous for their standards — a case at least some social scientists, then as now, would have volunteered to make for them. But Roscoe Pound and Benjamin Cardozo and Oliver Wendell Holmes, Jr., were indeed realists, and seemingly were prepared to make do with what was at hand, especially when there was such a correspondence with the spirit and structure of their own enterprise.

In 1908, Roscoe Pound in a seminal article, "Mechanical Jurisprudence," declared in the *Columbia Law Review*: "We have ... the same task in jurisprudence that has been achieved in philosophy, in the natural sciences, and in politics.

We have to ... attain a pragmatic, a sociological legal science."

This passage suggests, of course, an alternative explanation for the easy acceptance of the social sciences by the lawyers: to wit, that Pound and his associates were not themselves intolerably rigorous. For what else are we to think of the suggestion, even in 1908, that philosophy and politics had been advancing arm in arm with the natural sciences toward some presumed methodological maturity!

Equally we may wonder at the legal realists' seeming perception of "natural law" as prescientific. It may have been for them, but it was nothing of the sort to the framers of the Constitution, for whom "natural law" and scientific law were parts of an integrated understanding of the behavior of both physical objects and human beings. As Martin Diamond has reminded us, the framers' respect for human rights, which constituted liberty as they understood it, was not an idiosyncratic "value" of a remote culture. Rather, liberty was seen as *the* primary political good, of whose goodness any intelligent man would convince himself if he knew enough history, philosophy, and science. Indeed, it was because our constitutional principles seemed so self-evident, so much at harmony with the results of enquiry in other fields, that the Founders felt such confidence in them.

But this is perhaps to cavil. The point is that as between the legal scholars and jurists of two and three generations ago, who were seeking to establish a "science of law," and those seeking to establish scientific principles and methods in, say, sociology, there was indeed that symmetry of technique and purpose which Paul Horgan has observed in the arts and sciences of most eras.

There was a corresponding bustle of organization and a discovery of likemindedness among persons who may have thought themselves quite alone in their new, and sometimes radical, purposes. At the same time that a new judicial philosophy was making its appearance, the social sciences were organizing themselves. The Anthropological Association was founded in 1902; the American Political Science Association in 1903; the American Sociological Association in 1905. The innovators in the legal and academic realms were, in the popular saying of the period, made for each other.

Even so, the process whereby social science argument became more prominent in the proceedings and decisions of American courts was gradual, and followed the equally gradual rise to ascendency of the "progressive realists," to use Alexander M. Bickel's term, from whom, as he wrote, "the Warren Court traced its lineage."

In its most famous decision, *Brown* v. *Board of Education* (1954), the Warren Court drew upon a spectrum of social science — ranging from discrete psychological experiments to broad-ranging economic and social enquiry — in reversing the Court's earlier ruling in *Plessy* v. *Ferguson* (1896), which had established the separate-but-equal standard in racial matters. Taking their lead from the Supreme Court, subordinate federal courts began to resort to social science findings to guide all manner of decisions, especially in the still troubled field of schooling. But they extended this to questions of tax policies, of institutional confinement and care, of crime and punishment, and a hitherto forbidding range of ethical issues.

From the time that Louis D. Brandeis began to argue facts and figures before various courts — arguing for judicial restraint in the face of legislation establishing minimum labor standards — judges had had to contend with social science arguments presented *to* them. Brandeis's data consisted in the main of social statistics, the early measurement devices on which most subsequent social research has been based. But it should be emphasized that the "Brandeis brief" did not assert that its view of the facts was totally accurate; its purpose was merely to demonstrate that the legislature, in acting as it did, had a reasonable basis, that the facts *might* prove, for example, that hours-of-work standards were necessary to protect workers' health.

The Supreme Court itself soon became accustomed to and comfortable with this kind of brief. The Court's capacity to cope with social science arguments was much on display, for example, in *Witherspoon* v. *Illinois* (1968). At issue was the constitutionality of an Illinois statute providing for the exclusion of jurors having scruples against the death penalty. Mr. Justice Stewart, for the Court, took note of the social science arguments presented by those contending that the statute was illegal: "To support this view, the petitioner refers to what he describes as 'competent scientific evidence that death-qualified jurors are partial to the prosecution on the issue of guilt or innocence.' "

The justice, in a footnote, took further note of the academic papers — nicely and accurately describing them as "surveys" — which the petitioners had presented. He went on, however, to declare: "The data adduced by the petitioner . . . are too tentative and fragmentary to establish that jurors not opposed to the death penalty tend to favor the prosecution in the determination of guilt." In a footnote to this passage, the justice commented on these studies in language that will be familiar to graduate student and thesis committee alike: "We can only speculate . . . as to the precise meaning of the terms used in those studies, the accuracy of the techniques employed, and the validity of the generalizations made."

Having thus acquitted itself in the matter of methodological rigor, and having in effect rejected the social science data presented by the petitioners, the Court went on to rule *for* them, and to rest its decision on *other* social science data! Specifically, Justice Stewart found that ours is a nation "less than half of whose people believe in the death penalty." To establish this he cited opinion polls for the year 1966, as compiled in the *International Review on Public Opinion*, and judged that an Illinois jury culled of "all who harbor doubts about the wisdom of capital punishment" would thus speak only "for a distinct and dwindling minority." Accordingly, the statute was deemed to fail under the Sixth Amendment.*

In these changed — or perhaps it were better to say developed — circumstances it would seem useful to suggest, from the point of view of the social sciences, something of the limitations of social-scientific information in the judicial process. If it is quite clear that the courts employ social science with considerable deftness on some occasions, then it must be allowed that on other occasions the courts have got themselves into difficult situations by being too casual, even trusting, about the "truths" presented to them by way of research on individual and group behavior. Here it is not necessary to get into the question of where the courts might have erred. If there are those who wish to challenge particular decisions, they are free to do so under the arrangements so ably, indeed wonderfully, presided over by the American judiciary itself. It is enough to state that the social science involved in a great many judicial decisions — including, for that matter, *Brown* itself — has been sharply criticized by social scientists with differing or competing views.

Hence there are two points which one would ask jurists to consider before deciding how much further to proceed, and in what direction:

The first point is that social science is basically concerned to predict future events, whereas the purpose of the law is to order them. In this respect both are unavoidably entangled with politics in an *argument* about the future. But where social science seeks to establish a fixity of *relationships* such that the consequences of behavior can be known in advance — or,

---

*It may be that few persons will think of public opinion polls as social science, but they represent one of our largest achievements in the field of direct measurement, having been developed largely by Paul Lazarsfeld and his colleagues at Columbia University in the 1930s and 1940s.

rather, narrowed to a manageable range of possibilities — law seeks to dictate future performance on the basis of past *agreements*. It is the business of the law, as it were, to order alimony payments; it is the business of social science to try to estimate the likelihood of their being paid, or their effect on work behavior and remarriage in male and female parties, or similar probabilities.

In the end social science *must* be a quantitative discipline and deal with statistical probabilities. Law, by contrast, enters the realm of the merely probable at some risk. For the law, even when dealing with the most political of issues, must assert that there are the firmest, established grounds in past settlements on which to order future settlements. The primary social function of the courts is to preserve the social peace embodied in such past settlements, and to do this by establishing a competent, disinterested forum to which parties in dispute can come, ask, and be told *what it was we agreed to.* Hence Justice John Marshall's dictum in *Marbury* v. *Madison*: "It is emphatically the province and duty of the judicial department to say what the law *is.*"

To restate, for emphasis: The courts are very much involved with the future; indeed, to declare the future is what they do, and not infrequently they do so in the largest conceivable terms. (Bickel writes that the Warren Court "like Marshall's, may for a time have been an institution seized of a great vision, that it may have glimpsed the future, and gained it.") But the basis for ordering the future is that which the judges conclude were the standards and agreements reached in the past for the purpose of such future ordering.

Hence, also, the concern of the courts to appear to be above politics. If they are to keep the king's peace they had best not be visibly involved in planning the king's wars. And so long as the courts confine their references to established *past* agreements — constitutions, customs, statutes, contracts — they are protected by the all-important circumstance that we have agreed that for legal purposes *the past is what the courts say it is*. It is all very well for others to have opinions about what the Sixth Amendment intends with respect to the composition of juries, but what Justice Stewart says, in the company of a sufficient number of his colleagues, goes, *and there is no way to disprove him*. What the court decrees to be the past thereupon has the consequence of *being* the past. On the other hand, when the courts get into the business of predicting the *future* by the use of various social science techniques, then others, not lawyers, much less judges, can readily dispute them, and events will tell who is right and who is wrong.

In this circumstance, perhaps the first thing a jurist will wish to know about the social sciences is: How good are they? How well do they predict? Have they attained to any of the stability that Pound observed in the natural sciences in the early years of the century? The answer must be that the social sciences are labile in the extreme. What's settled in one decade is as often as not unsettled in the very next; and even that "decent interval" is not always observed. (Consider, for example, the cycles of professional opinion concerning the desirability of putting persons with various behavior disorders in institutions, as against maintaining them in their communities.) True, there are some areas of stability. With a sample of 500 or so persons, a "psephologist" can predict the popular vote in a presidential election within a few percentage points. But who will foretell the fate of the administration that follows?

The unsettled condition of the social sciences represents something of a disappointment, even a surprise. It was thought, especially in economics, that matters were much further advanced than they now look. With respect to the slow progress, or nonprogress, of the social sciences a range of explanations is put forward: The subject matter is more complex than that of the physical sciences. Experimental modes are usually unattainable. The disciplines are relatively new and probably have not attracted their share of the best talent. Other reasons come readily enough to mind. But the fact of slow progress is clear enough. The judiciary is entitled to know this, for it needs to acquire the habit of caution, the more perhaps when the work presented to it declares itself to be the most rigorous and "scientific."

Consider the venerable, yet always troubled and constantly shifting "advice" which social science has to offer in the matter of crime and punishment, a subject of the greatest relevance to the judiciary. For the longest while, twentieth-century criminology, such as it was, tended to hold that capital punishment did not deter capital crimes. This tendency persisted until the 1960s, when a number of empirical analyses appeared which seemed to establish a "negative association between the level of punishment and the crime rate." Concepts borrowed from economics were employed, often with great elegance, and once again (!) it was discovered that as price goes up demand goes down. We began to talk of the "elasticity of the crime rate to changes in the probability of imprisonment." Next, studies appeared which seemed to establish that capital punishment *saved lives*, as it were, by preventing subsequent capital crimes. This important and responsible research bade fair to make a considerable impression on public and even judicial policy, coming as it did at a time when the courts were banning capital punishment and elements in the public began to demand its return.

In 1976, however, the National Academy of Sciences established a panel to study the relation between crime rates and the severity of punishments. Two years later, the panel concluded that "the available studies provide no useful evidence on the deterrent effect of capital punishment." Thus, research lends support to the decision of the Supreme Court in *Gregg* v. *Georgia* (1976), in which Justice Stewart, for the Court, declared: "Statistical attempts to evaluate the worth of the death penalty as a deterrent to crimes by potential offenders have occasioned a great deal of debate. The results simply have been inconclusive." Perhaps Justice Stewart was judging just a little ahead of the evidence, *Gregg* having preceded the NAS panel report by two years. But if it is accepted that the courts ought to be hesitant to the point of reluctance before accepting any social science finding as final, Justice Stewart's cautionary decision seems warranted indeed.

For it is a melancholy fact that even the most rigorous efforts in social science recurrently come up with devastatingly imprecise stuff. Thus, a few lines after the "Summary" of the National Academy of Sciences study informed us in plain enough language that execution may or may not deter murder, a surpassingly murky passage sums up the evidence on the effect of imprisonment on other kinds of crime:

Since the high crime jurisdictions that are most likely to be looking to incapacitation to relieve their crime problems also tend to have relatively lower rates of time served per crime, they can expect to have the largest percentage increases in prison populations to achieve a given percentage of reduction in crime.

As English composition, the sentence itself calls for punishment of some sort. To say that high crime jurisdictions can expect to "have" the largest percentage increases in prison populations, rather than to "require" them or some equivalent term, is to leave the reader with a sense of surpassing fuzziness that all manner of mathematical notation does not overcome. Or conceal. Thus, farther in the same study, we are told that the lower boundary on the probability of arrest for an "index" offense is given by the formula

$$q \wedge > \frac{\lambda q \wedge T\left(\frac{V}{A}\right)}{\frac{C}{A} \quad \frac{V_1}{A}}$$

and we are also told that if prison use is expanded there is a potential for "two to fivefold decreases in crime." Now one need not be much of a mathematician to know that a twofold decrease in anything will likely lead to a negative number, and that a fivefold decrease might well produce a black hole.

The profession, in a word, has a way to go.

The second point is that social science is rarely dispassionate, and social scientists are frequently caught up in the politics which their work necessarily involves. The social sciences are, and have always been, much involved with problem-solving and, while there is often much effort to disguise this, the assertion that a "problem" exists is usually a political statement that implies a proposition as to who should do what for (or to) whom. (This essay, for example, which suggests that social science can have limited value for the courts, will almost certainly be ransacked for clues as to whether its implications are politically liberal, or conservative.) Social scientists never reveal more of themselves than when challenging the objectivity of one another's work. In some fields almost *any* study is assumed to have a more or less discoverable political purpose.

Moreover, there is a distinct social and political bias among social scientists. In all fairness, it should be said that social scientists are quick to acknowledge this. It all has to do, one suspects, with the orientation of the discipline toward the future: it attracts persons interested in shaping the future rather than preserving the past. In any event, the pronounced "liberal" orientation of sociology, psychology, political science, and similar fields is well established.

This observation, however, leads us to one of the ironies of the present state of the social sciences. The explanatory power of the various disciplines is limited. Few serious permanencies are ever established. In a period of civilization when in the physical sciences the methodology of adequate proof is well established, and when discoveries rush one upon the other, there are not many things social science has to say. To the degree that social science strives for the rigor of the physical sciences, its characteristic product is the null hypothesis: that is, the discovery that two social phenomena are *not* causally related. In some circumstances this can liberate social policy. For example, few recent works in social science have had the immediate impact of James Q. Wilson's *Thinking About Crime*. After examining the research concerning the effect of rehabilitation programs on criminals in this country and abroad, Wilson concluded that no consistent effects could be shown one way or the other. All that he could establish for certain about the future behavior of criminals is that when they are in jail they do not commit street crimes. Two centuries of hopes collapsed in that proposition, and not a few illusions. But out of the wreckage came the idea that fixed and predictable prison terms are a sensible social policy. In short order this was being advocated across the spectrum of political opinion. Indeed, if anything, while social scientists tend to be liberal, the tendencies of social science *findings* must be judged conservative, in that they rarely point to the possibilities of much more than incremental change. In 1959 the Yale political scientist Charles Lindblom set this forth as a necessity, the one *law* of social change, in a celebrated article entitled "The Science of Muddling Through."

The political orientation of the social sciences has been particularly evident (and is, I believe, least objectionable) in the shifting fashions in research topics. One will find a score of books, mostly of the period 1910–1950, about trade unions and strikes for every serious study of a middle-class organization such as the American Bar Association. But these preferences change with some regularity. Trade unions, now that they are judged "conservative," do not get much written about. Of late, community organizations, such as those funded by government antipoverty efforts, have been in vogue. Tomorrow, doubtless, it will be something else again.

This is not to be understood to suggest any deliberate attempt to distort. One has little more than impressions to offer here, but it seems mostly to be a matter of a somewhat too ardent searching for evidence that will help sustain a hoped-for conclusion. Sometimes the search succeeds; just as often it does not. Where there is deliberate fudging in the research, success is brief and retaliation can be truly termed draconian. The social sciences are serious professions, seeking to become ever more professional. They are also highly competitive, at times perhaps damagingly so. Edward C. Banfield has described this as the Fastest-Gun-in-the-West Effect — anyone briefly on top of any particular subject matter knows that young graduate scholars dream of making their own reputations by bringing him down in a brief, violent encounter. Such efforts may or may not succeed. But *anyone* who brings questionable data or methodology into the various fields can expect to be severely challenged. And even the most impeccable work will be challenged simply because "it is there."

The prudent jurist, aware of this, will take it into account, as the Supreme Court did in its decision in *San Antonio School District* v. *Rodriguez* (1973). Here a class action on behalf of certain Texas schoolchildren was brought against school authorities, challenging the constitutionality, under the equal protection clause of the Fourteenth Amendment, of the state's system of financing public education. The San Antonio system relied heavily on local property taxes, which implied substantial differences in per-pupil expenditure. Now it happens that just a very few years before this issue came to the Court, a series of research findings devastated the previous assumption that achievement in education was more or less a direct function of spending. This new research seemed to show that, after a point, this just wasn't so.*

The *Rodriguez* case was the culmination of an effort, primarily the work of academics, to disestablish the general

---

*In the interest, as lawyers say, of full disclosure, I should state that this is the interpretation that Frederick Mosteller and I presented in a reanalysis of the Coleman data, in *On Equality of Educational Opportunity* (1972). Mr. Justice Powell cites our work, along with that of others, in a passage in his decision in *Rodriguez.*

American pattern of local school district financing in favor of statewide, or even nationwide systems, with uniform per-pupil expenditures. (Moving an issue *upward* in the federal system has been well documented by political scientists as a technique for effecting social reform.) In briefest summary, these scholars did not anticipate that their research establishing differentials in school expenditure would be vitiated, at least in part, by the enquiries that were simultaneously taking place which cast grave doubt on just what significance was to be attributed to such differences.

In any event, the matter did not escape the attention of Justice Powell, who, writing for the majority, observed:

On even the most basic questions in this area the scholars and educational experts are divided. Indeed, one of the major sources of controversy concerns the extent to which there is a demonstrable correlation between educational expenditures and the quality of education — an assumed correlation underlying virtually every legal conclusion drawn by the District Courts in this case.

Farther on, Justice Powell declared, "We are unwilling to assume for ourselves a level of wisdom superior to that of legislators, scholars, and educational authorities in 50 states," and found that the Texas system of school financing met the constitutional standard of the equal-protection clause. It is not necessary to side with either the majority or the dissenting justices in this latter judgment to state with some confidence that, if the district courts depended overmuch in their decisions on the existence of a "demonstrable correlation between educational expenditures and the quality of education" — which Justice Powell says they did, and no dissenting Justice said they did not — then the district courts either did not know their social science, or, perhaps, did not know their social scientists.

The attentive reader might well take pause at the somewhat

remonstrative suggestion that "the District Courts . . . did not know their social science." Since when, it might well be asked, have judges been required to know social science? Is it not enough to expect that they will know the law?

No, alas, it is not. Herewith we encounter the major impact of social science on law.

Though the social sciences may be at an early state of development, this has not in the least inhibited their assertiveness. For the moment their ambitions are truly imperial. There is little by way of human behavior that the social sciences do not *in theory* undertake to explain, to account for.

As a result, there are fewer and fewer areas of social behavior for which traditional or "commonsense" explanations will any longer suffice in serious argument. A cursory reading of the district court decisions which preceded *Rodriguez* suggests that the judges' views on the relation of educational expenditure to educational achievement were based on nothing more than commonsense everyday opinion. The point is precisely this: commonsense everyday opinion no longer persuades. Everybody asks: Who *knows*? If it is theoretically possible to know something — and there are few relationships about which it is not theoretically possible to know *something* — no one is in a very good position to speak until the research is done!

If we may adopt for a moment the lawyers' term *material*, then we may say that the range of what is material in lawsuits has greatly expanded — or will as the courts submit to the logic, and the spirit, of the social sciences. Some years ago Kenneth Boulding spoke of the advent of the social sciences as an historical event comparable for society to the beginnings of consciousness in human beings. That we may be only beginning this era does not at all limit what we expect of it; we may greatly exaggerate. But that changes nothing as yet. The Supreme Court in *Rodriguez* found there was *no evidence* to support the charges. Accordingly, the Texas school financing system was found Not Guilty. (Or was it a Scottish verdict: Not Proven?)

Thus does social science rend the "web of subjectivity," the phrase which Alexander Bickel used to describe the Warren Court's reading of the past. "On more than a few occasions," he wrote (in *The Supreme Court and the Idea of Progress*, 1978), "the Warren Court has purported to discover in the history of the Fourteenth Amendment, and of the Thirteenth, and of other constitutional provisions, the crutch that wasn't there." Now this can be seen to be a traditional enough critique. But where the Court essays to predict the *future*, which is the realm of social science, the idiosyncratic and the subjective are even more conspicuous, and more subject to criticism. Litigation concerning educational matters has illustrated some earlier propositions. It may also illustrate this last, most important one. Since the *Brown* decision, the Supreme Court has held that "education is perhaps the most important function of state and local governments." But a decade prior to *Brown*, the court ruled in *Everson* v. *Board of Education* (1947) that the First Amendment requires that government assistance to schools that are not in the public sector (schools that are defined as not operated by government) must be severely restrained, and as nearly as possible cut off.

It is common enough for the courts to be asked to determine what the Constitution decrees with respect to matters that clearly lay at a remote distance from the thoughts of those who drafted the document, including its various amendments. Anyone who will trouble to read the debates concerning this part of the First Amendment — and this will not entail a great deal of trouble, for the question was debated for the equivalent of about a day in each house of Congress, and the entire record in the *Annals of Congress* takes up only 119 lines — will find no mention of aid to education. Judges have had to interpret as best they could.

In the judgment of some, they have quite misinterpreted this history. Bickel chides the Warren Court for discovering things in the history of the Thirteenth and Fourteenth Amendments that simply are not there. Such scholars as Walter Berns, Michael Malbin, Antonin Scalia, and Philip Kurland find that, with respect to aid to nonpublic schools, the Court's interpretation of the establishment clause is nonhistorical. In *Religion and the Law* (1962), Philip Kurland writes: "Anyone suggesting that the answer, as a matter of constitutional law, is clear one way or the other is either deluding or deluded."

I quite agree with the critics of the Court in this matter. In my view, the only *truly* comparable situation is that long period when the Supreme Court repeatedly claimed to find in the Fourteenth Amendment a whole series of restrictions on the power of legislatures to enact labor legislation. Thus in *Lochner* v. *New York* (1905), the Court — striking down a sixty-hour-work-week law — said that it was not at all "a question of substituting the judgment of the Court for that of the legislature," but simply that there was "no reasonable ground for interfering with the liberty of person or the right of free contract." Now there was no real difficulty in 1905 in discovering the purposes for which the Fourteenth Amendment had been adopted, and establishing that it was in no wise enacted to prevent the New York State legislature from regulating the hours of bakers. But such nonsense had been solemnly invoked by the Supreme Court in *Allgeyer* v. *Louisiana* (1897) in the closing years of the nineteenth century and was not to be overruled until the fourth decade of the twentieth century. All but forgotten now, save by historians, it was once a burning issue of American politics — as it should have been.

In just this manner, the establishment clause has been held to prevent legislatures from providing various forms of assistance to church-related schools, even though that clause has the plain and unambiguous meaning and intention that Congress will not establish a national religion.

There are those who are not happy with this state of affairs, but few, one would venture, who are actively angry. We go through these things every so often, and have done so for generations. One day it will come to be seen that the Court's rulings on aid to private schools reflected a particular religious point of view — that is, that there is no public interest in the promotion of religion — which reached its peak of intellectual respectability in the 1920s and 1930s, the period in which most of the judges who made the decisions were educated.

I have stressed the shaky reliability of social science. A certain kind of fairness suggests that the infallibility of judges might also be questioned. The establishment-clause decisions are an intellectual scandal. Without intending it, the courts in the school aid cases have been imposing on the country their *own* religious views. This point was well understood in 1841 by John C. Spencer, Tocqueville's first American translator and New York's secretary of state and superintendent of public schools. To those who feared use of public funds for sectarian purposes, Spencer in an official report replied that all instruction is in some ways sectarian:

No books can be found, no reading lessons can be selected, which do not contain more or less of some principles of religious faith, either directly avowed, or indirectly assumed.

Even the moderate degree of religious instruction which the Public School Society imparts, must therefore be sectarian; that is, it must favor one set of opinions in opposition to another, or others; and it is believed that this always will be the result, in any course of education that the wit of man can devise.

All this will be borne with sufficient goodwill and even good humor. The greater problem is for the courts, and it is a problem much complicated by social science. For social science affects what the court *can* say. Thus the case of *Tilton* v. *Richardson* (1971), which is the decision controlling federal aid to church-related schools. The Higher Education Facilities Act of 1963 provided federal construction grants for college and university facilities. Tilton *et al.* sued, contending that grants to four church-related colleges and universities in Connecticut had the effect of promoting religion. The Court held that this was not so, even though it would never tolerate a federal statute that provided construction grants to church-related high schools or suchlike institutions. Colleges and universities, the Court said, are different from elementary and secondary schools where religious matters are concerned, and college students are different from high school students.

Before grappling with the decision of the majority, it will help to touch upon the dissent of Mr. Justice Douglas, who thought federal aid to church-related colleges to be unconstitutional. It was an impassioned dissent: in his own words, a despairing dissent. The respect, he said, "which through history has been accorded the First Amendment is this day lost." Before coming to this sad conclusion, he presented an argument which some may view as wrong, but which is also logically quite — or almost — unassailable. By contrast, the less idiosyncratic decision of the majority is nonetheless indefensible, and it is a weakness which the advent of social science has brought about.

There is *one* unimpeachable sentence in Justice Douglas's opinion. "The First Amendment," he writes, "bars establishment of a religion." Just so. There was to be no established religion such as the Church of England or the Church of Ireland of that period. The meaning and intent of the amendment was most clear in the version considered by the House of Representatives on August 15, 1789, which read "no national religion shall be established by law." Elbridge Gerry objected, as the word *national* was a matter of contention between Federalists and Anti-Federalists, and the final version emerged, accessible in meaning to anyone who can read English. No established religion. Surely this has nothing to do with construction grants made available to religious institutions of *all* denominations. A judge who is going to contend that it does had best give considerable thought to what kinds of available evidence will tend to prove or disprove his contention. On this score Douglas was unassailable. He advanced arguments that some will find curious, but which none can refute.

To begin with, he would brook no distinction between levels of "parochial schools." They all looked alike to him. There is, he stated, a "dominant religious character" to all such schools. He then introduced in evidence the work of Loraine Boettner. A passage from Boettner's book *Roman Catholicism* is reproduced in a footnote. It should be clear, Boettner writes, "that a Roman Catholic parochial school is an integral part of that church." The title of ownership is vested in the bishop as an individual, a person "who is appointed by, who is under the direct control of, and who reports to the pope in Rome."

Now this "pope in Rome" is a person much on Boettner's mind. Boettner's book was published in Philadelphia in 1962, by the Presbyterian and Reformed Publishing Company, but it could as well have appeared in Edinburgh four centuries earlier. To Boettner, the pope is an Antichrist; his church is an heretical church; its teachings utterly subversive of true religion. As for the followers of the pope, they are, in Boettner's view, to a greater or lesser degree, agents of papal subversion. In one passage in the book, for example, he states that Roman Catholics ought not to be allowed to teach in *public* schools. In Boettner's view Roman Catholic schools are heretical. In Douglas's view they are unconstitutional: that is, they are not *Presbyterian.*

Now this is a venerable view, entertained over the years by other Scotsmen as well.* Of equal interest is the passage that

---

*For what it may be worth, in Scotland today church-related schools, including Catholic schools, receive full state support.

Douglas quotes in his dissent in *Tilton* from an article by Dr. Eugene Carson Blake which appeared in *Christianity Today* in 1959, the year after Blake completed his distinguished eight-year tenure as stated clerk of the general assembly of the Presbyterian Church of the United States of America. Blake, who had studied in Edinburgh as a youth, had a lively imagination of the sort associated with that city. He had also, more rare, the gift of prophecy. It was his judgment that owing to the tax-exempt state of church properties "it is not unreasonable to prophesy that with reasonably prudent management, the churches ought to be able to control the whole economy of the nation within the predictable future." This alarmed him:

That the growing wealth and property of the churches was partially responsible for revolutionary expropriations of church property in England in the 16th century, in France in the 18th century, in Italy in the 19th century, and in Mexico, Russia, Czechoslovakia, and Hungary (to name a few examples) in the 20th century, seems self-evident.

Now, this is a range of historical reference which Gibbon would have admired, and in our time perhaps only Toynbee might have essayed. It is also of course gibberish, much as Boettner is . . . well, if not harmless, surely not serious. But these arguments are nonetheless powerful. Boettner thinks the pope is the Antichrist. Douglas cites Boettner. *Who is to disprove them?* Blake thinks rich monasteries caused peasant revolts. Douglas cites Blake. *Who is to disprove them?* Douglas chose his ground well. He asserted a range of particular values and ultimate truths which he claimed to find in the Constitution, and that was that.

By contrast, the majority of the Court chose to rest its decision on assertions of readily challenged fact. The chief justice, for the majority, stated that "there are generally significant differences between the religious aspects of church-related institutions of higher learning and parochial schools." Two particular differences are cited. First, that religiously affiliated colleges and universities do not attempt to indoctrinate their students, while religiously affiliated elementary and secondary schools do. Second, that college students are different, that "college students are less impressionable and less susceptible to religious indoctrination," that the "skepticism of the college student is not an inconsiderable barrier to any attempt to subvert the Congressional objectives and limitations."

Enter social science. For these are *researchable* subjects. It is no longer possible to make such statements and expect to be taken seriously unless one has proof.

The Court in a sense acknowledges this. Proofs are provided. But as in the evocation of the Dreyfus case in Anatole France's *Penguin Island*, this was fatal. For what the justices offered with respect to the assertion that "there are generally significant differences between the religious aspects of church-related institutions of higher learning and parochial elementary and secondary schools" is a *Harvard Law Review* article by Paul A. Freund. And what does Professor Freund report? He reports that "institutions of higher learning present quite a different question, mainly because church support is less likely to involve indoctrination and conformity at that level of instruction." The argument grows tautological. What is Freund's evidence? What studies? What survey data? *None.* No evidence of any kind. Freund is among the most distinguished legal scholars of the age. But it is not for anyone to describe the pedagogical practices of a group of colleges and universities without having inquired into the matter, preferably in accordance with reasonably well established methodological rules. "Less likely" will not do. A modern bench requires harder data than that. Social science establishes new standards for what it is that can be taken as "self-evident," what, to use the words of the Court, "common observation would seem to support." This of course is a special problem for the Supreme Court. One cannot imagine that the bloopers of *Tilton* would have survived review — but with the Supreme Court there is no review.

Consider the second assertion, that "there is substance to the contention that college students are less impressionable and less susceptible to religious indoctrination." The Court again offered in evidence a *Harvard Law Review* article, this by Professor Donald A. Giannella. Again the tautology: Church-related colleges, Giannella writes, do not "attempt to form the religious character of the student by maintaining a highly controlled regime . . . to attempt such control of the college students is highly inappropriate, and would probably prove self-defeating." Again, no evidence, no data.

This kind of assertion by the Court is bound to be challenged. Anyone with any experience of a liberal arts faculty would immediately suspect that psychologists would not have any reliable findings on a subject so vast as "impressionability to religious indoctrination." This almost surely would come under the heading of things researchable but not researched.

Indeed, in response to an enquiry on this specific question, the 1978 president of the American Psychological Association, Professor M. Brewster Smith of the University of California, replied:

There is no comparable comprehensive treatment of religious change over the high school years that I know of, and while surely a close search might turn up scattered studies, I think it is fair to say, in answer to your question, that solid evidence regarding the high school vs. college comparison in which you are interested *does not exist* [his italics].

Inasmuch as I have called the *Tilton* case into question in the course of Senate debate, allow me to be particularly explicit as to what I judge the Court to have done in this case. The Court's confidence in what some might call its "secularist" position on the establishment clause has declined steadily since it first pronounced on the matter in *Everson* in 1947. In

Tilton it was trying to find grounds for allowing a clear intent of Congress to be carried out, and did so by distinguishing between higher education facilities, which are the only ones affected by the law, and other facilities. The Court, in an effort to base its decision on contemporary modes of argument, was rigorous but not rigorous enough. On examination, there is no evidence with which to support its finding. Justice Douglas, arguing in a prescientific mode, made no such mistake.

Is this distressing? Not, I think, unless one is distressed by the modern age. Primitive man, presumedly, had an explanation for everything. There is a sense, of course, in which science has made ignoramuses of us all. So much is *not* known. But modern man still does know more than his ancestors, even immediate ones, and we would do well to recall the old saying "It's not ignorance that hurts, it's knowin' all those things that ain't so." Courts will learn to adapt to the changed conditions of evidence which social science imposes on contemporary argument. One would not be surprised, for example, to see the emergence of a group of lawyers trained in social science, much as there are now specialists trained both as lawyers and as medical doctors. Indeed, lawyers with no more than a good undergraduate grounding in social science methodology could have quite an impact in this area simply by establishing higher standards of cross-examination.

This would be no small thing. Consider the controversy which broke out in the late 1970s over the Equal Educational Opportunity Report, commonly known as the Coleman Report after its principal author, Professor James S. Coleman. In the late 1960s Coleman's data on pupil achievement were the basis for a number of major court decisions calling for school busing. Subsequently — in the familiar pattern — his initial interpretations were challenged. Much confusion and some bitterness followed. It is at least arguable that much of this might have been avoided had it been made clear to the courts, in the first place, either through exposition by plaintiffs or cross-examination by defendants, that Coleman had not found any race effect as such in his analysis of student body characteristics and educational achievement. He had found a social class effect.

Judges in the future should be able to look for such cross-examination. One hopes it does not transgress any boundaries to suggest that these developments might also encourage in the courts a somewhat more easeful acceptance that, in the end, law is after all only long-established preference, codified opinion. When Pound and Cardozo and Holmes began talking of the "science of law," perhaps they, too, were mostly trying to impose a different set of opinions from those then prevailing. But at least they were doing so in an effort to get the bench back to the business of interpreting opinion as *embodied in legislation*, rather than as embodied in the education and social class preferences of a particular body of judges. This was great wisdom, and this is precisely the import of Chief Justice Burger's decision in *Tennessee Valley Authority* v. *Hill* (1978), in which it was held that, inasmuch as the Tellico Dam would endanger the snail darter, it was prohibited by the Endangered Species Act. In civil but firm tones the Congress was informed that it must expect that, when called upon, the Court will enforce such laws as Congress enacts regardless of any individual appraisal of the wisdom or unwisdom of a particular course. Whether that was to be considered a warning or not will depend on one's judgment as to the balance of wisdom against unwisdom in congressional enactments. But that it is the policy of the present Court, none need doubt. We may all take pleasure in the nice touch of the Chief Justice who closed his opinion *not* with a citation of social science, nor yet of any "science of law," but rather of lines ascribed to Sir Thomas More by the contemporary playwright Robert Bolt: "The law, Roper, the law. I know what's legal, not what's right. And I'll stick to what's legal. . . . I'm *not* God."

9.
When the Supreme Court Is Wrong

An institution charged with the role which the Supreme Court has successfully filled for so many years is entitled to our respect and understanding. If one criticizes the Court (as people have always done in the past, and should continue to do in the future), it should be essentially for the purpose of trying to contribute to that respect and to that understanding. The debt which we all owe to the Court is far greater than any individual can repay. Criticism of decisions of the Court or opinions of its members should be offered as an effort to repay that debt, and with the thought that conscientious criticism may be an aid to the Court in carrying out its difficult and essential task.

— ERWIN N. GRISWOLD, 1963

IN ITS SPRING TERM OF 1979, the Supreme Court ruled in the case of *Gannett* v. *DePasquale* that the public does not have an independent constitutional right of access to a pretrial judicial proceeding. The case had been brought by the Gannett newspapers after one of their reporters was barred from a pretrial hearing in a murder case in upstate New York. Gannett argued that the guarantee of the Sixth Amendment to a "public trial" extended to the public at large, including, of course, the press. The Court held that this was not so. Mr. Justice Stewart's opinion for the majority of the Court declared: "The history upon which the petitioner and *amici* rely totally fails to demonstrate that the Framers of the Sixth Amendment intended to create a constitutional right in strangers to attend a pretrial proceeding. . . ."

Strangers? The press?

In a concurring opinion, Mr. Justice Rehnquist went further, and in such a manner as to highlight the fact that though, strictly speaking, *Gannett* concerned pretrial proceedings, the decision is easily construed as applying to trials as well. The Court's recitation, he said,

of the need to preserve the defendant's right to a fair trial . . . should not be interpreted to mean that under the Sixth Amendment a trial court can close a pretrial hearing or trial only when there is no danger that prejudicial publicity will harm the defendant. To the contrary, since the Court holds that the public does not have *any* Sixth Amendment right of access to such proceedings, it necessarily follows that if the parties agree on a closed proceeding, the trial court is not required by the Sixth Amendment to advance any reason whatsoever for declining to open a pretrial hearing or trial to the public.

The decision was the lead story of *The New York Times* the following day. It had, *The Times* reported, "aroused immediate strong criticism from both the press and the legal profession." The initiative of the Gannett newspapers in challenging the closing of a local court proceeding had been seen as a commendable effort to defend the rights of both the public and the press. The Edward Willis Scripps First Amendment Award for 1979 was presented to the Gannett Rochester Newspapers for pressing the suit and for their reporting and analysis of the issues involved. Allen Neuharth, chairman of the board of the Gannett newspapers and chairman of the American Newspaper Publishers Association, called the ruling "another chilling demonstration that the majority of the Burger Court is determined to unmake the Constitution." The American Civil Liberties Union declared that the decision "erected an iron curtain between the criminal process and the inquiring press."

Editorial comment was not less severe. Much emphasis was placed on the asserted departure by the Court from historical, even ancient standards of justice. A forceful *Times* editorial began:

For centuries the idea of open justice has been synonymous with justice itself. Before the Norman Conquest, before English judges spelled out the rudimentary rights of defendants, throughout the development of British and American jurisprudence, the tradition of open courts has been honored. Now a 5–4 Supreme Court majority has ordained an exception. . . .

In a commentary, Tom Wicker, associate editor of *The Times,* deplored the ruling. It would surely lead to miscarriage of justice, he wrote. Not just the press, but the general public would be barred from courts, discarding a standard "rooted in American history." For the Court "now to say that that tradition has no constitutional validity . . . shakes public confidence in institutions and rights long thought to be a citizen's birthright."

The most telling comment came from the Court itself. In a dissenting opinion, Mr. Justice Blackmun stated that in their constitutional argument the Gannett newspapers were right, and the majority of the Court was wrong:

The Sixth Amendment, in establishing the public's right of access to a criminal trial and a pretrial proceeding, also fixes the rights of the press in this regard. Petitioner, as a newspaper publisher, enjoys the same right of access . . . as does the general public. And what petitioner sees and hears in the courtroom it may, like any other citizen, publish or report consistent with the First Amendment.

In "rare circumstances," Justice Blackmun allowed, exclusion could be justified. But, he concluded, "Those circumstances did not exist in this case."

It is difficult to avoid the judgment that Justice Blackmun was right and the majority of the Supreme Court was wrong. If so, the question arises: What to do?

This is a question for which we have no clear answer and little theory. The Court is not supposed to be wrong. Even *The Federalist,* much given to emphasizing the frailty of human judgment, does not adequately treat this possibility. To be sure, the doctrine of judicial supremacy — of the Supreme Court's power to void acts of Congress by declaring them unconstitutional — is not explicit in the Constitution and was not generally assumed to be implicit until Chief Justice John Marshall established it in *Marbury* v. *Madison*. But Hamilton, who believed in it, and in *Federalist* paper number 78 made a strong argument for it, had to deal with the charge that "the errors and usurpations of the Supreme Court of the United States will be uncontrollable and remediless." In number 81, he suggests several reasons why this charge, upon examination, is "made up altogether of false reasoning upon misconceived fact," but all but one of his points are actually further arguments for the necessity and rationality of judicial supremacy. The sole check upon supremacy suggested by Hamilton, other than that of appeals to superior courts, is the power of Congress to impeach individual judges.

This is alone a complete security. There never can be a danger that the judges, by a series of deliberate usurpations of the authority of the legislature, would hazard the united resentment of the body intrusted with it, while this body was possessed of the means of punishing their presumption, by degrading them from their stations.

No other corrective is suggested. Rather, the argument is made with particular force that the judiciary is inherently and uniquely possessed of the necessary wisdom and disinterest to weigh the actions of the legislature and the executive on constitutional scales. But if the Court were wrong, what —

short of impeaching its members — would be the remedy? *The Federalist* does not say.

It happens, however, that we have a considerable practical experience of just this situation. For long periods of American history the Supreme Court has been wrong about one or another of the principal constitutional issues of the day. It has been wrong in the specific sense that there later came a time when the Court reversed itself, and either directly or implicitly stated that it *had* been wrong.* Nor has this been without consequence. Charles Evans Hughes, in his 1928 volume, *The Supreme Court of the United States,* could refer to the Court's having suffered from a succession of "self-inflicted wounds."

Thus from the last decade of the nineteenth century into the fourth decade of the twentieth century the Supreme Court repeatedly declared that the due process clauses forbade labor legislation. The Fourteenth Amendment was held to justify the *Lochner* decision. Under the Fifth Amendment, a District of Columbia Minimum Wage Act was held invalid (*Adkins* v. *Children's Hospital,* 1923).‡

This was solemn nonsense, as Holmes pointed out in his acid comment in *Lochner* that "the 14th Amendment does not enact Mr. Herbert Spencer's *Social Statics.*"† But the nonsense

---

*Strictly speaking, the Court could have been right the first time and wrong the second. Walter Berns contends, properly, that the standard against which we measure a decision in order to say whether the Court was wrong must be the Constitution itself, not what the Court says about it. Still, experience is the life of constitutional law also, and I would hold that where the Court has reversed itself it has almost always done so to correct an observable error.

‡In *Erie R.R. Co.* v. *Tompkins* (1937) the Court reversed *Swift* v. *Tyson,* acknowledging that they were abandoning a doctrine widely applied ". . . throughout nearly a century. But the unconstitutionality of the course pursued has now been made clear and compels us to do so."

†Holmes's suggestion appears to be misleading. The Court was not trying to enact anyone's social theories but its own. In James Q. Wilson's phrase, the Court had an idea as to what a "good economy" would be, and it was against this standard that statutes were measured. A considerable body of labor legislation and business regulation was in fact upheld by the "Laissez-Faire Court." My point is simply that there was precious little constitutional warrant for any of this.

persisted, thwarting for almost half a century the major social movement of the time. Then, as suddenly as it had begun, it stopped. Writing somewhat later, Mr. Justice Douglas declared in *Williamson* v. *Lee Optical Co.* (1955):

The day is gone when this Court uses the Due Process Clause of the Fourteenth Amendment to strike down state laws, regulatory of business and industrial conditions, because they may be unwise, improvident, or out of harmony with a particular school of thought.

Or, as Mr. Justice Black put it in 1963 in *Ferguson* v. *Skrupa:*

The doctrine that prevailed in *Lochner, Coppage, Adkins, Burns,* and like cases — that due process authorizes courts to hold laws unconstitutional when they believe the legislature has acted unwisely — has long since been discarded.

Of these episodes in American history, the most notorious was the *Dred Scott* decision of 1857, which held the Missouri Compromise to be unconstitutional, a matter in which the Court was, again, plainly wrong. The most pernicious was *Plessy* v. *Ferguson* (1896), which held that the Fourteenth Amendment permitted separate but equal public facilities segregated by race, a doctrine that persisted until *Brown* v. *Board of Education* (1954).

Apart from the *Dred Scott* decision, which was, in effect, overturned by the Thirteenth Amendment, the essential fact in all these cases is, however, that the time came when the Court discovered its error and reversed itself.* This may

*To be sure, the Sixteenth Amendment, permitting a progressive federal income tax, had the effect of reversing the Supreme Court's five-to-four decision in *Pollock* v. *Farmers' Loan and Trust Company* (1895), which had struck down such a tax. But many commentators feel that in this instance the Court was accurately interpreting Article I, Section 9, of the Constitution, and that changing circumstances in fact called for a constitutional amendment. The contrary view, expressed by some members of Congress during debate on appear much too optimistic, even pietistic, a reading of American history, but there it is for those to refute who will. The question I would address is how these reversals have come about. It is a process not now described in political or juridical science. As a beginning contribution I would offer a simple hierarchy of response which in one or another combination has commonly led the Court to change its position in those instances in which it has been wrong. In ascending order: Debate, Litigate, Legislate.

(In theory the ultimate recourse of those who feel the Constitution has been misread is an amendment settling the issue. But this has *never* happened. It has never proved necessary. Apart from the evolving idea of Federalism that was needed to correct *Chisholm,* the exceptional circumstances that followed *Dred Scott,* and the changed circumstances that caused a graduated income tax to appear more reasonable in 1913 than in 1787, sooner or later the justices have rectified their mistakes. That is not the least ground for the loving fealty we owe the Court.)

As a "case history" I will first present in some detail the history of the issue of state aid to nonpublic schools. I will argue that the Supreme Court was wrong in its interpretation of the Establishment Clause in its decision *Everson* v. *Board of Education* (1947), but that after a generation the conditions are developing in which it may (will?) now reverse itself. That time is a considerable element in this process will be of small consolation to those now most distressed by the decision in

---

the Sixteenth Amendment, is that the Court *was* wrong but had recognized this and was already diluting the effect of the *Pollock* decision and that the proposed amendment was therefore superfluous.

The Eleventh Amendment, ratified in 1795, which denied the Supreme Court original jurisdiction in lawsuits brought by citizens against individual states, responded to the Court's decision in *Chisholm* v. *Georgia* (1793) that it had such jurisdiction. But this could reasonably be described as part of the completing of the federal structure embodied in the Constitution itself.

Gannett v. *DePasquale,* but this also appears to be the general experience.

Some weeks before the lengthy *Gannett* decision was announced to the consternation of so many, the Supreme Court in twenty-six words announced its decision in *Byrne, Brendan T. et al.* v. *Public Funds for Public Schools*: "The judgment is affirmed. The Chief Justice, Mr. Justice White, and Mr. Justice Rehnquist would note probable jurisdiction and set the cases for oral argument." Thus yet another effort by a state government, in this case New Jersey, to provide a measure of assistance for nonpublic, mostly denominational schools was found to violate the establishment clause of the First Amendment, and hence to be unconstitutional.

This in itself was nothing noteworthy. From 1947, when the Court in *Everson* ruled on a state school-aid status (also of New Jersey), to *Byrne* there were altogether some forty-six cases brought to the Court dealing with aspects of this subject. As the circuit court in the most recent New Jersey case stated in the opening sentence of the majority opinion, each of these presented "recurring and troublesome questions concerning the relationship between religion and government."

Withal, the 1979 action by the Supreme Court received some attention, for it involved tuition tax credits. New Jersey had enacted a state income tax to provide funds for public education. Included in the statute was a deduction for parents of children in nonpublic schools, it being reasoned that through tuition they contribute to the secular objective of education, and could receive some partial recompense. (For a parent earning $20,000, the total savings was to be $20.)

A more general, and national, measure, providing tuition tax credits at all levels of education — which is to say including college and university as well — had passed the House of Representatives in 1978. The postsecondary portion passed the Senate as well, while the elementary and secondary provisions failed by only fifteen votes. This indicated considerable national support for such assistance, but in the New Jersey case the circuit court declared itself bound by a 1973 Supreme Court decision, *Committee for Public Education* v. *Nyquist,* which struck down a New York measure allowing a taxpayer with a dependent in a nonpublic elementary or secondary school to deduct an amount from his gross income, and thus pay less state income tax. The Supreme Court had held that this had the primary effect of advancing religion and that therefore — following the constitutional "tests" established in prior decisions from *Everson* through *Lemon* v. *Kurtzman* (1971) — the state law and the deduction it established necessarily failed.

But the notable aspect of the New Jersey event went altogether unremarked. In a separate opinion of the circuit court, Judge Joseph F. Weis declared that while clearly the Supreme Court decision in *Nyquist* governed the case, just as clearly the *Nyquist* decision was wrong. It had been a split decision (as almost all these decisions have been) and in Judge Weis's view, "the dissenters have far the better of it in the *Nyquist* opinion. . . ."

Those dissenters — Chief Justice Burger and Justices White and Rehnquist — had written a trio of powerful opinions, observing *inter alia*:

While there is no straight line running through our decisions interpreting the Establishment and Free Exercise Clauses of the First Amendment, our cases do, it seems to me [the Chief Justice], lay down one solid, basic principle: that the Establishment Clause does not forbid governments, state or federal, to enact a program of general welfare under which benefits are distributed to private individuals, even though many of those individuals may elect to use those benefits in ways that "aid" religious instruction or worship. . . . The essence of all these decisions . . . is that government aid to individuals generally stands on an entirely different footing from direct aid to religious institutions. . . . However sincere our collective protestations of the debt owed by the public generally to the parochial school systems, the wholesome diversity they engender will not survive on expressions of good will.

Rather, as with the dog that Sherlock Holmes observed did *not* bark, the significant fact in the New Jersey tuition-deduction case is that the high court chose *not* to hear an appellate judge tell it that it was wrong.

Here close attention is required. There are two senses in which it may be argued that the Supreme Court has been wrong in this area. The first concerns the basic *Everson* decision itself, set forth by Justice Hugo Black, which announced a rule of law in the widest sense:

The "establishment of religion" clause of the First Amendment means at least this: Neither a state nor the Federal Government can set up a church. Neither can pass laws which aid one religion, aid all religions, or prefer one religion over another.

The key elements of the rule, as Michael J. Malbin has written, are that Congress cannot give nondiscriminatory aid to religion and that neither can the states.

This is the basic ruling of the Court and it endures three decades later. It has not been challenged, albeit (in my view) wrong. Instead, the *Everson* doctrine has been the basis for numerous challenges to state efforts to channel modest amounts of aid into nonpublic education through one means or another, efforts which persist. (The actual holding in *Everson* itself was that New Jersey *could* provide bus transportation to parochial school students.) The challenges have always been brought by persons opposed even to such small efforts and determined to maintain the *Everson* doctrine in as strict a form as possible.

This opposition has been organized (the list of plaintiffs in the recent New Jersey case begins: Public Funds for Public Schools of New Jersey, American Civil Liberties Union of New

Jersey, Inc., Americans for Democratic Action . . .) and vigilant. As states have devised new forms of aid to accommodate each succeeding Court decision, the organizations have typically challenged the statute, leading in time to yet another decision by the Court. Thus there has followed from *Everson* a great number of interpretive, or exegetic, rulings which not infrequently have been wrong, if you will, in their own right.

The result has been an intellectual shambles: one confused and convoluted decision requiring a yet more confused and convoluted explanation or modification. Professor Antonin Scalia of the University of Chicago Law School, former assistant U.S. attorney general, Office of Legal Counsel, and in that capacity perhaps the senior constitutional authority in the executive branch, testified before the Senate Finance Committee in 1978: "It is impossible, within the time allotted, to describe with any completeness the utter confusion of Supreme Court pronouncements in the church-state area." Professor Philip Kurland, also of the University of Chicago Law School, writes that "the Court is thoroughly unprincipled in the area," meaning, of course, that there is no coherent principle to be found in the ever-lengthening series of decisions.

Such incoherence has invited challenge from persons with no greater interest than intellectual rigor in the high court. Challenges to this secondary, exegetic body of decisions from Supreme Court justices themselves, have become increasingly frequent, even as challenges to the primary decisions have remained rare. The notable quality of the Weis opinion is that it challenges both.

Judge Weis's opinion treats first the exegetic decisions:

An analysis of the cases touching upon state assistance to nonpublic schools could proceed at length, but would merely illustrate the lack of a principled and logical thread. The reality is that the Supreme Court has marked out a series of boundaries and points of departure on an ad hoc basis. Thus, school books may be loaned to pupils, *Board of Education* v. *Allen . . .* (1968), but weather charts may not, *Wolman* v. *Walter . . .* (1977). Buses may be provided to allow for transportation of pupils to school, *Everson* v. *Board of Education . . .* (1947), but not for field trips to courthouses or museums, *Wolman* v. *Walter, supra.* Financial aid for the construction of buildings may be given to colleges, *Tilton* v. *Richardson . . .* (1971), but grants to provide needed maintenance to parochial schools in slum neighborhoods are forbidden, *Committee for Public Education* v. *Nyquist, supra.*

The Weis opinion turns then to what is the fundamental constitutional issue:

In many of the opinions in this area, I am struck by the frequent use of the metaphor that the first amendment was intended to erect a "wall" between church and state. E.g. *Committee for Public Education* v. *Nyquist, Everson* v. *Board of Education.* Insofar as this concept expresses a guiding principle for constitutional adjudication, I find it unfortunate and historically inaccurate.

My first reservation is semantical. So often a wall implies fear and hostility, as the infamous structure separating East and West Berlin so dramatically demonstrates. No such emotions should dominate the relationship between government and religion and the use of a metaphor that encourages such concepts is not desirable.

A more fundamental objection, however, is grounded in the history of the Establishment Clause. Although an accurate description of the Framers' intent is beyond our grasp, it is dubious that the Madisonian-Jeffersonian concept of absolute separation was widely accepted by the draftsmen. . . .

Commenting upon the checkered constitutional history of the Establishment Clause, one scholar has noted: "[I]t remains at best ironic and at worst perverse to appeal to the history of the Establishment Clause to strike at practices only remotely resembling establishment in any core sense of the concept." (L. Tribe, *American Constitutional Law.*)

Yet that is what has been done in using the "wall" concept to justify a policy of judicial hostility towards state aid to nonpublic schools.

Perhaps a more accurate appraisal of the purpose of the first amendment is that the state is to be neutral in its relationship with religion. And so if a particular legislative enactment, particularly in the field of taxation, provides clearly observable secular benefits, then religious institutions should not be barred solely because of their status. See *Walz* v. *Tax Commission*.

Finally, constitutional adjudication requires that the courts read aparticular clause with its historical context in mind, lest the fears and prejudices of an earlier age serve to distort the problems of today. As Justice Powell, who wrote the *Nyquist* opinion, noted some four years later:

> It is important to keep these issues in perspective. At this point in the 20th century we are quite far removed from the dangers that prompted the Framers to include the Establishment Clause in the Bill of Rights. See *Walz* v. *Tax Comm'n.* The risk of significant religious or denominational control over our democratic processes — or even of deep political division along religious lines — is remote, and when viewed against the positive contributions of sectarian schools, any such risk seems entirely tolerable in light of the continuing oversight of this Court. Our decisions have sought to establish principles that preserve the cherished safeguard of the Establishment Clause without resort to blind absolutism. *Wolman* v. *Walter.*
>
> These cases require a realistic approach, not an exaggerated response to nonexistent threats. Simple justice would require that the court honor the decision of the New Jersey legislature where the *quid pro quo* weighs heavily in favor of the state. But as the majority correctly concludes, the narrow legal issue in this case is whether *Nyquist* or *Walz* governs. Although it seems to me that the dissenters have far the better of it in the *Nyquist* opinions, I cannot in all intellectual honesty say that case differs from the one *sub judice.* I am bound to follow the holding of the majority of the Supreme Court and I therefore concur, albeit reluctantly. . . .

". . . [J]udicial hostility towards state aid to nonpublic schools." It has now been stated from the federal bench.

Whence does this hostility derive? (Assuming, of course, that it exists, and this brief is clearly written from the partisan view that it does.) It does *not* derive from the Establishment Clause of the First Amendment. The Supreme Court is wrong. This is the heart of it. The matter must begin here.

The Establishment Clause is simplicity itself. It states that Congress may not set up a national church.

There are two ways to get at this meaning. The first is to acquire a moderate facility with the English language, and in particular with one word that has somewhat gone out of usage. The clause states: "Congress shall make no law respecting an establishment of religion. . . ." The term *establishment* referred to a state church, such as the Church of England, an altogether familiar concept at the time, and rather a familiar institution.

All thirteen colonies had established churches or other official involvement with particular denominations at some point in their history. At the outbreak of the Revolution, the Church of England was officially established in five southern colonies (Virginia, Georgia, South Carolina, North Carolina, and Maryland); the Congregational Church enjoyed official status in Massachusetts, Connecticut, and New Hampshire; and the Anglican and Dutch Reformed churches both had similar status in New York. This pattern remained in flux for some time. (Virginia, for example, took steps toward disestablishment in 1776 and 1786 but did not eliminate the vestiges of the previous arrangement until 1802.) When the First Amendment was ratified, three states gave preference to particular denominations, Anglican, Congregational, and Dutch Reformed; four states gave special status to the Protestant religion; three required adherence to Christianity among public officeholders; and three granted full religious freedom.

The term *establishment* has become somewhat unfamiliar in the intervening two centuries simply because there are no longer any established churches around. (In much the same fashion the provisions of Article III that "no Attainder of Treason shall work Corruption of Blood" would puzzle many persons simply because we don't do that much anymore.) But the meaning of the term *establishment* as used in the First Amendment is altogether accessible and quite unchanged. The first definition given in Webster's second edition is: "The establishing by law of a church or religion, etc." It is not too much to ask that persons who profess to care about the Constitution take the trouble to learn the language in which it is written.

Neither, if Mr. Justice Powell is to be believed, is it too much to ask that such persons learn a little of American history. To be fair, this may be stated with perhaps more insistence today than three decades ago when the *Everson* doctrine came into being. For the longest while, the meaning of the First Amendment was clear to everyone concerned. Then a curious sequence took place. In the second half of the nineteenth century a movement arose to prohibit aid to Catholic schools. It was assumed that the Constitution would have to be amended to do this. But the "Blaine amendment," first proposed in 1876, was never adopted by Congress. (For what it may be worth, a clause in the amendment provided that "This article shall not be construed to prohibit the reading of the Bible in any school or institution. . . .") But somehow when the Court came to rule in 1947, it took the political attitudes of the late nineteenth century to be the constitutional purposes of the late eighteenth. In the Court's defense it may be said that in 1947, there wasn't much formal history to direct it otherwise.

This has now changed. In a predictable manner scholars have been drawn to the issue. In what may also have been predictable, it took them a good while to get the facts organized. In *Beyond the Melting Pot* (1963), Nathan Glazer and I may have helped to reconstruct the early history of state aid to education. (In New York it went exclusively to church-related schools, as there were none other.) In *The Garden and the Wilderness* (1965), Mark DeWolfe Howe commenced a careful examination of the meaning of the First Amendment and the intentions of those who drafted and ratified it. Of the line of church-state decisions begun with *Everson,* he wrote:

The Supreme Court, in my judgment, has gravely erred in its reading of two chapters of American history. An impulsive eagerness to find that the state and nation were subject to the same disabilities so far as religion was concerned, led the justices to make the historically quite misleading assumption that the same considerations which moved Jefferson and Madison to favor separation of church and state in Virginia led the nation to demand the religious clauses of the First Amendment. . . . Furthermore, it permitted the Court to fill the space from which it had removed the vivid complexities of the eighteenth century's political philosophy with a simple and false absolute — all aid to religion is unconstitutional.

Howe's analysis was followed, and powerfully reinforced, by Walter Berns in his splendid volume *The First Amendment and the Future of American Democracy* (1976) and by Michael J. Malbin's extensive essay *Religion and Politics: The Intentions of the Authors of the First Amendment* (1978). Although Berns and Malbin use different evidence, they reach similar conclusions, as summarized by Malbin:

As the Court has espoused its doctrines, it has relied on an incredibly flawed reading of the intentions of the authors of the First Amendment. . . . Aid to religion was to be permitted as long as it furthered a purpose the federal government legitimately could pursue and as long as it did not discriminate in favor of some sects or against others.

The research continues, and we are gradually acquiring a solid understanding of the relationship between church and state that obtained in 1791, of the assumptions and intentions of the Founding Fathers, and of the practices that prevailed through much of the nineteenth century. Among the work now in progress is a comprehensive history of the First Amendment by Professor Robert L. Cord of Northeastern University.

In his dissent in the *Gannett* case, Justice Blackmun stated that the Sixth Amendment established "the public's right of access to a criminal trial and a pretrial proceeding" and that of the press also. Those who would persuade the majority of the Court of this view must begin by reconstructing the history of that Amendment and of the First Amendment. This is not as direct a matter as might be thought, but it is entirely doable. It has now been done with respect to the Establishment Clause.

The Bill of Rights was adopted in something of a hurry: debate on the Establishment Clause took up about one day in each chamber. The standard, if somewhat shaky, record for the House of Representatives is the *Annals of Congress,* first published in 1834, taken from contemporary newspaper accounts and from the shorthand notes of a reporter, Thomas Lloyd. It is not complete, but is the only serviceable record of the proceedings of the First Congress. An essential fact is that the texts of successive versions of the clause, in each body, are available and these make the intention of the Congress conclusively clear. James Madison introduced two amendments in the House on June 7, 1789. The first of the amendments read:

"The Civil Rights of none shall be abridged on account of religious belief or worship, nor shall any national religion be established, nor shall the full and equal rights of conscience be in any manner, nor on any pretext infringed."

And the second:

"No state shall violate the equal rights of conscience or the freedom of the press, or the trial by jury in criminal cases."

Malbin notes that Madison's language prohibited both states and the federal government from infringing on the rights of conscience. "In contrast, the Establishment Clause was to apply only to the federal government."

How so? Because, as noted earlier, various of the states still *had* established churches. This is the lesson Perry Miller has taught: that if there was no very great love of religious tolerance in eighteenth-century America, given the profusion of religious denominations there was a very great need of it.

Alas, it was this very fragility of the Union which led ultimately to the substitution of the present language for Madison's explicit prohibition against "any national religion." Malbin reminds us that "federalism was *the* overriding issue throughout the Congress." It was still a lively issue as to whether the Constitution had created a new nation, or merely a federation of states. The Federalists, insisting that the latter was the case, carefully left the word "nation" out of the Constitution. But they were suspected (correctly!) of having a nation in mind and of being determined to forge one. Accordingly, in the debate in the First Congress the Anti-Federalists seized on the word *national* in Madison's draft, declaring that the gigantic conspiracy, the massive subterfuge, was at last revealed. Feelings were intense. Gerry recalled that at the Philadelphia convention of 1787 the two factions were designated Federalists and Anti-Federalists. They should, he said, have been called "rats" and "anti-rats": that is, ratification and antiratification. The phrase *national religion* promptly disappeared. Otherwise the theme of the debate, which took place August 15, was set rather by the opening address of Peter Sylvester of New York, who apprehended that the clause "might be thought to have a tendency to abolish religion altogether."

Senate debate was secret at this time. (The doors of the Senate chamber remained closed until 1795, and no record of the debates is available until 1802, when journalists were admitted to the Senate floor. The official transcript embodied in the *Congressional Record* did not begin until 1873.) But the Senate *Journal* records the texts which were considered on September 3. The first substitute offered for the House lan-

guage began: "Congress shall make no law establishing one
religious sect or society in preference to others. . . ." The final
language sent back to the House read: "Congress shall make
no law establishing articles of faith or a mode of worship or
prohibiting the free exercise of religion." A conference committee settled on the present language.*

A century and a half later, when the Supreme Court in
Everson turned its attention to this subject the justices did not
accept the Establishment Clause at face value, as meaning
what it said, nor yet did they inquire into this history. Rather,
as much as we can judge, they inquired as to the views of
Madison and Jefferson, and came up with the well-known "wall
of separation." This surely will not do. The question is not what
Madison or Jefferson may have thought; the question is what
the Congress did. It is perhaps not wholly irrelevant that
Jefferson was not a member of the First Congress; he was
Secretary of State at the time, and quite uninvolved. (He had
spent most of the previous five years on diplomatic missions in
Western Europe.) Madison was floor manager of a complex
piece of legislation which required compromise. Compromise
he did. What more evidence is needed than that his original
draft in no way reflected his own, and for the time somewhat
extreme, views?

If it be the case, in Judge Weis's words, that "an accurate
description of the Framers' intent is beyond our grasp," are we
not then well advised simply to take the plain language for
what it plainly says? No establishment of religion, period.

Does not the burden of proof rest with those who assert that
it says more? The legislators of the early American Republic
were entirely friendly to religion and religious purposes. The

---

*Not at issue here is the "incorporation" doctrine, whereby the prohibitions
imposed on Congress by the Bill of Rights have been expanded by the Supreme
Court to cover the actions of states. The Supreme Court interprets the
Fourteenth Amendment to bind the states as well as Congress when they
legislate "respecting an establishment of religion."

House passed the ten amendments of the Bill of Rights on September 24, 1789. The *next* day the House passed a Joint Resolution calling upon President Washington to issue a Thanksgiving proclamation. The Senate passed the Bill of Rights on September 26, and on the twenty-seventh passed the Joint Resolution. It called for "a day of public Thanksgiving and prayer, to be observed, by acknowledging, with grateful hearts, the many and signal favors of Almighty God, especially by affording them an opportunity peaceably to establish a constitution of government. . . ." The first Congress wanted to encourage religion, but in no circumstances to establish a church so as to prefer one to the other. Chaplains were appointed to the armed forces. Both House and Senate began — and still begin — each day with a prayer by a clergyman. The Northwest Ordinance of 1787, reenacted by Congress in 1789, set aside federal lands in the territory for schools: "Religion, morality, and knowledge," the law read, "being necessary to good government and the happiness of mankind, schools and the means of learning shall forever be encouraged." If they were to aid education, how could they do otherwise? Who, in 1789 in the United States, could imagine a school that did not teach some religious belief or other?

Madison and Jefferson, say the justices, and there the matter rests. The inferior courts follow, as they must. Early on, the majority opinion in the recent New Jersey case invokes the declaration of former Chief Justice Warren that the First Amendment "underwrote the admonition of Thomas Jefferson that there should be a wall of separation between church and state." This well-known phrase of Jefferson's first occurs in his letter to Danbury Baptists in 1802.* How could it be said to underwrite an amendment to the Constitution which had been

---

*Although others — starting with Roger Williams in the seventeenth century — had employed this and similar constructions, a fairly systematic search of the literature indicates — and biographers of Jefferson concur — no prior appearance of this phrase in Jefferson's own writings and utterances.

written eleven years earlier? But this has not infrequently
been the level of argument used against aid to nonpublic
schools.

The constitutional facts are obvious enough. The state, at
any level, is allowed to cooperate with religious groups in a
nondiscriminatory manner in the furtherance of acceptably
secular purposes. Further, this is precisely what now happens,
with the single exception of elementary and secondary schools.
Thus city, state, and federal funds, in the usual baffling mix,
provide most of the support for the Jewish Hospital in
Brooklyn. Federal foreign-aid funds provide much of the
resources for the relief work in developing nations of Church
World Services, a Protestant agency. The federal government
provides money to improve the curriculum and the teaching
methods of Marist College, a Catholic institution in Pough-
keepsie. And so it goes.

The exception, to repeat, is that of elementary and secondary
schools with religious affiliations. (*Not* colleges and universities with such affiliations.) Slowly, however, this anomaly is
emerging. Slowly, the hierarchy of responses that arise when
the Court is wrong is beginning to appear.

1. *Debate.* This is the first and in every way crucial response.
When the Court is wrong there must be those who will say so.
Often as not this will be a dissenting member of the Court
itself. But to be effective the question must become a political
issue of the day. In his grand study *The Least Dangerous
Branch,* Alexander M. Bickel described Lincoln's response to
Dred Scott:

The principle that the Court proclaimed was that slavery was not
only legal in states which had it but was constitutionally guaranteed
in unorganized territories as well. In the debates with Stephen A.
Douglas in 1858, Lincoln said that he was against this decision, that
he thought it wrong, that he feared its consequences, that he deemed
it altogether deplorable. Douglas, on the other hand, without admit-

ting that he necessarily thought the decision right, dwelt heavily on the argument that "whoever resists the final decision of the highest judicial tribunal aims a deadly blow at our whole republican system of government." "I yield obedience," Douglas said, "to the decisions of that Court — to the final determination of the highest judicial tribunal known to our Constitution." To this Lincoln countered by deriding the notion that a decision of the Supreme Court is a "Thus saith the Lord." The Court, he said, can be wrong. There is nothing sacred about the Court's decisions. Men may properly differ with them.

As the initial decisions regarding state and church involved Catholic schools, the first arguments in opposition to *Everson* and its progeny came, generally, from Catholics. This made for difficulties (as the press, perhaps, will now find), it being easy for others to dismiss or ignore arguments that are necessarily self-interested. It may be Catholics were deficient in the skills and the access needed to mount a debate of this sort; it may also be that an element of prejudice worked against them. Surely there are episodes in this generation-long history that raise this latter question. Consider the instances in which Justice Douglas supported his opinions in *Tilton* v. *Richardson* (1971) and *Lemon* v. *Kurtzman* (1971) with references to Boettner's *Roman Catholicism* volume, characterized by Douglas Laycock of the University of Chicago Law School as an "elaborate hate tract." Boettner's views on Catholicism generally may be summarized in the following brief quote:

Our American Freedoms are being threatened today by two totalitarian systems, communism and Roman Catholicism. And of the two in our country Romanism is growing faster than is communism and is the more dangerous since it covers its real nature with a cloak of religion.

That particular passage is not cited by Mr. Justice Douglas, but here is one he quotes in footnote 20 of his concurring opinion in *Lemon* v. *Kurtzman:*

In the parochial schools Roman Catholic indoctrination is included in every subject. History, literature, geography, civics, and science are given a Roman Catholic slant. The whole education of the child is filled with propaganda. That, of course, is the very purpose of such schools, the very reason for going to all of the work and expense of maintaining a dual school system. Their purpose is not so much to educate, but to indoctrinate and train, *not to teach scripture truths and Americanism,* but to make loyal Roman Catholics. The children are regimented, and are told what to wear, what to do, and what to think. [Emphasis added.]

Ponder Boettner's charge that Catholic schools do not teach "scripture truths."

As it happens, a number of Catholic laymen and clergy pondered just that and at the time tried to draw attention to the peculiarity of such a tract being cited as a reference work in an opinion of a Supreme Court Justice. Had Douglas in some similar connection cited the Protocols of the Elders of Zion, or a Kommunication from the Grand Kleagle of the Ku Klux Klan, there would have been some notice taken. But there was no response whatever to these citations. There is a climate of presumption, and it must be worked against. (Thus, on April 3, 1979, reporting that the Supreme Court would hear a challenge to yet another state statute providing bits of aid to parochial schools, a New York law providing expenses for state-required testing, *The New York Times* noted: "The Federal Constitution specifically forbids state aid to parochial schools. . . .")* The dynamic of scholarship, which is both truth-seeking and competitive, at length responds to this kind of imbalance. Already the time is at hand when law clerks will

---

*This case, *Committee for Public Education and Religious Liberty et al.* v. *Regan,* was decided in favor of the State of New York, which had chosen to reimburse private schools for the costs of state-required tests. Mr. Justice White, for the majority, held that such reimbursement was permitted by *Wolman* v. *Walter.* Mr. Justice Blackmun, who wrote the opinion in *Wolman* v. *Walter,* dissented, stating that the majority was misinterpreting him. Mr. Justice Stevens also dissented, asserting:

have learned as law students that the *Everson* decision is disputed. In time there will be judges who learned it as students also. Just as important, Presidents may come to office committed to change. Roosevelt made no secret of his desire to appoint to the Court justices who would not block New Deal legislation on the basis of a flawed reading of the Fourteenth Amendment. It would be unthinkable today for a justice to be appointed who held to the *Plessy* doctrine.

The same may come to be true of *Everson*. This is a constitutional check on the Court: justices are appointed by the President. Already both major parties have endorsed aid to nonpublic schools. It is becoming a familiar position for presidential candidates since Senator George S. McGovern endorsed tuition tax credits in his 1972 campaign. It remains for a President to come to office either committed to the proposition as a matter of justice, or able, as a matter of politics, to balance the claims of the nonpublic schools with the fears of the public schools that they will lose whatever the other system gains.

Opinion polls indicate that the great majority of American people believe that educational pluralism is a principle deserv-

---

Rather than continuing with the sisyphean task of trying to patch together the "blurred, indistinct, and variable barrier" described in *Lemon* v. *Kurtzman,* I would resurrect the "high and impregnable" wall between church and state constructed by the Framers of the First Amendment. See *Everson* v. *Board of Education.*

Things are getting out of control. Mr. Justice Black, in *Everson,* stated that "the First Amendment has erected a wall betweeen church and state." An unspecified wall, that is. Conceivably a serpentine wall. But then *he* said: "That wall must be kept high and impregnable." Now Justice Stevens says that such was the wall constructed by the Framers. If *Everson* envisioned such a wall, why then did the actual decision uphold the New Jersey legislation providing bus transportation for children in private schools? But then the Court, in *Everson,* did seem *disposed* against the state. In a dissenting opinion, Mr. Justice Jackson observed:

The case which irresistibly comes to mind as the most fitting precedent is that of Julia, who, according to Byron's reports, "whispering 'I will ne'er consent,' — consented."

ing of active governmental support. And it is well to bear in mind Robert G. McCloskey's observation, in his magisterial study *The American Supreme Court* (1960), that "the Supreme Court has seldom, if ever, flatly and for very long resisted a really unmistakable wave of public sentiment. It has worked with the premise that constitutional law, like politics itself, is a science of the possible."

Debate on the *Gannett* decision began immediately, and soon became almost formal. The Associated Press, for example, distributed to its news staff a prepared statement to be read aloud to a judge who has announced the closing of a courtroom. The statement, described by Louis D. Boccardi, executive editor and vice president of the Associated Press, as "concise and legalistic," objects to any closed proceedings, sets forth the reasons why, and asks for time for further argument before a decision is made. This would appear to be a model reaction, if the validity of the Debate, Litigate, Legislate model is assumed.

2. *Litigate*. The exemplar of litigation as a tactic for bringing the Court back to the Constitution is the prolonged but in the end triumphant effort of the National Association for the Advancement of Colored People to reverse the *Plessy* decision. This is more difficult with *Everson*, for the effect of that ruling is that things don't rather than do happen, and it is not easy to challenge a nonexistent regime. Still, experience argues that those who feel aggrieved need to take initiatives. A former United States attorney, now teaching law, asks his class in constitutional law to explain why the United States government is *obligated* to provide financial aid to church- or synagogue-related schools. The answer, evidently, lies in the Free Exercise clause of the First Amendment: an interesting thought, and worth a lawsuit. Harry J. Hogan, retired counsel to the House Subcommittee on Elementary, Secondary, and Vocational Education, has pointed to the potential inherent in the growing practice of teaching "values" in public schools. "The fascinating possibility is that as soon as public schools

and universities are required to teach values, then church-related schools and universities will be able to demand equal access to state and federal tax funds."

The risk of litigation is that it divides. In the end *no* schools may receive support for ethics courses. But, as no other process, it educates the courts.

3. *Legislate.* Legislation is the most direct and open way for the Congress and President to advise the Court of their reading of the Constitution, views which have equal standing under the Constitution, albeit they do not have equal effect. This issue arose directly in the Lincoln-Douglas debates. Lincoln said: "If I were in Congress and a vote should come up on a question whether slavery should be prohibited in a new territory, in spite of that *Dred Scott* decision, I would vote that it should." Douglas was scornful, saying, "[I]f you elect him to the Senate he will introduce a bill to re-enact the law which the Court pronounced unconstitutional. . . . I never heard before of an appeal being taken from the Supreme Court. . . ." Lincoln replied that Douglas "would have the citizen conform his vote to that decision; the member of Congress, his; the President, his use of the veto power. He would make it a rule of political action for the people and all the departments of the government. I would not." Commenting on this exchange, Bickel allows that while deference to the Court is surely in order from the other branches, this cannot be absolute:

The functions cannot and need not be rigidly compartmentalized. The Court often provokes consideration of the most intricate issues of principle by the other branches, engaging them in dialogues and "responsive readings"; and there are times also when the conversation starts at the other end and is perhaps less polite. Our government consists of discrete institutions, but the effectiveness of the whole depends on their involvement with one another, on their intimacy, even if it often is the sweaty intimacy of creatures locked in combat.

That Congress can abuse its power, should cause no surprise. Indeed it has. Reacting to the Supreme Court decision in *Engel*

v. *Vitale* (1962), which forbade school prayer, the Senate on
April 5, 1979, and again on April 9, by margins of 47 to 37 and
51 to 40, respectively, voted to deny the Supreme Court
appellate jurisdiction in such cases. This can be done under
Article III, Section 2, at least with respect to cases in federal
court. (It is contended that the power was intended as Congress's restraint on the Court, corresponding to the President's
power of appointment.) But in this case the power was surely
misused. Publicly prescribed prayer, voluntary or not, is
precisely what "an establishment of religion" is all about and
that is what the First Amendment forbids. (In the course of the
debate, one Senator rose "to speak as a Christian" about what
he called the "secular humanism that abounds in our children's schools today." He did not like this and thought "we
Christians" should do something about it. One is reminded,
from time to time, that this is a Protestant country.)

For all this, legislation is unequaled as a means to influence
the Court. Labor legislation was finally accepted by the Court
only because state legislatures kept passing bills. Even the
venerable Charles Evans Hughes at last was converted.
Writing for the Court in *West Coast Hotel Co.* v. *Parrish* (1937),
he derided the "freedom of contract" argument: "What is this
freedom? The Constitution does not speak of freedom of
contract. It speaks of liberty and prohibits the deprivation of
liberty without due process of law."

Similarly, the Congress through legislation has commenced
the undoing of the *Everson* decision. First, in the Elementary
and Secondary Education Act of 1965, provision was made for
compensatory services in schools with high proportions of
"deprived" children, of which denominational schools have a
more than sufficient share. (In New York City, nuns initially
had to teach the children to operate the television sets thus
provided, as they themselves were forbidden to touch them.
But even such silliness makes its impact.) Similarly, the
Higher Education Act of 1965 provided federal funds for

"strengthening developing institutions." These were understood to be, in the main, black colleges in the South. But federal administrators, in the manner of bureaucracies, found that denominational colleges in the North often met the criteria and they were given grants accordingly. Half the private colleges and universities in the nation have religious affiliations, and most seem to take part in the now considerably complex system of federal aid to higher education. Mild tensions persist. It was reported that at the First National Congress on Church-Related Colleges and Universities, held at Notre Dame in the summer of 1979, there were complaints of "federal officials who question whether theology should be taught in classrooms built with federally guaranteed loans." But this is the point. Federal officials are now merely nervous about support for activities which, if one were to read *Everson* and nothing more, it would be assumed are altogether forbidden. What is happening, of course, is that American practice is coming in line with that of the other English-speaking democracies, where government support is provided to any bona fide educational activity, and the communal peace, on this score at least, is maintained.

There will remain the issue of public policy. *Should* eighteen-year-olds receive assistance? That is a different question altogether. It has never been satisfactorily resolved, mostly because opponents have always succeeded in interposing the constitutional question. But it is not a constitutional question.

Legislation is not always to be advised. The press, for example, will want to be cautious indeed before deciding that it wishes Congress to make a law respecting its freedom. On the other hand, it may find it useful for Congress to make laws protecting the Sixth Amendment right of the public to be present at trials. To those who say the Court has decreed that no such right exists, there is Lincoln's retort that a Supreme Court decision is not a "Thus saith the Lord."

Has this analysis any predictive power? The *Gannett* case will provide a test. As with most cases in which the Supreme Court would seem to be wrong, debate began promptly and it may be forecast that a good deal of litigation will follow. In the manner of *Everson,* one decision will lead to another: clarifying, adjusting, half-apologizing. Legislation will be contemplated: most likely dealing with the public's right to access to the courts, rather than that of the press as such. In the end the Court either will reverse itself, or set forth rules for the closure of courts so narrow and restricted in their application that the controversy will go away. It may be hoped that it does not require a generation for this to come about.

THREE

In a transport, possibly, of Bicentennial excess, I ran in five elections in the course of 1976. Each was contested; some were close. I ran, first, from the Bronx, to be a delegate to the Democratic National Convention. Then I ran for a place on the platform committee. My next "campaign" was for membership on the drafting committee for the platform. Thence to the senatorial primary in New York, and finally to the Senate election itself.

Save for Robert Kennedy in 1964, I was the first Democrat to win a New York Senate race since 1950. Thus it may be said the outcome of the campaign was different; but so was the campaign itself. Or so I judged, and I had been involved in most of the Senate campaigns in New York since 1950. If there was a theme to those campaigns, it was the celebration of past glory. Smith, Roosevelt, Lehman. The coming of the New Deal. The magic, however, had slipped out of the incantation.

I approached the campaign differently, and what I said may be of some interest. Meaning just that: what I SAID. *There is a certain amount of writing in politics still, and some of it gets into the newspapers. But for candidates as well as for voters, the real campaign, the authentic experience, is almost wholly embodied in the stump speech. Morning and night, day after day, in —just as the formula has it— in union halls in Tonawanda, in senior citizens' centers in the Flatlands of Brooklyn, by swimming pools in East Hampton, in drawing rooms high over Fifth Avenue, in basement halls in the South Bronx, in cafés in the southern tier, in taverns in the Norther Country, down to the last homecoming rally at Pindars Corners, this is what I said:*

The dilemma for liberals in New York is that we face unprecedented government problems, which, however, have come about under the auspices of impeccably liberal governments in New York City and in New York State. Not merely liberal, but most often patrician liberal. There has been a great coalescing of progressive forces, and government has truly been given a free hand to do all that it could do. And all that it did was go bust. New York City is in default. Its powers of self-government, intact since 1664 except for a brief spell under General Howe, have been significantly taken from it, and given to persons little known to us and certainly not chosen by us. Some, impervious to evidence, blame this on Washington, where a Thermidor or worse is said to have set in. But such an evasion will not survive scrutiny of the federal budget, which has grown enormously, mainly to solve problems which New York is finding insoluble.

None of this, I said, was helping the reputation of liberalism. Indeed, during the presidential primary, when Congressman Morris K. Udall came to New York, he disowned the term. This led Senator Henry M. Jackson to remark that he might not be a liberal, but he was the only candidate willing to call himself one. Jimmy Carter won the primaries by speaking continuously of "the horrible, bloated, confused bureaucracy" in Washington. So it wouldn't do us too much good to blame tightwads in Washington. And there was no point getting nasty blaming ourselves. What we needed to do, I said, was to sort out our situation and to be as honest about it as we dared.

It was the Bicentennial, I would continue, not just of the

American Revolution, but also of Gibbon's Decline and Fall, *and I would cite the theme of the later chapters: "the leakage of reality." Something like that had been happening to public discourse in New York, and we must resist it — but not to the point of imprudence, because there are some realities that are simply too painful to confront.*

I would then describe our situation in terms of three interconnected and reinforcing crises: a crisis of government, a crisis of the economy, and a crisis of social organization.

The essential of the government crisis, I said, was that New York City could no longer maintain its present level of operations. This situation threatened the state and other jurisdictions already sufficiently shaky. Raising taxes to meet rising costs, as we had done in the past, would lead to the loss of taxpayers and reduced income. The subway syndrome: higher fares, fewer riders, less revenue, greater deficit. In part this crisis derived from the honorable tradition of New Yorkers making a decent provision for one another. In part it derived from folly. We had become a people who know the value of everything and the price of nothing. This posture presents itself as highly moral; but Reinhold Niebuhr, if alive, would soon enough reveal the coercion involved in all that preachiness. "If we can send a man to the moon. . . ." In any event, it was a crisis very much of our own making. If we decide to pay twice what Texans pay for the same thing, we must expect to suffer twice the tax.

The decline of government is inexorably associated with the crisis of the economy. The economy of the Northeast is stagnant. In New York City itself there has been a crashing decline. Since 1969, 640,000 private-sector jobs had been lost — enough to sustain a normal metropolitan area of 2,000,000 persons. The Hudson Valley was asleep, the Mohawk Valley was drowsy. Buffalo had lost more than one fifth of its population in the past twenty years. New York State was losing population. We had had only 2 percent of the nation's housing starts. An executive in Manhattan could increase his real income by almost a quarter merely by moving to Dallas, most of the difference being in reduced taxes. But such an executive, firm, or industry might want to move away because the decline of government services in New York City was making our area a less attractive place to live in; and the rise of social disorganization was making it a positively dangerous place. Even loyalists like George Kennan were declaring the city "no longer fit for civilized living."

The crisis of social organization in 1976 was the easiest to describe but the hardest to analyze. And even though it was easy to describe, few in public life cared to do so, because the crisis was now so far advanced that merely to describe it was to suggest how little it was likely to respond to public policy. I call it Weaver's Paradox, from a memorandum Paul Weaver wrote in 1968 on New York City. The social fabric of New York, he wrote, was coming to pieces. "A large segment of the population is becoming incompetent and destructive. Growing parasitism, both legal and illegal, is the result; so, also, is violence."

This parasitism (I would argue) is to be found at every level of society, and not least in the horde of New Yorkers who live well looking after the poor. Feeding the sparrows by feeding the horses. But Weaver's point, and mine, was that no one sensed the threat to freedom caused by this growing dependence.

I would quote the economist Arthur Cecil Pigou: "Environments . . . as well as people have children." We therefore must expect our present situation to persist at least into the twenty-first century.

But this generational problem aside, the decline of the economy itself would increase dependency. Dependency of women and children probably would grow because of the shift in the job market away from male-defined jobs. Of 11.2 million new jobs created in the country over the eight years before 1976, 8 million were white-collar, 2.5 million service, and 1.5 million blue-collar. The number of farm jobs actually declined. Of the 8 million white-collar jobs, 72 percent went to women. Women "received" 59 percent of new professional and technical jobs and 50 percent of new managerial and administrative jobs. Only among the blue-collar occupations — barely a tenth of the new jobs — did men get most of the new jobs.

The growth of government was beginning to divide the population. This is most readily seen in an upstate, rural county such as the one I have called home since the early Kennedy years. The farmers there had been pretty much in the mud in those days, and pretty much still were. But a whole new class of public-sector employees had entered the scene, and it appeared we were well on our way to becoming a society of public affluence and private squalor; until the crisis of government arrives and the future becomes more problematic.

That was my stump speech. Does it seem bearish? Despairing? Illiberal? It did not to my audiences. It seemed true. They told me so. I ran as a liberal willing to be critical of what liberals had done. If we did not do this, I contended, our liberalism would go soft. I never yielded much on this. I even got close to belligerent when, in the primary-election debates, it was suggested that the budgetary crisis could be resolved by cutting $30 billion from defense appropriations. (Presumably the savings would be turned over to New York.) It would be the final corruption of our tradition to tilt the balance of world power in favor of the totalitarians in order to continue to pay for the subsidies we had voted one another.

This sort of talk caused convulsions in some New York City circles. But there was nothing illiberal about it except in the perspective of a liberalism that had indeed gone soft. In the general election some perspective was restored when a (thoroughly honorable) Republican/Conservative opponent called for my defeat so that liberalism would never again show its "ugly head" in New York. Conservatives know.

I genuinely was concerned to identify the excessive moralizing of our politics, and to resist it. Everywhere I quoted Renata Adler: "Sanity . . . is the most profound moral option of our time."

I also tried to argue against the apocalyptic voices that have *begun to be heard in circles once so overconfident. Murphy's Law applies only in the short term, I said. I would invite attention to the large complex of empty buildings on Ward's Island in the East River visible to anyone using the Triborough Bridge. These were built in the 1950s to warehouse the mentally ill from Manhattan. At that time the rising resident population of New York State's mental hospitals — doubled in the previous quarter century, likely to quadruple in the next — was our most pressing social problem. But there seemed no answer except to build more hospitals, and then more, until half the population would be confined in them, as Isaiah Berlin had once jocosely predicted, and the other half working in them. Then in 1955 Governor Harriman authorized the large-scale use of the tranquilizing drugs developed at Rockland State Hospital under Governor Dewey. The next year and then every year for the rest of the decade, the population of the mental hospitals went down. The new buildings were never occupied. What seemed at mid-century the most pressing crisis of state government — the housing of the mentally ill — today is nearly forgotten as a crisis. (Although problems of the care of the mentally ill persist.)*

When there was time, I went on a bit. Reputations were at stake. The reputation of New York, of an intelligent liberalism, Republican as much as Democratic. If it came to be judged in the nation that such politics lead to ruin, how would we be judged? It was time we recognized, even if no one else would, what New York means. Trying to describe what Venice meant to the Mediterranean world of the fifteenth or sixteenth century, the French historian Fernand Braudel writes: "Venice dominated the 'Interior Sea' as New York dominates the western world today." And if New York should collapse . . . what then of the West? What then of the Constitution? Of all the features of the American federal system, one of the most important (I would say) is one not at all provided for, but which evolved directly from the constitutional preoccupation with the separation of

power. This is the separation between New York and Washing-
ton. Hamilton and Jefferson struck the agreement: the political
capital would move to Washington. For all other purposes the
first city of the nation would be New York. Those other purposes
have been well served by New York, and none more faithfully
than in preventing the behemothic amalgam of government,
finance, business, industry, and culture which the Founders
most feared. It would not take much for Wall Street to move to
Connecticut Avenue; for NBC and Time, Inc., to follow; for
Broadway to give way to the Kennedy Center; for the Washington Post *to become the national paper. In the long sequence of*
generations of New Yorkers, I would conclude it had fallen to
ours to defend the city against a collapse that would bring down
a political tradition with it.

An interval of four years has not much altered the condition
of the city, nor yet my view of the situation save for the extra-
ordinary insights offered by a paper presented by Mancur
Olson at the American Political Science Association meeting
in 1978, entitled "Pluralism and National Decline: The Political
Economy of Comparative Growth Rates." Why, he asked, have
the economic growth rates of Great Britain in recent genera-
tions been so much lower than those of other industrial nations,
and why in particular have Germany and Japan so outper-
formed the British from the time of their defeat in the Second
World War? He located the problem in just that place where
no one else had looked: in the very stability — and freedom —
of British society.

He began by distinguishing between the "sources" and the
"causes" of growth. The sources are well known: for example,
increased capital investment, improved training of the work
force, technological innovation. But what causes such develop-
ments to take place? As most of the developed democracies have,
broadly speaking, had the same opportunities available to them,
why does one society take more advantage of its opportunities
than others? It is Olson's suggestion that "in many societies and

regions there are unusually obdurate retardants *to growth: socially derived obstacles that unintentionally but substantially delay or deflect, at times even dam up, the flow of economic progress."*

And what are these obstacles? In brief, they are the common-interest organizations — professional associations, trade unions, cartels, cooperatives, and whatever — which can make their own members better off by reducing the efficiency of the economy as a whole. "The most important way in which common interest organizations reduce the rate of growth is by limiting entry into the industries and occupations which they control." Whence it follows that "those countries which have had democratic freedom or organization without upheaval or invasion the longest, will suffer the most from growth repressing organizations and combinations." Of the industrial democracies, no nation has had a longer record of military security and democratic stability than Great Britain. France, with its long history of invasion and upheaval, had by 1970 a per-capita income decidedly above that of Britain and only a fourth lower than that of the United States.

And what of the United States? There is a direct and negative relationship between years-since-statehood (or in the case of former Confederate states, years-since-the-Civil-War) and economic growth rates.

And of New York? New York has governed itself without interruption since 1664 save for a brief period under the British during the Revolution. By coincidence, during 1976 Norman Macrae of The Economist published an essay entitled "Little Britain in New York," suggesting the parallels between our decline and Britain's. Olson suggests that it is worth asking whether the special problems of New York City, "one of the very oldest of the large American cities, are in part due to the logic" of his hypothesis. And not just of New York, for in any comparison of developed economic growth rates since the Second World War, only Britain ranks lower than the United States.

There are, again, more than a few difficulties with Olson's hypothesis, but at least it directs our attention to that aspect of our circumstances, which is to say, our stability, which we are least accustomed to associating with any of our difficulties. As the 1970s closed the political voices heard in the land (it is, after all, a time of "peace") called for less government, not more. This represents almost a complete reversal from the atmosphere at the end of the 1960s. As I was something of a dissenter then, so now. But nothing but good can come from a little more attention to just what it is that makes for the wealth of nations.

If I have got it right, certain of our ideas have been flawed. In essence there developed in our thinking a radical disjunction between the production of wealth and its distribution, with the accompanying view that the former takes care of itself and that the task of government is to see to the latter.

Professor Bruno Stein of New York University suggests that this disjunction goes back to John Stuart Mill. No one any longer reads Mill; but it would be a profound mistake to suppose that we are no longer influenced by him. His was the formative intellect of the modern liberal state, and that, by the grace of God, is what we are and will continue to be. (Few of us any longer read Hamilton or Jay, but their spirits walk this chamber, being the more comfortable perhaps, as New Yorkers.) The Principles of Political Economy, With Some of Their Applications to Social Philosophy *(to give its full title) begins with Book I, devoted to the subject of "Production." That matter having been disposed of, Book II turns to "Distribution." Chapter I, "Of Property," begins:*

The principles which have been set forth in the first part of this treatise, are, in certain respects, strongly distinguished from those on the consideration of which we are now about to enter. The laws and conditions of the production of wealth, partake of the character of physical truths. There is nothing optional or arbitrary in them. Whatever mankind produce, must be produced in the modes, and under the conditions imposed by the constitution of external things, and by the inherent properties of their own bodily and mental structure.

Production, in other words, was the realm of science and of necessity. How very different that of distribution.

It is not so with the distribution of wealth. That is a matter of human institution solely. The things once there, mankind, individually or collectively, can do with them as they like. They can place them at the disposal of whomsoever they please, and on whatever terms. . . . The distribution of wealth, therefore, depends on the laws and customs of society. The rules by which it is determined, are what the opinions and feelings of the ruling portion of the community make them, and are very different in different ages and countries; and might be still more different, if mankind so chose.

Thus the dolorous disjunction arose; the rationale, as Stein puts it, that those who worry about distribution need not worry about production. ". . . It became easy to view production as a grubby process that involved dirt and noise and exploitation and calculation, to be disdained by aristocrat and social reformer alike." Never mind that "what gets distributed is limited by what gets produced."

There would be several generations between John Stuart Mill and John Maynard Keynes, but Keynes, a figure very much of our own time, would add a scientific base to what was only an obiter dictum in his great Victorian predecessor. For to Keynes, distribution was the problem; an excess of savings the obstacle to recovery, the symptom of malfunction to be constantly watched for. Supply would take care of itself.

But of course supply does not take care of itself, and that which is produced is clearly affected, if not indeed determined by the manner in which it is distributed. The tax system is the nexus of the two.

For a period New York could escape any special consequences of such doctrinal confusion. As the nation's largest industrial state, our "production side" took care of the "supply side."

We spent more; but earned more. In approximate terms, per capita income in New York was about a quarter higher than that of the nation; and so was the amount we spent on ourselves through government.

In some areas we were slow to accelerate. As late as 1963, for example, per dollar of personal income, New Yorkers were spending 10 percent less than was the nation as a whole on state and local public welfare expenditures.

But then a fateful sheering process began. Our relative advantage in income began to move down and government costs to move up. By 1978, per capita personal income of New Yorkers was only 6 percent greater than the national average. By contrast, social welfare expenditures as a percent of income were 66 percent above the national average.

This was a fateful imbalance: it has led to a significant loss of freedom, which is to say of traditional self-government. It has diminished a great political tradition. Traces of the same process appear in the nation itself. It commands attention.

10.
Patterns of
Ethnic Succession

The Rise of Blacks and
Hispanics in New York City

ETHNIC SUCCESSION is one of the persistent rhythms in the life of New York City. Political scientists will recognize it as a variant of Pareto's circulation of elites, a measure of the vigor of our society and our capacity for self-renewal.

In the late 1950s Nathan Glazer and I, collaborating on a study of the ethnic groups of New York City, saw this as a central dynamic of the city's organizational life. At that time the Irish had dominated the political life of the city for generations; yet just as clearly they were departing that scene, and this was the opening observation in our chapter devoted to them. In the aftermath of the municipal elections of 1977 there was (for the first time in at least a century) not a single Irish name on the board of estimate, that central governing body of the city made up of the mayor, the comptroller, the president of the city council, and the five borough presidents.

Ethnic succession was not, however, the central theme of our study. We had as our more elemental purpose the mere assertion that ethnicity was still a force in the life of the city (and the nation) *and was not going away.* Our first proposition received grudging assent at the time. At election season

editorials deploring the persistence of the balanced ticket were
as predictable as the accompanying admonition to all citizens
to make certain to vote. But the thought that ethnicity was *not*
going away aroused alarm indeed. It conflicted with the then
near-universal view which held the ethnic group to be a
premodern, preindustrial phenomenon, rather to be deplored
and in any event soon to disappear. The view was espoused
with equal vigor by the two preeminent ideological schools of
the 1960s, the Marxists and the reformist liberals. That they
agreed on this, as on almost nothing else, gave extra weight to
the then-conventional wisdom which Glazer and I now called
into question.

The Marxist view was well known, encapsulated in the
slogan "Workers of the World, Unite!" Non-Marxists shared the
unstated assumptions which at this period Milton Gordon
described as the "liberal expectation," the belief that in the
normal course of events superficial traits, such as speech
accents and food preferences, would simply fade away, or
homogenize, and thereafter only individual characteristics
would be visible and significant. (Typically, neither Marxists
nor liberals paid overmuch heed to the persistence of religious
belief *and* difference.)

We called our study, which finally appeared in 1963, *Beyond
the Melting Pot: The Negroes, Puerto Ricans, Jews, Italians and
Irish of New York City*. We stated that, far from being
preindustrial, ethnic groups were very much a modern phenomenon, and, whether one liked it or not, should be expected
to persist.

The key to our analysis was the statement: "The ethnic
groups in New York are also *interest groups*." That individual
members had personal and family ties to one another was
obvious enough. But we argued that the group itself established ties to the larger society. As Daniel Bell later wrote,
"Ethnicity can combine interest with an affective tie."

That ethnic groups are interest groups suggests that they

will conflict (and combine) with one another from time to time, that from time to time one group will overcome a second in one sphere or another, and thereupon what we call ethnic succession will follow.

In 1975 Glazer and I published a much more ambitious undertaking entitled *Ethnicity: Theory and Experience,* the result of a two-year seminar at the American Academy of Arts and Sciences. By this time the persistence of ethnicity was no longer much in dispute, and aspects of it were rather in favor. But we persisted merely in trying to be descriptive. Obviously ethnicity persisted in New York. "In this city it often seems that ethnic is all," the *New Yorker* City Hall reporter, Andy Logan, wrote in 1978. But we were struck by how much it had come to the fore in the world at large — not just in the United States but everywhere, including, quite graphically, the United Kingdom.

We now essayed a more general theoretical exposition. The ethnic group had plainly become a focus of social mobilization throughout the world, from preindustrial regions to postindustrial. (*A* focus, not *the* focus.) We offered a twofold explanation.

First, the evolution of the welfare state in the more advanced economies and the advent of the socialist state in the underdeveloped ones. In either circumstance the *state* becomes a crucial and direct arbiter of economic well-being and political status. In such circumstances the ethnic group acquires great strategic efficacy both as a way of making claims for benefits derived from the state, *and* as a channel by which the state distributes such benefits. (This latter point, not much noticed, seemed to us to be an important one. The state finds it helpful for the population to organize itself along ethnic lines for it makes it possible to confer distinct as against general benefits. This, presumably, enables the state to appear to be efficacious. Hence, we hypothesized, as the world becomes more industrial and more collectivist, there will be an enlargement of ethnic claims.)

The second part of our explanation had to do with the social dynamics that lead to ethnic claims, and concerned the fact and the nature of inequality. If men are everywhere equal in theory, they are rarely equal in condition. Neither, we observed, are ethnic groups. There is a constant churning, which in Ralf Dahrendorf's words "serves to keep social structures alive." In this view "inequality always implies the gain of one group at the expense of others: thus every system of social stratification generates protest against its principles and bears the seeds of its own suppression."

We also, in this work, took some pains to call attention to David Schneider's concept of the "desocialization" of ethnic groups, which is to say the increasingly similar cultural content of different ethnic groups in the United States, which by our lights would reduce ethnic content. But differences persist, and so do loyalties. Loyalties themselves constitute a kind of conflicting norm.

Hence, of course, the pattern of ethnic succession which in part consists of the displacement of established groups (established in a neighborhood, a profession, a church, a sport, a trade union) by another group and also — I stress — the attainment of one group to the "higher" condition of another.

So much for theory. How has it worked out in practice for the two ethnic groups, blacks and Puerto Ricans, which in *Beyond the Melting Pot* we described as the newest groups in the city? They are no longer the newest groups. A rather distinctly Asian cohort — Korean, Chinese, Filipino, and Vietnamese — has come in behind them. How then are the blacks and Puerto Ricans doing? If our theory holds up, both ought to be moving up (and being pushed up), to be actively challenging the norms of previous groups, and also to be emulating them. If history holds up, they ought to be having some success.

Both things seem to be so. Their challenge is well established. The mere assertion that there ought to be, for example, "racial" balance in the major institutions of city government — the emergency financial control board, the board of estimate — is a challenge to the previous norm of "ethnic" balance which typically excluded these two groups. Curiously, the achievement of that balance constitutes a diminishment of differences. But that, to repeat, is the dynamic of it all.

To appreciate the extent of the success of blacks and Hispanics, we must recall the dimensions of the black and Hispanic migration that occurred. Between 1960 and 1970, New York City's black population grew by more than half a million — giving us the largest black community in the Western Hemisphere, and one of the largest in the world. Once, New York had more Jews than Jerusalem, more Irish than Dublin, and so on. It could be said that New York today has more blacks than the populations of three great African capitals combined — Nairobi, Dakar, and Khartoum. In 1970, New York had more citizens of Hispanic origin than the combined population of Puerto Rico's three largest cities. Blacks now probably comprise almost 24 percent of New York City's residents, while persons of Hispanic origin make up almost 18 percent. The proportion of non–Puerto Rican Hispanics also grows.

New York's blacks and Hispanics tend to be considerably younger than the population of the nation, and to have higher proportions of females — which means they often have more difficulty finding employment, and often make greater claims on certain kinds of government services. In the public schools, for example, nearly 40 percent of the pupils enrolled in 1978 were black, and almost 30 percent were Hispanic.

Our schools, for all their troubles, are still the essential agency of ethnic succession. The Census Bureau's March 1978 Current Population Survey showed that the median of years of school completed was 11.4 for blacks in the United States compared with a median of 12.0 years for blacks residing in the New York metropolitan area. The median number of school years completed by all persons residing in the New York metropolitan area was 12.3 — only a few points higher than that for metropolitan New York blacks. Hispanics were still behind, with 10.2 years in the New York metropolitan area, compared to a national level for Hispanics of 10.4 years, but there are signs that they are beginning to press forward. *The Undergraduate Ethnic Census for the City University of New York* for the fall of 1977 showed that Hispanic enrollments had nearly doubled since 1972 — from 13,563 to 25,351 — while black enrollment increased by 12 percent — from 44,031 to 49,313.

No immigrant group ever arrives at the right time. That is a staple of immigrant history. In this respect blacks and Puerto Ricans were no different. We think of them as entering the labor force in particularly large numbers beginning in the 1960s, not long before job opportunities in New York ceased to grow and began to decline. Roy Bahl at the Maxwell School of Syracuse University has shown that employment in New York City grew by only 0.6 percent in the twelve years between 1960 and 1972. This contrasts with an increase of 31 percent in the rest of the state and 34.2 percent for the nation. Trends since 1972 made New York's relative situation even worse than that pictured in Professor Bahl's gloomy figures. Between 1969 and 1977 New York City lost over 600,000 manufacturing jobs — a number larger than the entire work force of many states.

New York's labor force participation rates — the percentages of people working or seeking work — are lower than those of the rest of the nation both for whites and blacks. In part, this is because many potential New York workers are still in school or college. There is also reason to suspect a *consequence* of New York's chronically high unemployment rate — in time, people just stop looking for work. Yet while the unemployment rate for New York City's blacks in the second quarter of 1978 was a high 10.1 percent, that was virtually two percentage points lower than the national rate for blacks, while unemployment here was two and a half points higher than the national rate for whites. All these numbers are dismaying — but they do suggest that New York's unemployment may not be quite so inequitably distributed as is often the case elsewhere. The unemployment level of Hispanic men in New York, our data suggest, in recent years has moved closer to the unemployment level for black men, while Hispanic women's unemployment levels are still considerably higher than those of both white and black women — perhaps evidence that the allocation of labor between men and women within an ethnic group varies according to the group's position in the line of ethnic succession.

Quite apart from employment rates, there has been a marked upgrading of the work force. The percentage of employed blacks in the New York metropolitan area listed by the census as "professional and technical" has tripled (from 5 percent to 15 percent) since 1960, and the percentage of Hispanics in similar job classifications more than doubled (from 2 percent to 5 percent) between 1960 and 1970. While 61 percent of New York's whites had white-collar jobs in 1976, so did 51 percent of New York's blacks. The distribution of blacks through the various classifications of employment in the New York area is growing remarkably similar to that of Washington, D.C. — long thought of as the capital of the black middle class. And among persons of Hispanic origin born in the mainland United States, the ever-improving employment distribution that the ethnic succession model would suggest is likewise beginning to emerge. Just as other ethnic immigrants overcame the proposition that there should be distinctively ethnic occupational castes, so too have blacks and Hispanics — at least in New York City.

Minority incomes in New York, like those of blacks and Hispanics throughout the country, have risen significantly since the mid-sixties. In New York City, it seems, they have risen higher than in most places.

The Census Bureau's Survey of Income and Education (SIE), a survey conducted in mid-1976, reported the income status of respondents for the preceding calendar year (1975). The sample size was sufficiently large to permit some data for New York City to be broken out for comparison to national findings. The census officials who have made this data available warn that because of the limited size of the sample, such data must be used with caution. With this caveat, I offer the following:

1. Despite the harsh recession of the mid-1970s, and the additional troubles that afflicted New York City's economy, the ratios of black to white family incomes in New York City are higher than those of black to white families in the nation at large. For New York City, the ratio of black to white median family incomes in 1975 was .73. For the United States as a whole, it was .62. For all large cities taken together, it was .65.

2. Families of Hispanic origin are making some income gains in New York City, but are not gaining so rapidly as blacks. This is in keeping with familiar patterns of ethnic succession, for compared to blacks, New York City's Hispanics are relative newcomers to the United States, and tend more frequently to return to their places of origin after having amassed some savings. Hispanics in California and the Southwest — who often are long established in the communities where they live — have higher incomes than New York Hispanics.

3. Among those not living in family units, the black-white median income ratio is about the same in New York as in the nation as a whole.

4. In 1970, some 25 percent of the black households in New York City had incomes above the median income for all New York metropolitan area households — putting them indisputably in the middle class. By 1975, that proportion had risen to

30 percent. In 1970, some 16 percent of the city's Hispanic households were middle-class by this definition. By 1975 that proportion had grown to 20 percent. It should be kept in mind that these gains occurred during a period in which white income here and in the nation at large was not rising at so rapid a rate. Some of the progress of our poorer minorities is therefore a relative matter. But there was progress, both relatively and absolutely. This trend toward equality was not simply a benefit conferred by the working of the market economy. Politics and government played an important part.

5. New York City has growing numbers of blacks and Hispanic families with incomes over $20,000. About 20 percent of black New York families are in this bracket.

6. Mean female incomes for blacks and Hispanics in New York City are significantly higher than female incomes for whites in the nation at large — surely an important factor in the economic standing of New York's black and Hispanic families.

7. A comparison of poverty rates for whites, blacks, and Hispanics in New York in 1975 shows that while whites and Hispanics have somewhat higher poverty rates than those of corresponding groups in the nation at large, black poverty rates are lower than the national level.

Housing shows the most promising trends of all, albeit ones with troubling features of their own. Blacks — especially those who are entering into the main currents of the city's economic life — are leaving the old neighborhoods of Central Harlem and Bedford-Stuyvesant (both were Jewish neighborhoods two generations ago) in a quickening stream. But while other cities show a trend toward increasing black movement toward the suburbs, New York City is seeing the resettlement of working-class and middle-class blacks within the city itself — for instance, in Flatbush and in Laurelton, Queens. In 1970, according to an analysis by Professor Emanuel Tobier of New

York University, 86 percent of the black middle-class house-holds in the New York region — the city and five counties closest to it in the state — were located in New York City. Five years later that figure had not changed. Blacks — and, to an increasing extent, Hispanics — are buying up the sound, older housing stock in the outer boroughs. Blacks owned and occupied eight times as many homes in 1978 as they did in 1950 — an increase in black home ownership of a hundred thousand. More than three quarters of the homeowners are in Brooklyn and Queens. If housing values hold up — and, regrettably, this is no certainty — the growth of these neigh-borhoods could turn out to be one of the most heartening aspects of our city.

Cynics will believe that whites are leaving these neighbor-hoods because blacks are coming to them. But there may be a more innocent reason for this. Whites may be leaving because the better jobs have been leaving. Here we encounter a factor which may prove to be a serious obstacle to those following the old routes of ethnic succession in New York City. For, unlike those of earlier migrants, the wave of the postwar era has made its advances in large measure through its successes in obtaining government employment. And while the effects of economic decline may reach government somewhat belatedly, when they do arrive, they strike with brutal and concerted force.

In a paper drafted for the National Commission on Manpow-er Policy in 1976, Andrew F. Brimmer presented powerful facts: only 15 percent of white workers work for the govern-ment, while 22 percent of blacks work in the public sector. And only 17 percent of all white earnings come from the govern-ment, while 26 percent of all black earnings do.

In the decade since 1968, according to the Office of the Chancellor of the New York City Board of Education, blacks increased their proportion of the professional staff of the New York City school system from 9.7 percent to 10.7 percent. But overall cutbacks in education meant that, despite the energy expended, there are, in absolute numbers, several hundred fewer blacks employed today in the school system. Government was half a decade behind in feeling the effects of the sharp economic downturn of the late sixties and after.

In the three years between 1974 and 1977, according to New York City's Department of Personnel, black employment in the so-called mayoral agencies in New York City declined by almost 13,000, and that of Hispanics declined by almost 5,000. A similar pattern seems to hold in the uniformed services. And if the White House and the Congress cut back federal funds for public service employment, these losses will be compounded.

The politics of ethnic succession brought considerable progress over the past decade and a half — but we cannot neglect to note that what government can do, it also can undo. The gains that were achieved must be consolidated by widening the foundation upon which they rest. In a 1978 speech, Professor Brimmer warned that: ". . . too much hope is being placed on the expected expansion of public service jobs. Instead, we must look to greater efforts to increase openings on private payrolls."

That, surely, is part of the answer. But there is yet an important role for government. Government must plan for an orderly adjustment to the circumstances we face. It can do a great deal both to counteract further decline in the private sector and to foster the kinds of economic development that still are possible. New York must learn to pursue economic development the way others do. We must establish in our political culture a concern for economic development — a concern not unlike that demonstrated by the governors of the states of the Sun Belt in the previous generation, one of whom, a Georgian, is now our president. But it should be possible for us to do this without sacrificing the better-than-average accomplishments made by those who came here to reenact the experience of ethnic succession that New York City has provided to so many generations of Americans.

The social programs of the 1960s, overpraised at the time (and woe it was for those of us who at the time suggested that), are now generally overcriticized. I believe the record of ethnic succession in New York City in the 1960s belies so pessimistic a summary. There is achievement alongside failure, and the achievement matters more.

Years ago I was introduced to Langston Hughes in a restaurant on 125th Street. I said to him that I thought he was the best political satirist writing since Finley Peter Dunne. "That is high praise," he said. But he accepted it, for he knew his own worth. And surely, Hughes's character, Simple, was a fitting successor to Mr. Dooley, an altogether happy ethnic succession. But both are gone, and neither has a successor. There is little social science has to say on this, the more important subject.

11.
The Politics of
Regional Growth

THE FIRST OBSERVATION to make about the 1977 White House Conference on Balanced Growth and Economic Development, the first of its kind, is that although it was nominally concerned with the subject of regional growth, the fact of regional decline actually engaged its concern. We don't summon White House conferences to discuss issues that are going well.

To be sure, the federal government has pursued policies of regional growth from the earliest days of the Republic. Think of Gallatin's *Report on Public Roads and Canals* in 1808. Through the nineteenth century the central theme to all such activity summed itself up in the notion of westward expansion.

In the twentieth century, and especially with the coming of the New Deal, the national government also began to direct its concerns to the South as a region. The development of agriculture had dominated westward expansion. Now it was believed that agriculture was holding on too long in the South, while industrialization was not proceeding rapidly enough. As President, Franklin D. Roosevelt very much associated himself and his administration with this belief. We are reminded by Frank Freidel, in his book *FDR and the South,* that Roosevelt was "a New Yorker who liked to think of himself as also a Georgian by adoption," because of his association with Warm Springs. In 1938, Roosevelt responded to the National Emergency Council's *Report on Economic Conditions of the South* thus:

It is my conviction that the South presents right now the nation's No. 1 economic problem — the nation's problem, not merely the South's. For we have an economic unbalance in the nation as a whole, due to this very condition of the South's. It is an unbalance that can and must be righted, for the sake of the South and of the Nation. . . .

Now the remarkable thing about national policies toward the West and the South is that both were remarkably successful — or, if you wish, were accompanied by remarkable success. The West developed, if not beyond anyone's imagining — in the era of Manifest Destiny, Americans had mighty imaginations! — then at least in line with expectations. And the South has truly risen again. It is too soon to declare the effort completed. The South is still relatively poor in many public services, and the people of the region have chosen to forgo a considerable range of "public goods" in order to build a solid industrial base. But the industrial base now exists.

In a 1977 paper, "The New Deal and the Decline of New York State," Bernard Gifford, of the Russell Sage Foundation, stated:

In the decade just before the 1929 Depression, per capita personal income in the industrial Mideast and Great Lakes region grew at a rate faster than the overall average for the nation. New York State's rate was even greater than the growth rate for the Mideast region. Georgia's growth rate was some 14 percent slower than the nation's.

After the Depression, these relationships were reversed, and they remained so until this very day. . . . The Southeast is the *only* region whose per capita income growth rate has consistently outpaced the rest of the nation for the entire post-Depression period.

Per capita personal income in New York has remained higher than that in Georgia, but only if the cost of living is not taken into account, as Gifford demonstrates. Using an index on which the United States average is 100, the Bureau of Labor Statistics gives the 1976 cost of living (the "intermediate family budget") in New York as 116 and in Atlanta as 91. Adjusted for this differential, the per capita income figure for New York is $4,612, and for Atlanta, $4,613. "Real" income in these two cities is the same.

Of course the government services available to a New Yorker are considerably greater in volume, and surely in cost, than those available to a Georgian. Even so a period is at hand when the national government will think of the Northeast as a region with problems. In October 1976, just prior to the presidential election, Jimmy Carter accused the incumbent Republican administration with having "deliberately turned its back on the Northeast." Forty-two years earlier, he said, a Democratic President had seen that "the poverty of the South was the greatest long-term obstacle the nation had to overcome. . . ." He then proposed to follow "Franklin Roosevelt's example" and rebuild the Northeast as earlier the South had been rebuilt. Once he was elected, there was not much of this in evidence in Carter's programs. Federal aid to New York City, for example, was actually reduced by 11 percent in constant dollars in the fiscal years 1977–1980. But the campaign promise was thought worth making and was made.

A large cycle of economic change and political response is involved here. The changes that the Northeast seems to be undergoing remind us of the experience of Great Britain in an earlier period. In the simplest terms — and these may be the simplest of patterns — the age of coal and iron and steam began where the coal beds and iron ranges were to be found;

when, after a century and some, the economy began to outgrow this connection, those regions declined. Economists began to describe this process as "changes in the structure of the national economy." In Britain in the 1920s exceptionally high levels of unemployment appeared in Scotland, the north of England, and Wales, the centers of coal mining, iron and steel, ship building, and textiles. As the economy dropped off, emigration to the south and east of Britain commenced as a trickle and became something of a flood. In 1934 the national government designated "special areas" in an attempt to reverse these changes, and the effort has continued. The results have not, I believe, been impressive. Few sites are more forlorn than the industrial parks dedicated by George VI in the late 1930s in the North Country. Planners seem to have thought that new industries would set up rather like shops, all in tiny spaces along neat village paths. In truth, the very design of these centers *declared* that industry was past in that part of Britain. What governments design, as against what they say, is what they really mean — a point that always seems to escape the contemporaries who could presumably put the information to some use.

This pattern of regional decline and national response first appeared in the United States a generation or so later, in the great coal mining regions of Appalachia, more specifically of West Virginia. National response came in the aftermath of John F. Kennedy's dramatic 1960 primary victory in that state and his subsequent election as President. I imagine he thought of West Virginia as somehow being either Southern or Western or both, as the name suggests, but of course, it is an Eastern state (and is so designated in the Democratic Senate caucus, for example). Wheeling, West Virginia, lies forty miles from Pittsburgh. West Virginia coal helped industrialize the Northeast. But in time, the structure of the economy began to change and the region to decline. The first natural-gas pipeline reached the East from Texas in 1944, and thereafter the decline of Appalachia became precipitous. In 1911, the United

States coal industry employed 728,000 coal miners. By 1970, there were 144,000.

In the most humane sense this change in the structure of the economy achieved the great result of bringing half a million men out of those holes in the ground. Coal mining was the curse of industrialization. Without anybody trying much to end it, it dropped off greatly as an employer of the work force. But what was to be done with the people and the regions, who may well have been delivered from one form of thralldom to a worse one, from hideous exploitation to being just as cruelly discarded?

President Kennedy obtained passage of the Area Redevelopment Act, and various bureaucracies took over. On the curious insistence of the Bureau of the Budget, the major federal investment in Appalachia took the form of highway construction. We can now say that conditions in Appalachia have improved: population is no longer declining, fewer people live below the poverty line, and per capita income has risen rapidly. But we cannot claim that federal programs had very much to do with any of these. James Sundquist and Hugh Mields, Jr., note in their paper "Regional Growth Policy in the United States":

While the [Appalachia Regional] Commission feels that its activities have contributed to improving conditions in the area, it makes no claims to having been the decisive factor — the turnaround in the demand for coal is probably the most conspicuous contributing cause. . . .

In the meantime, concern about the Appalachian region has expanded to a general concern about the whole industrial region of the Northeast, with special attention to its cities.

One fundamental imperative faces us. We must not politicize the question of relative regional growth, or, for that matter, regional decline.

To do this would be easy, and calamitous, especially if the White House Conference were to mark the formal beginnings of, in Meg Greenfield's wonderful image, "colonizing" the "problem." A big politicized bureaucracy could emerge, whose expansion would depend on the problem's becoming ever more political. The mind-numbing agenda prepared by the small and temporary staff of the White House Conference suggests, alas, that there are hands eager for the work.

Why should we fear politicization? Why try to avoid it? First, it would be contrary to the spirit of the Constitution for the federal government to intervene in our economy to try to prevent the natural movements of capital and people from one state or region to another, if a free choice is made by those concerned. The Constitution imposes such restraints on state governments by the interstate commerce clause, and surely the federal government should not act in a manner the Constitution forbids to the states. The founders of this nation understood that our political freedoms and national stability very much depended on our becoming a single economy with the freest possible movement of capital and labor across state and regional borders. The Supreme Court had more than once reaffirmed that commitment. Now is scarcely the time to go back on it.

Second, we like to tell one another, and we are right, that this nation of immigrants is made up of persons either whose ancestors or who themselves came to the United States to improve their lot, and did so. For just those very reasons today, some people leave Georgia and go to New York, and some people leave New York and go to Georgia. And everyone dreams of going to Hawaii. This mobility is our right as citizens, and it should not be impaired by efforts of the federal government to keep us where we will be less well off.

But this will certainly happen, as Professor Sidney Sufrin suggests, if the federal government begins to make a great series of uneconomic investments in places that can no longer attract investment on their own. Governments faced with economic decline typically resort to what can only be called sympathetic magic. They try to induce natural change by imitating it. Not to put too fine a point on it, the Yule log is burned to get the sun going again. So was housing policy when it started, based on what Robert Fishman has called "the narrow simplicities of the doctrine of salvation by bricks alone — the idea that physical facilities could *by themselves* solve social problems." So were those industrial parks King George VI was always opening. So will half the job development programs of a new national urban policy, supposing we ever get one. Some of this sympathetic magic does no harm. But to the degree that resources are put to a less than optimal use, there will be a less than maximum return, and almost everyone will be a little worse off. Sometimes it is necessary to think like an economist.

A third consideration. Try as it will, government cannot do much to prevent economic shifts between regions. Perhaps this should be rephrased: There is not much government *will* do. For it is all very well to promise to help one region. But when helping to prevent the losses of one region is perceived as depriving another region of its expected gains, the politics gets difficult, while the rhetoric becomes more earnest.

For one thing, the problem is simply too complex. I hazard that there was not a single speaker or participant at the 1977 White House Conference who read one half the material the staff prepared and none who ever will.

If one wants an example, there is a rather painful one on display in Washington. In 1977 the President appointed an Urban and Regional Policy Group ("URPG," if you can imagine) to produce a national urban and regional policy for him. Months passed. Nothing happened. We learned that a great consummation was approaching. At length a huge, leaky document began circulating within the government. I called a friend in the Treasury Department to ask if I could see a copy. He declined, on the honorable grounds that the work was so poor he did not wish to embarrass the administration by having an outsider read it. The administration was embarrassed anyway, for it was next learned that the document had been offered without success for the President's approval. After a year's work no one could agree on an urban or regional policy for the State of the Union message or the President's budget. In December 1977 we were told to expect something in March 1978. But in the printed message that accompanied the State of the Union message in January 1978 we were told merely to expect something "in the spring." When at length it was made public there was nothing there.

Surely the President would not be happy with a Defense and Foreign Policy Group that at the end of his first year in office was still promising to come up with a program on the Middle East or nuclear proliferation "sometime next spring." But the plain fact is that the matters are so complex and the interests conflict so variously that the federal policy system just can't respond with anything very ambitious.

Consider again the Appalachian program. Unlike President Roosevelt's program to develop the South, which worked *with* the economic forces of the time, President Kennedy's program worked against them. (Or it did until the price of oil quintupled.) The program did succeed in stopping the decline in the population of West Virginia, for example, which in 1978 is, once again, as large as it was in 1960. But it will be a long time, if ever, before the state returns to its population of 1950.

The reason politicization is dangerous is, simply, that there is just so much government can do. But if it does nothing, if an otherwise prospering nation should suddenly appear to be indifferent to the declining regions of the Northeast, a huge loss would follow. Not only would the Northeast lose the benefits that an intelligent government policy might bring about, we could well lose the political tradition that has sanctioned such efforts in the past.

The political tradition of the Northeastern states goes far

back into our history but is associated in recent times with the activist national liberalism of the New Deal. I am unabashedly a product of that tradition. It incorporates an ethic of collective provision, to cite George Will, that has triumphed politically and, just as strikingly, has triumphed in the goals it set for itself. We are a vastly stronger, more united, and happier nation thanks to Franklin D. Roosevelt and the ideas he stood for. Those ideas, in *his* time, involved a very considerable transfer of resources from his region of the country — my region — to the South and West. It was all very well for him to think of himself as an "adoptive Georgian," but the vast outpouring of programs and aid for the South were for him the expression of a national purpose, which knew little of regional power, but concentrated greatly on regional need.

What will become of this tradition of national liberalism if the region from which it emerged should look up two generations later and find that, while other regions were willing enough to accept a transfer of resources when they were in need, no such reciprocal impulses will appear now that the Northeast is in need? What if it turns out that the New Deal was a one-way exchange? That resources flowed south, but never north? What if, on closer examination, we find that the social security system and tobacco price supports made their way to North Carolina, but not the Wagner Act? What if it comes to be believed that the policies of the New Deal brought about the downfall of the region that nurtured them and gave them to the nation?

I fear there will be a response of bitterness and reaction that will approach in duration if not in intensity the response of the South to its defeat in what we now call the War Between the States. It would be one thing to lose, as it were, the Northeast. It would be a very different and vastly greater blow to lose the tradition of national liberalism that the Northeast did so much to give the nation. It is not a point easily understood, and it will be fiercely resisted. Yet *that* is what is at issue.

What, then, is to be done? Two things, both of them large, but both quite within our political and organizational capacity. First, the federal government should stop exacerbating the economic problems of the Northeast. This will take some time. But the second thing the federal government can do it must persist in doing: this is to prevent the bankruptcy of New York City. These two actions are not unrelated; indeed there could be no clearer indication of the earnest intention of the federal government to attend to the economic decline of the Northeast than a firm commitment to ensure the solvency of the nation's largest city.

Government should not make things worse. Government should not artificially induce the decline of the Northeast in favor of other regions. This is the reciprocal, if you will, of the principle that government should not promise too much to make things better.

The federal government has for some time been making political decisions to induce development in the South and West, without clear economic justification and occasionally with economic costs. The most conspicuous example is that of the heavy concentration of defense facilities in the South.

This pattern of congressional influence dates back to a time of severe deprivation in much of the South, and of relative ease in the North. No one should in the least blame the South for using its opportunities, especially as no one, North or South, protested much at the time. But that pattern of congressional politics and presidential acquiescence should now be put behind us.

Just as important, the federal government *seems* to have contributed a good deal to economic imbalance without especially intending it, but without resisting it, either. Frank Lloyd Wright once remarked that everything in the country seemed to have come unstuck and to be sliding to California. A careful statement of this proposition has come from George Peterson, of the Urban Institute, in a paper written with

Thomas Muller, "The Regional Impact of Federal Tax and Spending Policies":

. . . [F]ederal spending for purchases of goods and services is more strongly skewed toward the rapidly growing regions of the country than are total federal outlays. On a per capita basis, the Pacific states receive more than twice as much federal revenue as the Great Lakes states and 80 percent more than the Mid-Atlantic states.

Although a detailed examination of federal spending would be necessary to establish the point conclusively, [data] strongly suggest that federal employment, goods and service acquisition, and direct capital investment have been shaped by the same cost and profitability considerations that have influenced private sector demand for regional output.

Obviously we could run the risk of significantly sanctioning uneconomic practices. Sufrin's principle that we should not invest in sympathetic magic should apply to purchases as well. But it may be that the great imbalance of federal expenditures at the present is *not* dictated by the market. The federal government has the responsibility to find out.

The federal government ought now to give some concentrated attention to finding out just what it *is* doing. We never do anything much about a problem until we learn to measure it. Perhaps government doesn't *want* to know very much about this problem. May I suggest that this unwillingness to measure effects shows how easy it would be for the problem to become politicized, and how much a calamity that could be? The more government conceals facts that could be known, the more lurid will be the conjecture about what is being concealed.

Nobody may have intended such a deception but when I first came to the Senate, I learned from a series of federal publications (known as the Federal Outlay series) that the federal government expended $40.6 billion in New York State in fiscal year 1976. On examining the tables, however, I found New

York had been credited with $14 billion in foreign aid payments and interest on the public debt. (The explanation was that these funds are deposited first in New York banks, or in the Federal Reserve Branch in New York.) I took this matter up with President Carter, who most courteously and deliberately undertook to reconsider the matter. It took six months, and it should have taken six months, this being a matter of no small issue. At length, in January, 1978, the executive branch agreed that it was not appropriate to credit these sums to New York. But, after deducting them, the state was left with federal outlays of $26.3 billion for fiscal year 1976 — as against personal and corporate income tax payments, and social security tax payments, *to* the federal government, of $33.7 billion. The federal government has in fact been deflating the economy of New York state, ever since federal spending began to rise in the late 1960s. This may be why, of all the states, only New York has not recovered its levels of employment prior to the recession of 1969 (much less those of the recession of 1973). Or so I *believe* — without any real competence in the economics of the matter. But I believe it anyway, and I would suggest that it is now up to others to disprove the case!

Here I must insert a word of caution. We are not likely ever to learn anything definitive about this subject — or at least I shall be surprised if we do. Social science, including economic science, just isn't capable. One of the reasons, surely, that the President's Urban and Regional Policy Group, a group of able and experienced persons, couldn't come up with anything acceptable to the President was that after ten or fifteen years, and half a billion or three quarters of a billion dollars of federal money spent in research on urban problems, we haven't really learned anything that tells us "what to do." We *have* learned a good deal about what *not* to do: in particular, we have learned that a great many problems of cities in America today arise from decisions made by the federal government — the interstate highway program and the VA and FHA mortgage programs are examples. As James Coleman has pointed out, these are "policies that destroy cities," for they lead persons to move away from them. But what would "make" them move back?

There is one concrete *and manageable* goal of urban and regional policy that the federal government should set for itself, and, if I am not mistaken, should accomplish — must accomplish. This is to prevent the bankruptcy of any major Northeastern city.

First, it is something government *can* do. I make much of this. I admit to being one of those who began to write of "the limits of social policy" in the middle 1960s. I bore no antagonism to the goals of social policy of that period (although some chose to think I did). My concern, and that of most of those who wrote in the same vein, was to prevent the great disillusionment with government that would predictably follow from proclaiming goals that would not be met. The economist Alfred Marshall laid down the guidelines for finding a satisfactory balance:

Government is the most precious of human possessions; and no care can be too great to be spent on enabling it to do its work in the best way: A chief condition to that end is that it should not be set to work for which it is not specially qualified, under the conditions of time and place.

I happened to be a graduate student at the London School of Economics when Michael Oakeshott succeeded to the chair of Harold Laski in 1950, and I was struck by a line from Oakeshott's inaugural lecture. "To try to do something which is inherently impossible," he said, "is always a corrupting enterprise." Almost two decades later, in 1969, I found myself in a commencement address at the University of Notre Dame speaking to the same point:

What is it that government cannot provide? It cannot provide values to persons who have none, or who have lost those they had. It cannot provide a meaning to life. It cannot provide inner peace. It can provide outlets for moral energies, but it cannot create those energies. In particular, government cannot cope with the crisis in values that is sweeping the Western world. It cannot respond to the fact that so many of our young people do not believe what those before them have believed, do not accept the authority of institutions and customs whose authority has heretofore been accepted, do not embrace or even very much like the culture that they inherit.

Now this is not so very different from the passage in President Carter's 1979 State of the Union message:

We need patience and good will, and we need to realize that there is a limit to the role and function of Government. Government cannot solve all our problems, set all our goals, or define our vision. Government cannot eliminate poverty, provide a bountiful economy, reduce inflation, save our cities, cure illiteracy, provide energy, or mandate goodness. Only a true partnership between government and the people can hope to reach these goals.

And yet this statement goes farther than I would: it is not as far in the direction I feared some president would have gone by this time, but it is *in* that direction. For the government *can* eliminate poverty — that is, poverty defined as income below a certain level. A good welfare reform bill would do that. This is precisely the kind of thing government *can* succeed in doing. It *cannot* "mandate goodness." But it *can* "save our cities" — if not from sin, then surely from bankruptcy. If New York City goes bankrupt, it will be in large measure because the federal government allowed it to.

My second reason for insisting that we must avert the bankruptcy is that otherwise *the issue of regional imbalance would certainly become politicized*. The bankruptcy of New York City or Philadelphia or Chicago would be to the Northeast what Sherman's march was to the South. It would also be a seismic event in the world at large.

It would be, and would be perceived as, a failure of democratic government of an altogether ominous degree. It would be an event of constitutional consequence. Already, the people of New York, after three-and-one-half centuries of self-government (interrupted only briefly by Lord Howe), have had to turn over their governance, on the issues that matter, to an Emergency Financial Control Board, made up, for the most part, of businessmen and state officials, and empowered to reject its budgets and financial plans, its proposed borrowings, and all its major contracts. Under Article VI, Section 4, of the Constitution, the United States guarantees to every state in the Union "a Republican Form of Government." No such guarantee extends to cities. But surely we tamper with the spirit of the Constitution at our peril. Can we imagine Jefferson or Hamilton or Franklin or Jay content with a situation in which a city with twice the population of all the original thirteen states is governed by a "control board"?

New York City, for example, has a debt of about $14 billion, which it cannot repay on the terms that now exist. The city is vibrant enough in most respects. If it did not have this huge debt — debt service alone comes to $2.3 billion a year — it would get along well enough. The debt itself, in absolute terms, isn't that huge. (Shall we call it seven tenths of 1 percent of our two-trillion-dollar GNP?) New York's budget shortfall isn't that great, about $1 billion.

Now how did this come about? If I am not mistaken, two essential causes govern.

First, New York City has had a powerful political culture of its own, which has disposed it to high levels of public provisions and to maintaining its independence from state government. One hears a good deal about the responsibility of the state to do its share for the city — to pick up welfare costs, for example. But the fault is not really that of the state. The city refused to allow this transfer of functions, for reasons based on self-interest disguised as eleemosynary concern. There is a welfare class in New York City, but, more conspicuously, there is a class of welfare administrators. Had the state taken over, what would have happened to the New York City commissioner, and the deputy commissioners? And the deputy deputy commissioners? And the union? And the union pension fund?

When Governor Nelson A. Rockefeller was elected in 1958, he set out to build a true state university, which until then had existed mostly on paper. This was obviously the moment for the city government to turn over to the state system its four city colleges, including my alma mater, City College of New York, the first free urban college in the world. The state system desperately needed these wonderfully established institutions. The City of New York could no longer afford to run them. But what did the city do instead of yielding to the state? It formed a university of its own, the City University of New York, and added a graduate center to it: CUNY to compete with SUNY. Within a half dozen years, of course, CUNY was near to bankruptcy: the treasured free tuition was abandoned shortly thereafter. Much of the splendor of the original four colleges seems to have vanished. Is not that part of the corruption that Oakeshott spoke of? "To try to do something which is inherently impossible"?

The second and obviously related point is that at the outset of the 1960s the traditional party structure of the city was broken, and a succession of middle-class coalitions took office. Capital funds began to be used for current expenses, and the present crisis began to build. New York celebrated its new governing style, and quite deprecated the older ones, with their more traditional, more down-to-earth fear of debt. It was very much the fashion of the 1960s in New York to deplore the then mayor of Chicago, the nation's second largest city. But by 1974, per-capita debt in New York was $1,767, while in Chicago it was $427. Most workingmen could pay off $427. Few can swing $1,767. And that is really all there is to say on the subject.

Except for one final observation, absolutely central to understanding the present situation, which the federal government must perforce face up to.

In 1975, when the city almost went bankrupt, and did indeed default on some of its debt, emergency measures were taken to prevent complete bankruptcy. The accumulated debt of the city was refinanced, but the ongoing deficit in the city's budget, which amounts to at least $1 billion a year, was not limited. It continues, and if anything, will grow. The city reached a seasonal loan agreement with the federal government that made it possible to manage these deficits for a three-year period. But nothing was done about the deficits themselves. Why? Why for a period of three years?

The answer is that those who put the emergency arrangements together assumed that in three years' time — in 1978 — there would be a Democratic administration in office, which would take care of the problems with a massive infusion of federal funds. But why make this assumption? An explanation must be sought beyond the superficial fact that the persons involved were Democrats. Something much larger was involved.

In the last generation there have been two distinct periods in which the expenditures of the federal government grew by huge amounts. Samuel P. Huntington has called them "the defense shift" and "the welfare shift." It is curious that both commenced under Democratic administrations but continued to grow under Republican administrations. The defense budget began to grow during President Truman's last years in office, but was truly enlarged and consolidated under President Eisenhower. The budget for social spending began to grow during President Johnson's last years, but was truly enlarged and consolidated under President Nixon.

To use a term from the academy, this series of events was counterintuitive. Since the time of the New Deal, Democrats have been supposed to increase budgets, and Republicans reduce them. Each party has rather approved of its reputation in this regard. So the huge increase in social spending during the early 1970s was kept something of a political secret. As a result, those who might have been expected to take pleasure in it, and by such exceptional innovations as revenue sharing with state and local governments and a guaranteed income for the aged, the blind, and the disabled, either ignored the existence of these programs, or believed that they definitely had not been enacted. Some even claimed the advent of a great social counterrevolution. The press, possibly in an effort to be neutral, gave about equal attention to both sides of the argument, although in fact one side had no argument at all. In 1975 responsible administrators imagined that with a change of administrations there would be a great release of funds.

Well, this just didn't happen. I don't know whether political economy has any special insight in these matters, but there does seem to be a point where enough is enough, and political systems respond accordingly. Thus in his Economic Message for 1978, President Carter observed that in fiscal 1976, federal outlays amounted to 22.5 percent of the gross national product. He proposed to *reduce* this proportion: "With good management we can, I believe, achieve our nation's important social goals and still reduce over time the share of gross national product committed to federal expenditures to about twenty-one percent." In 1980 Secretary of Labor Ray Marshall would declare that the administration's tight 1981 budget would be acceptable to the Democratic Party's liberal wing because "we radically lowered expectations last year." So much for the Northern New Deal.

But to revert to my earlier theme: the great object of the

federal government must be to prevent the issue of regional imbalance from being politicized. In 1964, it fell to me to write portions of the first draft of the Democratic national platform. As with most first drafts, little survived in the final version. But I dare to think it significant that as the draft passed from the lowliest White House scribbler on upward to Lyndon B. Johnson himself, no one took out my opening paragraph, which stated simply: We are one nation, one people.

12.
Government and the Ruin Of Private Education

WHAT MAY PROVE to be among the more important debates on education in recent American history began quietly with three days of Senate hearings in January 1978. Senator Bob Packwood and I had introduced a bill to provide tax credits to help pay the tuition costs of parents with children in nonpublic schools and colleges and universities. Our bill was distinctive in that fifty senators cosponsored it — twenty-six Republicans and twenty-four Democrats, ranging from Senator George McGovern to Senator Barry Goldwater.

The hearings resonated with the strength of the views expressed. Middle-income Americans felt they had this measure coming to them. They had put up with and supported a chaos of government programs designed in aid of other classes and, for that matter, other worlds. This was something for *them*. For *education*. Certain constitutional lawyers and scholars testified with equal force that in their view tuition tax credits are wholly constitutional as a form of assistance to nonpublic elementary and secondary education. Catholics testified; but so did Lutherans, and representatives of Hebrew schools and Baptist schools. A generation gap ago this was a

Catholic issue but not any longer. The issue reflects a broad revival of interest in religious education, and an upheaval in constitutional scholarship, but principally a pervasive sense that government has got to stop choking the life out of other American institutions that compete with it.

The response of the Carter administration came the following month. As is now routine, in the preceding election the party out of power and the President in office had pledged themselves to aid nonpublic elementary and secondary schools. Just as routinely, whoever wins the election breaks the commitment when the possibility of keeping it arises. The response of the Carter administration was distinctive only in that the President, in a White House news conference, announced that he was prepared, as a substitute for tuition tax credits, to expand existing programs of *college* student assistance by $1.2 billion. This came just days after his first budget message had provided next to nothing for schools. You have got to not want something pretty badly to be willing to spend $1.2 billion to keep from getting it. As for aid to elementary and secondary schools, HEW Secretary Joseph A. Califano, Jr., at the same press conference, allowed that, *tant pis,* Republican Presidents had promised tuition tax credits also — and hadn't delivered.

In the contest between public and private education, the national government feigns neutrality, but in fact it is anything but neutral. As program piles atop of program, and regulation on regulation, the federal government has systematically organized its activities in ways that contribute to the decay of nonpublic education. Those responsible have most likely not recognized this; they think themselves blind to the distinction between public and private. But of course they could not be. Governments inherently, routinely, automatically favor creatures of governments. They know no other way. Joseph Schumpeter's gloomy prophecy that liberalism will be destroyed through the steady conquest of the private sector by the public sector bids fair to come true in the United States. In no domain of our national life is this clearer or seemingly more inexorable than in education.

It is surprising that the bureaucracy gets away with this, for at the political level nothing is clearer than the avowed support of the parties and their leaders for private education, and for federal policies to buttress it. In its 1976 platform, the Republican party stated:

We favor consideration of tax credits for parents making elementary and secondary school tuition payments. . . . Diversity in education has great value. . . . Public schools and nonpublic schools should share an education fund on a constitutionally acceptable basis.

The Democratic party platform in the same year:

renew[ed] its commitment to the support of a constitutionally acceptable method of providing tax aid for the education of all pupils in nonsegregated schools in order to insure parental freedom in choosing the best education for their children. Specifically, the party will continue to advocate constitutionally permissible federal education legislation which provides for the equitable participation in federal programs of all low- and moderate-income pupils attending the nation's schools. [*In the interests of full disclosure, let me say I wrote the plank.*]

In 1973, on behalf of the Nixon administration, Secretary of the Treasury George P. Shultz testified before the House Ways and Means Committee in support of a tax credit for nonpublic school tuitions. "The nonpublic school system plays a vital role in our society," Shultz said.

These schools provide a diversity of education in the best of our traditions and are a source of innovation and experimentation in educational advances which benefit the public school system and the public in general. In many American communities, they are an important element of stability and civic responsibility. However, education costs are rising, the enrollment in the nonpublic schools is declining, and an important American institution may be in jeopardy.

Tax credits, he flatly predicted, would help "reverse this trend."

During his 1976 presidential campaign, Jimmy Carter said almost precisely the same thing in a message to the nation's Catholic school administrators:

Throughout our nation's history, Catholic educational institutions have played a significant and positive role in the education of our children. . . . Indeed, in many areas of the country parochial schools provide the best education available. Recognization [*sic*] of these facts must be part and parcel of the consciousness of any American President. Therefore, I am firmly committed to finding constitutionally acceptable methods of providing aid to parents whose children attend parochial schools.

In a major address, President Carter's new Education Commissioner Ernest L. Boyer echoed this sentiment. "Private education is absolutely crucial to the vitality of this nation," Dr. Boyer averred, "and public policy should strengthen rather than diminish these essential institutions." Yet the moment it appeared that public policy should actually do this, and legislation was proposed, the Commissioner of Education changed sides. He was quoted: "We would be saying for the first time that the extra costs of private education are deserving of governmental support."

The essential point of those opposed to measures such as tuition tax credits is this: Government has no responsibility to any form of education that government does not control. It is a modern doctrine, and not always honestly argued. The "extra costs" of "private" schools, which for the most part are neighborhood Catholic, Protestant, and Jewish schools, require about one fourth of the per-pupil expenditure of their neighboring public schools. But the opponents of aid to such schools are fierce and unshakable in their conviction that *theirs* is the cause of true liberalism, and that those who disagree are the instruments, witting or no, of divisiveness and privilege. No argument is too weak to be advanced. The Secretary of Health, Education and Welfare did not send an education official to testify at the Senate hearings. One of his assistant secretaries for legislation supplied the boiler plate for the occasion: "An elementary-secondary tuition tax credit could undermine the principle of public education in this country." *Undermine.* Church-related schools existed and thrived in the United States generations before the public schools as we know them came into being!

If there is an argument, it is that the public schools are a threat to the existence of church schools. But this is not really what HEW meant. It meant that private schools undermine the principle of state monopoly. If the bureaucracy were to say that private schools challenge and even defy that principle, then well and good. But the educational bureaucracy is never open, and often truly dishonest. The hapless assistant secretary was forced to say that our bill would "dry up local and state money for education." If there is one clear correlation in American education, it is that wherever a large proportion of students attend nonpublic schools, public expenditures for public schools are very high indeed. New York City is a prime example.

The Tuition Tax Credit Act of 1977 would have enabled a taxpayer to subtract from the taxes he owes a sum equal to 50 percent of amounts paid as tuition. The credit was limited to $500 per student per year, which is to say that after tuition charges pass $1,000 per student, no additional credit is allowed. If the taxpayer in question owes no taxes, or does not owe the full amount, the Treasury would pay the difference to him.

This is by no means the only feasible approach to the matter.

Senator Abraham Ribicoff had pressed a formula whereby the credit would be a varying percentage of tuitions, thus giving additional benefit to those paying higher tuitions. Another variation offers a flat tax credit for whatever the tuition may be, up to a cutoff point.

Almost any formula would entail legislation on the scale of the Servicemen's Readjustment Act of 1944 (the "G.I. Bill"), the National Defense Education Act of 1958, and the Elementary and Secondary Education Act of 1965, placing it among the half dozen great educational statutes of our history.

The first reaction at the Senate hearing was quiet: curiously, a positive sign. Rabbi Morris Sherer of Agudath Israel of America, a sixty-five-year-old international orthodox Jewish movement, observed that when he first testified on this subject — seventeen years ago, during the administration of President Kennedy — it was "so shocking," as he put it, that *The New York Times* put his picture on the front page. But in the interval, he suggested, the climate had changed, the idea of public support for nonpublic schools had become so widely accepted, that he was sure "today . . . seventeen years later, it will be relegated to page 99." He spoke better than he knew. Not a line about the three days of hearings made it onto any page of *The Times*. But the rabbi made his point: There has been a vast change in attitudes on this subject. It might reasonably be described as an idea whose time has come, which has made its way into that realm of political ideas so "self-evident" that few bother to express what almost everyone takes for granted.

Two thirds of the tax credits that would be paid under the legislation would have gone to defray the tuition costs of persons attending colleges and universities. A very considerable sum is involved; the bill would have cost the Treasury some $4 billion annually, and the bulk of these funds would go to maintain diversity in higher education. But there is certainly no constitutional issue involved at the college level, and not much political argument either. The House Ways and Means Committee had not previously wanted to commit the money, and economy is always a perfectly respectable contention. But middle-income Americans have come to feel a genuine grievance over this matter.

These parents pay most of the taxes in America and get relatively few of the social services. In the main, this has been acceptable to them. The social legislation of the past generation has been enacted primarily by legislators who represent such constituents. But in the last decade it has come to be seen that the level of taxes is beginning to conflict with the education of their children, and this they will not have. In this sense, our bill was straightforward, and consonant with the same objective that Americans have agreed upon since the Northwest Ordinance of 1787.

The Carter administration's alternative was not bad legislation. It raised the income limits of a good program, the Basic Education Opportunity Grants, from $15,000 to $25,000. (Full disclosure again: I drafted the presidential message that first proposed this program.) Senator Claiborne Pell has been a devoted and skilled advocate of BEOGS, or as they are known, Pell Grants. But they leave many families out. They put all *other* families under a means test. One must see the application form to believe it. Is it really necessary to let the federal bureaucracy dig that much deeper into our private lives? (Tax credits work directly through the Internal Revenue Service and need involve nothing more than an extra line on form 1040.) But the administration's response left out elementary and secondary schools altogether.

Ours was a distinctive measure. It would have provided support to elementary and secondary schools that are outside the public school system. Here we enter a dark and bloody ground where battles have raged for generations. And yet here, too, there is every sign that finally the matter may be resolved. This would be an achievement of social peace that goes well beyond education policy, and requires a certain elaboration.

The accepted interpretation of the Constitution is in the process of change. It is changing back to its original meaning and intention, which in no way barred public support for church-related schools. After more than a century — a period in which religious fear, and religious bigotry, distorted our judgment about the nature of constitutionality — we are getting back to the clear meaning of the plain language in which the Constitution and the Bill of Rights are written.

Most notably, we are demystifying the First Amendment. Demystification is anything but a plain word with a clear meaning, but it is a useful concept that first appeared in Marxist literature, and is now making its way into more general circles. It suggests that social groups commonly conceal *from themselves,* as well as from others, the true motives and interests that account for their behavior. All manner of myths grow up to explain and justify actions rooted in a reality that for one reason or another no one wishes to acknowledge. Social change often begins by "demystifying" such action, to reveal the true sources of behavior.

Education in colonial America was almost exclusively an activity of religious sects. As Bernard Bailyn writes (in *Education in the Forming of American Society*), "sectarian religion became the most important determinant of group life. . . . And it was by carefully controlled education above all else that denominational leaders hoped to perpetuate the group into future generations." In the diverse school systems of the time, we see a now-familiar phenomenon at work. Eighteenth-century Americans didn't necessarily *want* religious toleration; they simply had no choice, such was the number of religions. Public support for all manner of church schools was common and unremarked because, in the colonial economy, there was no effective way to endow church schools. Back in England, endowments meant land, which meant tenants, which meant rents. But with free land on the frontier, rent-paying tenants could not be found, and so colonial church schools came to be supported by taxes.

With the founding of the American republic, this arrangement continued. Change first appeared in New York City. At the turn of the nineteenth century, public funds from New York state's "Permanent School Fund" supported the existing church schools and four private charitable organizations that provided free education for needy youngsters. In 1805, however, the state legislature chartered the New York Free School Society, which shortly obtained a "peculiar privilege," not shared by the other groups, of receiving public funds to equip and construct its school buildings.

This favored status was challenged in the 1820s by the Baptists, whose schools were experiencing financial difficulties in the aftermath of a depression. The Free School Society responded by challenging both the integrity of the Baptist school organization and the legitimacy of *any* public money going to support schools associated with religious denominations. "It is totally incompatible with our republican institutions," the Society argued, "and a dangerous precedent" to allow any public funds to be spent "by the clergy or church trustees for the support of sectarian education."

Although New York Secretary of State John Van Ness Yates urged the legislature to support the Baptist position, his advice was rejected, and in 1824 the state turned over to the New York City Common Council the responsibility of designating recipients of school funds within the city. In 1825, the council ruled that no public money could thereafter go to sectarian schools. The following year, as if to reinforce the claim that it alone represented nonsectarian "public" education, the Free School Society changed its name to the New York Public School Society. Although it remained a private association with a self-perpetuating board of trustees, the society obtained what amounted to legal recognition that only its version of education — nonsectarian but Protestant — would thereafter receive public support. The phrase *public school* that endures in New York — as in P.S. 104 — is a legacy of this nomenclature.

By 1839, the Public School Society operated 86 schools, with an average total attendance of 11,789. In that year, the Catholic Church also operated seven Roman Catholic Free Schools in the city, "open to all children, without discrimination,"* with more than 5,000 pupils in attendance. "Nonetheless," as Nathan Glazer and I wrote in *Beyond the Melting Pot* in 1963, "almost half the children of the city attended no school of any kind, at a time when some 94 percent of children of school age in the rest of the state attended common schools established by school districts under the direction of elected officers."

Catholics in the city began clamoring for a share of public education funds, but were turned down by the Common Council, notwithstanding Bishop John Hughes's offer to place the parochial schools under the supervision of the Public School Society in return for public money.

As tempers rose, in April, 1841, acting in his capacity of ex-officio superintendent of public schools, Secretary of State John C. Spencer submitted a report on the issue to the state senate. Spencer was a scholar (as noted earlier, he was Tocqueville's first American editor) as well as an authority on the laws of New York state. He began by asserting the essential justice of the Catholic request:

It can scarcely be necessary to say that the founders of these schools, and those who wish to establish others, have absolute rights to the benefits of a common burthen; and that any system which deprives them of their just share in the application of a common and public fund must be justified, if at all, by a necessity which demands the sacrifice of individual rights, for the accomplishment of a social

*New York Register, 1840, p. 336.

benefit of paramount importance. It is presumed no such necessity can be urged in the present instance.

As for avoiding sectarianism by abolishing religious instruction altogether: "On the contrary, it would be in itself sectarian; because it would be consonant to the views of a peculiar class, and opposed to the opinions of other classes."

The Catholics got no satisfaction from the legislature, but the Public School Society was, in effect, disestablished as early as 1842. The legislature was persuaded, chiefly by Democrats of a Jacksonian persuasion, that the Society was a dangerous private monopoly over which the public had no control. The new school law allowed the Society to continue to operate its schools but only as district public schools under the supervision of an elected board of education and the state superintendent of common schools. The system that persists to this day was thus established: including a "private" Catholic school system enrolling about one fifth of the city's school population.

Soon, a specifically anti-Catholic nativist streak entered the opposition to public support for church-related schools. President Ulysses S. Grant, looking around for an issue on which he might run for a third term, seized on the danger of papist schools. The Republican platform of 1876 declared:

The public school system of the several states is a bulwark of the American republic; and, with a view to its security and permanence, we recommend an amendment to the Constitution of the United States, forbidding the application of any public funds or property for the benefit of any school or institution under sectarian control.

Observe. In 1876 there were those who thought that public aid to church schools should be made unconstitutional. But at least they were clear that the Constitution would have to be amended to do so. It is extraordinary how this so obvious fact got lost in the years that followed. We may hope that the matter has now been settled by Walter Berns in his devastatingly clear historical account, *The First Amendment and the Future of American Democracy.* To repeat yet again, what Congress intended by the First Amendment was to forbid the preference of one religion over another.

It is necessary again to insist that, though the First Amendment does not prohibit aid to church schools, it does not follow that the authors of the amendment favored aiding them. Some did, some did not. Madison surely would not have. Aid was left as a political choice, as an issue of public policy to be resolved however we chose, and changed however often we might wish.

A friendly word for the nativists. Early Americans were considerably suspicious of non-English immigrants. Bailyn reports that even Benjamin Franklin was "struck by the strangeness . . . of the German communities in Pennsylvania, by their lack of familiarity with English liberties and English government." He helped to organize the Society for the Propagation of the Gospel to the Germans in America. George Templeton Strong in New York City of the 1860s wondered what would come of the flood of Catholic Irish, not half of whom, probably, spoke English. Yet he expressed himself more fearfully about the Central and Southern Europeans who followed, none of whom spoke English, none of whom came from a country where political liberties existed. How could he *not* have suspected the Pope of Rome? The only perceptible political preference of the papacy in the flood tide of republicanism was for monarchy. In 1870, as if for the purpose of outraging the rationalism of the age, the Vatican Council of Bishops, after nineteen centuries of blessed unawareness, discovered that the pope was infallible — a curious doctrine, and singularly out of harmony with the era.

Nor at the turn of the century, would an American libertarian have felt great confidence in the Russian and Polish Jews who were then arriving, with a religious faith that had never shown any great interest in political democracy. Their nonreligious elements were all too well versed in the latest antidemocratic doctrines of the continent. *But it all worked out.* German Protestant and Italian, Polish Catholic and Polish Jew have all produced recognizably American progeny, enough to calm the fear and perhaps even to arouse the patriotic pride of the most nervous nativist of generations past. Political anxieties that were at least understandable a century ago make no sense today.

What, then, holds us back from educational equality under law? The answer, simply, is the Supreme Court. For generations state legislatures have been passing bills that provide various kinds of aid to church-related schools, but for the last generation the Court has been declaring these unconstitutional in whole or in part.

The decisive case, the first of its kind, was *Everson* v. *Board of Education* in 1947, involving a New Jersey statute authorizing school districts to reimburse parents for bus fares paid by children traveling to and from schools. Although sustaining the statute as such, the Court went on to hold that neither Congress nor the state legislature might "pass laws which aid one religion, aid all religions, or prefer one religion over another." Nor might any tax "in any amount, large or small . . . be levied to support any religious activities or institutions, whatever they may be called, or whatever form they may adopt to teach or practice religion." Now this was simply wrong. Again, to cite Berns: "It does not accurately state the intent of the First Amendment." Mr. Justice Black, who wrote the opinion, depended primarily on views of Madison and Jefferson, who, in 1784, had been much exercised over a bill reported favorably by the Virginia legislature "establishing a provision for teachers of the Christian religion." The late Mark DeWolfe Howe of the Harvard Law School put it that in *Everson* the justices made "the historically quite misleading assumption that the same considerations which moved Jefferson and

Madison to favor separation of Church and State in Virginia led the nation to demand the religion clauses of the First Amendment." This, he wrote, was a "gravely distorted picture."

The Supreme Court had no sooner ruled in *Everson* than it began to retreat from its ruling. Slow at first, this of late has become a genuine rout, and in all truth something of an embarrassment. In the Senate hearings of 1978, perhaps the most passionate statements came from legal scholars who pleaded that the Court has got to be relieved of this enterprise in which it has got itself hopelessly mixed up. Pass a bill, the scholars urged; declare it to be constitutional; the Court will be only too willing to agree.

The alternative is the present confusion, verging on scandal. Not five years after *Everson*, recalling the evident duty of all American institutions to foster piety, the Court held:

We are a religious people whose institutions presuppose a Supreme Being. . . . When the state encourages religious authorities by adjusting the schedule of public events to sectarian needs, it follows the best of our traditions. For it then respects the religious nature of our people and accommodates the public service to their spiritual needs. . . . The government must be neutral when it comes to competition between sects.

From that not especially enlightening passage (*Zorach* v. *Clauson* [1952]), the justices seemingly abandoned their own standards of evidence, and even the dictates of reason, to justify the unjustifiable. In *Tilton* v. *Richardson* (1971) the Court was required to pass upon the constitutionality of the Federal Higher Education Facilities Act of 1963 insofar as it applied to church-related colleges and universities. Most of the statute was found constitutional, but only four justices could agree in an opinion. On their behalf, Chief Justice Burger noted that "candor compels the acknowledgment that we can only dimly perceive the boundaries of permissible government activity in this sensitive area of constitutional adjudication."

It was necessary, of course, for the Court to find a serviceable distinction between church-related elementary and secondary schools and sectarian colleges and universities. Venturing toward those dimly perceived boundaries in his judgment for the plurality, the chief justice asserted that "there is substance to the contention that college students are less impressionable and less susceptible to religious indoctrination."

Now surely this "contention" is an empirical statement whose "substance" is susceptible to verification. The justices state that something is so. Their statement, then, must rest on evidence. The justices know about this sort of thing. When in *Brown* v. *Board of Education* (1954), they held that segregated schools were *educationally* inferior to integrated schools, they cited evidence. One may argue how good the evidence was. But the Court had no doubt that it needed evidence if it was going to say things like that. Very well, then. What is the state of the evidence concerning the impressionability, with respect to religious indoctrination, of seventeen-year-olds as against nineteen-year-olds, or rather, high school students as against college students? There is, as noted earlier, no evidence one way or another.

But the justices did not rely solely on this contention. "Many church-related colleges and universities are characterized," the chief justice wrote, "by a high degree of academic freedom, and seek to evoke free and critical responses from their students." What an extraordinarily patronizing endorsement! Would the justices have said the same of "many state universities"? Of "many Ivy League campuses"? What about "many elite preparatory schools"? Obviously not "many Catholic elementary schools"!

The Court has been given the thankless task of finding constitutional legitimacy for the religious bigotry of the nineteenth century. The quality of its decisions suggests the misgivings with which the deed has been done.

On June 24, 1977, the Court handed down its decision in *Wolman* v. *Walter,* which tested an Ohio statute dealing with expenditure of public funds to provide aid to students in nonpublic elementary and secondary schools. A three-judge district court panel had upheld the statute, and citizens and taxpayers had appealed. Mr. Justice Blackmun handed down what may be the most embarrassing decision in the modern history of the Court. It concludes: "In summary, we hold constitutional those portions of the Ohio statute authorizing the State to provide nonpublic school pupils with books. . . . We hold unconstitutional those portions relating to instructional materials. . . ."

Observe the state of opinion of Mr. Justice Blackmun's brethren in *Wolman*:

Chief Justice Burger concurred in part and dissented in part.

Mr. Justice Rehnquist and Mr. Justice White concurred in the judgment in part and dissented in part.

Mr. Justice Brennan concurred in part and dissented in part and filed an opinion.

Mr. Justice Marshall concurred in part and dissented in part and filed an opinion.

Mr. Justice Powell concurred in part and dissented in part and filed an opinion.

Mr. Justice Stevens concurred in part and dissented in part and filed an opinion.

In his *Wolman* opinion, Mr. Justice Stevens cites with avowed deference Clarence Darrow's argument in the Scopes trial on the great harm that comes to both Church and State whenever one depends on the other. This is not without charm, but must we really accept Mr. Darrow as a constitutional authority in such matters? Darrow was virtually a professional agnostic whose great triumph in the Scopes case was to elicit the admission from William Jennings Bryan that the Silver-tongued Orator believed every word in the Bible to be true. Well, so does the thirty-ninth President of the United States, and no one thinks it especially hilarious. None of us knows as much as we knew in those fine old times in the hills of Tennessee. Even Darwin is having troubles these days.

In rather striking contrast, the political realm has acted in a far more pluralist and, if you will, liberal spirit in these matters. In 1875 President Grant addressed the Army of Tennessee in Des Moines, exhorting his old comrades that no money should "be appropriated to the support of any sectarian schools. . . . Leave the matter of religion to the family altar, the church, and the private school, supported entirely by private contributions. Keep the Church and State forever separate." The following year, as anticipated in his party's platform, Representative James G. Blaine (Republican — Maine) proposed a constitutional amendment to this effect. It failed in the Senate. Altogether, between 1870 and 1888 there were eleven separate amendments proposed, five in the House and six in the Senate. All were rejected. State and local governments continued to provide support of one sort or another to sectarian schools, and continue to do so to this day. According to an authoritative survey by the Congressional Research Service, thirty-seven states supplied some aid to nonpublic schools as of January 1977, although often in tiny amounts, for sharply limited purposes, and through quite roundabout means. The public has been a good deal more perceptive about the First Amendment than have been the courts.

After World War II, support began to develop for federal aid to elementary and secondary education, which President Kennedy first proposed to Congress in 1963. It failed of passage because the Catholic hierarchy argued that church-related schools should share in the program, and the Congress could reach no agreement. In 1964 I negotiated a plank in the Democratic platform which stated:

The demands on the already inadequate sources of state and local revenues place a serious limitation on education. New methods of financial aid must be explored, including the channeling of federally collected revenues to all levels of education, and, to the extent permitted by the Constitution, to *all* schools. [Emphasis added]

The Catholic bishops had agreed that on these terms they would support a bill, and the Elementary and Secondary Education Act of 1965 followed directly. But church schools got precious little of the federal funds that followed, and today private school students receive only dribs and drabs of the services to which they are presumedly entitled. With respect to Title I, for example, which is the major ESEA program delivering remedial educational services to disadvantaged youngsters, a recent study conducted for the National Institute of Education by Dr. Thomas W. Vitullo-Martin concludes that "the program reaches only 47 percent of the nonpublic school students who should be eligible for it, and provides them with only about 18 percent of the services they should receive." In most communities, Vitullo-Martin continues, "children with the same level of educational disadvantage have less chance of receiving Title I services if they are enrolled in private schools, and will receive fewer and poorer services."

Now a new element appears. The Catholic issue recedes, as it emerges that all manner of Protestant and Jewish groups want to be able to maintain or establish *their* schools. They said as much at the Senate hearings. What we now have is a fight for educational pluralism, with a growing awareness that something precious to this society is being lost. A spokesman for CORE testified that his organization has "begun a community school in the Bronx. In this school, children read, on the average, at approximately grade level, while in the public schools of District 9, which services the area, children are over a year behind by grade five and almost two years behind by grade 8." This experience reinforces Professor Thomas Sowell's research findings attesting to the importance of private schools in the education of black youngsters. "One of the great untold stories of contemporary American education," Sowell stated in testimony to the Senate Finance Committee in January 1978, "is the extent to which Catholic schools, left behind in ghettoes by the departure of their original white clientele, are successfully educating black youngsters there at low cost."

The cost differences *are* significant. In the 1975 hearings, witnesses from one city after another offered statistics indicating that the parochial schools in their community customarily educate their students at 25 to 40 percent of the cost of the local public schools. Without students, these schools will vanish. And with them will vanish a large measure of the diversity and excellence that we associate with American education. (The CORE-operated school in the Bronx, cited above, closed, in 1979, mostly because CORE seemingly fell apart.)

I take pluralism to be a valuable characteristic of education. We are many peoples, and our social arrangements reflect our disinclination to submerge our inherited distinctiveness in a homogeneous whole. The point is surely obvious enough.

Private schools and colleges embody the values of diversity. They provide enrichment to the society, choices to students and their parents, and an array of distinctive educational offerings that even the finest of public institutions may find difficult to supply, not least because they *are* public and directed to embody generalized values.

Diversity. Pluralism. Variety. These are values, too, and perhaps nowhere more valuable than in the experiences that our children have in their early years, when their values and attitudes are formed, their minds awakened, and their friendships formed. I do not believe it excessive to ask that these values be embodied in our national policies for American education.

Tax credits for school and college tuitions furnish an opportunity to support these values. And they do so without raising any unresolvable question of constitutionality. They are not a sufficient recognition of private education. But they are a necessary beginning, and a sound example of a public policy idea whose time, one hopes, at last has come.

If we don't act, the question is likely soon to become moot. The conquest of the private sector by the public is well advanced. As a result of its inequitable treatment at the hands of the national government, private education in the United States has taken a drubbing in the past quarter century. Everyone knew that elementary school enrollments would decline between 1965 and 1975 — it was a demographic inevitability. But nonpublic schools accounted for 98 percent of the entire net enrollment shrinkage, and this loss of one million students represented more than one fifth of their total enrollments.

At the college level, private institutions accounted for a majority of all students enrolled in 1951. Twenty-five years later, more than three quarters of all college and university students were in public institutions.

At the elementary and secondary level there is surely a revival of Protestant and Jewish education, but Catholic spirits have flagged. Some dioceses — New York is a prime example — press on. In others, the bishops have seemingly come to think that schools are not really part of the vocation of the church. It would be ironic for them to give up just as the climate of liberalism was changing in their favor; but it could happen.

Tuition tax credits were not enacted by the 95th Congress. The matter was not concluded until the very last hours of the Second Session. In a curious way, the Senate hearings appear to have aroused the House of Representatives more than the Senate, and a measure applicable to all levels of education first passed in the House. After a three-day debate in the Senate, tax credits for colleges and universities were overwhelmingly approved, but credits for elementary and secondary schools were defeated by a vote of 41 to 56. A House-Senate Conference

Committee accepted this limitation, but the House itself thereafter insisted that all levels of education be included. Opponents in the Senate insisted they would filibuster, and, with the Congress scheduled to adjourn within hours, it seemed the better part of wisdom to let the bill be defeated by a voice vote.

But this was not a measure to be adopted by maneuver in the closing hours of an exhausted legislature. It is a major issue of public policy, and deserved the fullest scrutiny and openness. The debate in the 95th Congress, if you will allow for my obvious bias, turned out rather to the advantage of the proponents. For one thing, the merits of our position could only be elided by the threat of filibuster. More important, the opponents of tuition tax credits, from the President to the Secretary of Health, Education and Welfare to the leaders of the opposing debate in the Senate and House, *never* argued against the measure on its merits. Instead, they hid behind the issue of constitutionality. The measure, they said, was unconstitutional. To this the proponents replied that if this were so the opponents had nothing to fear, for the Supreme Court would so declare and the matter would be concluded. (The proposed legislation actually provided for direct review by the Court, and postponed elementary and secondary school credits until such a review would have taken place.) The next response after that was the threat of filibuster.

American liberalism will almost certainly undergo a test in this matter. In the course of the 1978 debate organizations issued statements opposing tuition tax credits that scarcely suggested the openness that one would hope for in liberal spokesmen.

The Americans for Democratic Action called elementary and secondary tuition tax credits "reprehensible," and claimed that "approximately four times as much federal aid would go to the private or parochial school student [as] would go to the public school student," although the opposite would have been a more accurate statement. Further, the ADA charged, the proposal "could encourage segregation along religious, racial and class lines."

A group styling itself the National Coalition to Save Public Education made the extraordinary statement that "aid to nonpublic schools carries with it the danger that public funds will be used to support sectarian purposes or ideological viewpoints in violation of the Constitution and American principles." It did not say what those "principles" are, but among the thirty-four signatories were leaders of the American Civil Liberties Union, the League of Women Voters of the United States, the NAACP, the United Auto Workers, the National Council of Churches, and the National Urban Coalition.

Such views were characterized by Norman S. Miller in the pages of the *Wall Street Journal* (December 14, 1978) as a "subtle form of anti-Catholicism." The segregation charge was called "shameful" for "in truth, Catholic schools in many dioceses were integrated long before the public schools." "It is difficult," the writer added, "to explain the indifference toward outright anti-Catholic bigotry and the more widespread insensitivity toward the Catholic viewpoint except in terms of the historic nativism that has afflicted the American Catholic minority."

It is time liberalism examined its purposes in the area of education. State monopoly is not more appropriate to liberal belief in this field than in any other.

13.
Two Tax Revolts

O N MARCH 3, 1858, *The New York Times* reported from
Albany that eighty-six state senators had presented
a petition "so brief and so explicit" that it was given
entire:

The undersigned, citizens of the State, would respectfully represent:
That owing to the great falling off of the Canal revenue, as well as the
increasing drafts upon the State Treasury, and the large expenses of
carrying on the several departments of the State Government,
thereby swelling up the taxes; therefore, with the view of relieving
the people from the large amount now unnecessarily expended to
sustain the Executive and Legislative Departments, and to secure the
honest and better administration thereof; your petitioners respectfully ask that your Honorable body pass an act for calling a Convention
to so alter the Constitution as to abolish both the Executive and
Legislative Departments, as they now exist, and to vest the powers
and duties thereof on the President, Vice President, and Directors of
the New York Central Railroad Company.

The proposal, *The Times* Special Correspondent explained,
was "intended as a joke." But, he continued, "it conveys a bitter
satire, a satire which is deserved and just." There followed a

discourse on the villainy of the railroad, a detailed indictment of the ruling Democrats, a somewhat less specific assault on the opposition ("When the Republicans have ascendency it is — well, it is hardly worthwhile to mention.") and a prediction that the time would come when "after long suffering" the people would rise and "retaliate."

Whether intended as a joke or not, the proposition went on the ballot that fall, where it failed by only 6,360 votes.

A long-suffering people fed up with taxes is likely to resort to less well thought out modes of retaliation than commend themselves to Special Correspondents of *The New York Times*.

It was nothing new, even then. Shays's Rebellion had taken place in western Massachusetts in 1786. Shays was a responsible man, an ensign at Bunker Hill and a captain in the Continental Army, but he took to armed insurrection over the salary of the governor and related matters.

The adoption of Proposition 13 in California on June 6, 1978 — by a two-to-one vote, local property taxes were limited to 1 percent of market value, thereby reducing these by more than half — made clear to almost everyone that another tax revolt was in progress.

The "seismic" event in California was only the most recent in a series of essentially similar actions in other states. Neil Pierce, who has distinguished himself in journalism by following these issues, which seem so dreary until something blows up, has noted that in the years immediately preceding 1978, Tennessee, New Jersey, Colorado, and Michigan adopted "tax expenditure limits," which set a ceiling on state and local expenditure in terms of a percentage of personal income, or suchlike.

Nothing, as such, actually began with Proposition 13. But it is the *moment of perception* that is the important political event. Modern historians seem determined to demonstrate that nothing ever begins; that all events are rooted in the past and that continuity is all. Which is nonsense. Events build up, but there comes a moment when as a *political* fact the times are seen to have changed. A good historian will find more continuity than break between the administrations of Herbert Hoover and Franklin D. Roosevelt, but there were a few things Roosevelt did which by contemporary standards were new, were even radical, and the public saw this. Enter the New Deal.

Did the New Deal exit on June 6, 1978? A generation hence we might say yes, but for now we may content ourselves that something occurred of more than passing note. For example, Republicans were confirmed in a new strategy. For two generations, from the time of the New Deal, they had directed their opposition, especially in Congress, where they have been almost permanently *in* opposition, to the undesirability of Big Government. Whatever the merits of their case, the political appeal was minimal. Nothing more attested this than the huge increase in spending on social programs that took place in the Nixon and Ford administrations. Finally in Congress the idea struck: Was it not wiser instead to oppose high taxes?

It surely was. Nothing better demonstrated this than the conversion of the Democratic governor of California, who had opposed Proposition 13 with characteristic fervor, but, once it had passed, reversed his position completely and campaigned for reelection as a supporter of the measure. Victorious, he began his second term in 1979 with an inaugural address calling for a national constitutional amendment requiring that the federal budget be balanced. Such an amendment would surely put an end to the most conspicuous fiscal feature of American government introduced *as doctrine* by the New Deal, which is to say Keynesian-based countercyclical fiscal policies, policies accepted and deployed as much by subsequent Republican administrations as by Democratic ones.

It was, therefore, an event. Events need theories to explain them. Accordingly, I offer the thought that Proposition 13 had little to do with the supposed eccentricities of California politics, save some happenstance disparities between the recent revenues of state as against local government. Rather, the old experience of taxes interacted with the rise of a new social class. If the theory is right, it also helps explain why it has become so difficult to govern of late.

Begin with taxes. There is a certain cycle. Large events, especially wars, first lead to a sharp increase in taxes, which thereafter present a political and economic issue as the argument arises over cutting back. Jude Wanniski argues that a key to recent economic history has been the speed with which the different industrial nations reduced their tax rates following the First and Second World Wars.

For some while now the United States has been in just such a "postwar" situation. For one thing, there *was* a war. Long and costly, but now over. Just as important, there was an extraordinary demographic convulsion, also now over, during which American society had to cope with an unprecedented number first of babies, then of teenagers, then of young adults. This, too, was over by 1978. Many new social programs had been established, and government entered a number of essentially new areas such as environmental protection.

The result, in the words of the Advisory Commission on Intergovernmental Relations (1978), had been "an unparalleled expansion of government."

State and local governments in particular have grown rapidly, as demonstrated by the nearly threefold increase in their work forces from about 4.1 million to 12.2 million between 1953 and 1976, and the nearly tenfold increase in their own revenues during the same period, from about $27 billion to approximately $200 billion.

The unavoidable consequence was a huge increase in taxation, in tax levels, and *a quite astonishing convergence in the rate of taxes imposed on the average family, as against the high-income family*. The Advisory Commission calculates that in 1953 the average family earned $5,000 and paid 11.8 percent of income in taxes, including federal income tax, social security tax, and state and local tax. In 1975, this average family earned $14,000 and paid 22.7 percent of its income in taxes. The earnings of the high-income family went from $20,000 to $56,000, but its tax rate went only from 20.2 percent to 29.5 percent. As a result of inflation and social security increases, and whatever, the tax rate on the average family doubled in twenty-five years, and by 1978 average families enjoyed the doubtful distinction of paying an even higher rate of taxes than had the well-to-do a quarter century earlier.

Now to the rise of a new social class. Or New Class, as some refer to it. The term was first used by the Yugoslav dissident Milovan Djilas to describe the bureaucratic elite that battened on the "class-free" Communist society of his homeland. Next it began to be observed as a development in societies that were not in the least Marxist, and the question emerged whether the new class was a more general aspect of modernization. This indeed became something of a theme of the journal *The Public Interest,* which Irving Kristol and Daniel Bell founded in 1965. So much so that the socialist writer Michael Harrington took some justified pleasure in pointing out that the lead article in the first issue of *The Public Interest* "might be called a manifesto *for* the new class."(My emphasis.)

As it happens, I wrote the article in question, entitled "The Professionalization of Reform." I took the theme from Nathan Glazer, who just prior to the assassination of President Kennedy had commented in a British journal:

Without benefit of anything like the Beveridge report to spark and focus public discussion and concern, the United States is passing through a stage of enormous expansion in the size and scope of what we may loosely call the social services — the public programs designed to help people adapt to an increasingly complex and unman-

ageable society. While Congress has been painfully and hesitantly
trying to deal with two great measures — tax reform and a civil rights
bill — and its deliberations on both have been closely covered by the
mass media, it has also been working with much less publicity on a
number of bills which will contribute at least as much to changing the
shape of American society.

These had to do with such matters as mental health,
manpower training, area redevelopment, and welfare. While
public attention focused on the stalemate of Kennedy's most
publicized proposals, *these* programs, each considerable in
itself, and very much so in combination, were quietly moving
through Congress. Few observers other than professionals
noticed. (Few amateurs, I remarked, could as much as keep the
names of the programs straight.) For indeed the initiative for
these programs came mostly *from* professionals, and the
deliberations in Congress concerning them had begun to take
on the atmosphere of consultations *among* professionals concerning matters about which outsiders were — well, not really
qualified.

I was then Assistant Secretary of Labor for Policy Planning
and Research, a new position President Kennedy had established. Until then when the Labor Department needed a policy,
it sent out for one, as you might say, from the AFL-CIO. I had
been part of the group that had planned the "War on Poverty."
There were three aspects of the poverty program I observed, in
"The Professionalization of Reform," which distinguished it
from earlier efforts of that kind: "The initiative came largely
from within. The case for action was based on essentially
esoteric information about the past and probable future course
of events."

This was something new to government and politics, I
suggested, and was based on three large developments. First,
what I termed "the econometric revolution." Men were "learning how to make an industrial economy work." This, I held,

was a genuine discontinuity. The old schemes for how to keep an economy going would be replaced by agreeably allocating a predictable rise of federal revenues, some $4 to $5 billion a year, to useful purposes. "The singular nature of the new situation in which the Federal government finds itself is that the immediate *supply* of resources available for social purposes might actually outrun the immediate *demand* of established programs." This was the then notorious problem of "fiscal drag," the expectation that the graduated income tax brought money rolling in faster than Congress would agree to roll it out.

Well, we are all young once. The second development to which I referred was "the professionalization of the middle class," the movement away from business as the prime pursuit of middle Americans, toward the burgeoning professions and semiprofessions. Third was "the exponential growth of knowledge." Put them all together and you have a new politics.

As a first approximation, this was not the worst. Whatever it was I was trying to describe, it was real enough. Soon the term *professional-bureaucratic complex* came into use, corresponding to the earlier *military-industrial complex*. In his 1977 presidential address to the American Political Science Association, Samuel H. Beer declared that a "public sector of the polity" had emerged, and that this was changing the nature of Federalism. The polity, like the economy, he asserted, has a public sector. "It consists of people in their public capacities trying to influence government action." Like the public sector of the economy, it was growing and changing the way we do things:

I would remark how rarely additions to the public sector have been *initiated* by the demands of voters or the advocacy of pressure groups or the platforms of political parties. On the contrary, in the fields of health, housing, urban renewal, transportation, welfare, education, poverty, and energy, it has been, in very great measure, people in government service, or closely associated with it, acting on the basis of their specialized and technical knowledge, who first perceived the problem, conceived the program, initially urged it on president and Congress, went on to help lobby it through to enactment, and then saw to its administration.

Sociologists were as much or even more absorbed with the subject. Daniel Bell provided the master concept in his 1976 work *The Coming of Post-Industrial Society*. In such a society, he held, the crucial people are those who handle information: their numbers and their influence grow. Everyone agrees on the extraordinary influence of higher education. Without much noticing we had become a society in which there were 600,000 professors. Everett Carll Ladd, Jr., put it that the upper middle class in America, formerly a business class, had become an intelligentsia. This new class was attracted by the public sector in just the way its predecessor had been alarmed and even repelled by it.

Politics changed. In his superb analysis in *Fortune* in 1977, Ladd showed that university graduates who forty years ago were dependably Republican have just as predictably become Democrats today. But Democrats are not the same anymore. Ladd has shown a second crucial transformation. A large segment of the working class became middle class, in Ladd's term, a "stability endorsing new bourgeoisie." Workers have bought houses and acquired pensions and have become a conserving party. Working people have become increasingly suspicious of the growth of government; professional people less so. "Old Class" Democrats, for example, consistently favor less government spending than the college-educated "New Class" Democrats, who want more except for crime, drug addiction, and national defense. (On these issues the "Old Class" wants more.) All in all, quite a change.

Back to California, 1978. What happened? California is preeminently a place where working people can buy a home and honestly expect to accumulate a little something in the course of their working lives. What they acquire is the value of their house, the most important investment most people ever make. *Real* property. To lose it, would be as tormenting as in the old days "to lose the farm," which is to say to lose everything. In California inflation was driving up land values, and assessments and taxes followed. In Sacramento a quintessential New Class state government was running a surplus of some $5 billion a year, and, presumedly, thinking of new and interesting things to do with it. Proposition 13 was to settle whether the surplus would be used for firehouses and libraries.

The view that property taxes had become insupportable in California would not seem warranted, at least by contrast with other states. We really are becoming an information-rich society — and, as it happens, we know something about this. In 1962, the economists Selma J. Mushkin and Alice M. Rivlin developed a mathematical model by which to measure tax capacity and tax effort in state or local jurisdictions. The "representative tax system" first determines the national average for a particular tax, as for example, residential property tax. Next it determines the tax base for a particular jurisdiction — on the basis of residential property value. Multiplying the average rate against the tax base produces the tax potential. When compared with actual tax collections, the result is a measure both of capacity and effort. Simple. All good ideas are simple once somebody has taken the trouble to think them up.

D. Kent Halstead, for the National Institute of Education, has computed the tax wealth of all fifty states and the District of Columbia for 1975. The results are striking. States scatter all over the place, but distinct clusters can be seen. The South remains a region with low tax capacity and low tax effort. The Northwest and the high Plains are resolutely average, or you might say, sane. (The State of Washington has a tax capacity of 100, which is to say, exactly average, and a tax effort of 101.) Only two states, Hawaii and California, show both a high tax capacity and a high tax effort. California has a tax capacity index of 110 and a tax effort index of 120.

This argues that Californians are somewhat better off than most, and also tax themselves at an even higher rate than their position might warrant. *Except* for residential property taxes. Here California's tax capacity rates at 143, third highest in the nation, but California has a tax effort of 126, high, but not higher than tenth in the nation. Farm property is walloped in California, with a capacity index of only 64, but an effort index of 189. Public utilities, with a capacity of 80, have a tax effort of 138. Commercial and industrial property shows the same pattern. But homeowners do not seem *that* badly off save for older persons whose incomes rise much more slowly than others. There are many such persons, but they do not explain a two-to-one vote.

Nor can the vote be explained in terms of a great wave of reaction rolling out of California. If Californians had wished to be reactionary, they could have chosen, in the primary election of that year, a Republican candidate for governor who announced as a reactionary. Instead they chose Evelle Younger, a moderate, experienced man who was not mad at anybody.

Proposition 13 did not bring out a traditional Republican/ Democratic division in the electorate so much as a division between the "Old Class" Democrats — the Roosevelt coalition — and "New Class" Democrats. People whom a progressive social and economic system had enabled to buy homes, voted to conserve the very real gains they have made — not just individually but as a class.

The example of New York very likely had some influence on the California outcome. New York and California are the primary centers of the political culture of the New Class, with Massachusetts, Wisconsin, and Minnesota perhaps also belonging in the group. Taxes are bad enough in the three other states, but in New York they have become a disaster. From the mid-sixties to the mid-seventies, government in New York, at the city and state level, thought up new modes of spending and raised taxes to incomparably the highest level in the nation's history. New York, in Halstead's computation, has only an average level of tax capacity, with an index of 102. But its index of tax effort is 152, half again the national average. At the other extreme, Texas has a capacity index of 113 and an effort index of 68. With a greater tax capacity than New York, Texas collected from its citizens in 1975 $492 per capita in state and local taxes. New York collected $991.

Taxes destroyed jobs and drove them out of New York. From 1969 to 1977 the city lost 663,400 jobs. (There are 17 states in which the entire labor force is not that large.) This decline was offset only slightly by a 30,000 increase in municipal employment. With the city's economy collapsing, the tax system could not produce as expected. On June 30, 1975, it was revealed that the city had a cumulative deficit of $5.1 billion and was insolvent. The city went into receivership. A centuries-old system of self-government was put aside. The most recent legislation contemplates the restoration of self-government on or about the year 2008. In the words of *The New Yorker* commentator Andy Logan, the city had been reduced to "recidivistic beggary." Is it not possible that the citizens of California saw a lesson here?

I hold no brief for the specific of Proposition 13, which for flexibility and prudence compares approximately with the proposal to turn the government of New York state over to the New York Central Railroad. Local government revenue in California was reduced from $12 billion to $5 billion. School districts lost half their present funds. Only a third of the tax cut applied to owner-occupied residences. The big bonanza was to landlords, farmers, and corporations, who no doubt supported Proposition 13. But surely they could not have supplied the huge plurality of 1,837,075. There is a further irony. By fiscal year 1980 the federal government expects an additional $900 million in taxes from Californians who have until now been deducting much larger property taxes. But then a lot of Californians were mad.

According to our theory, the Californians were mostly mad at the wrong people. Sacramento did not originate their troubles, but Washington. The Advisory Commission on Intergovernmental Relations in effect made this point in a recent statement on "Significance of Fiscal Federalism":

. . . While the size and scope of state and local responsibilities have grown, policy initiatives, allocational decisions, and administrative authority increasingly have been centralized at the national level. Paradoxically, this shift began to accelerate at a time when two national administrations were proposing policies designed to facilitate decentralization.

Translated, what the commission is saying is that the great expansion of state and local government has come increasingly at the behest of the national government, although recent Presidents have openly opposed this trend.

What we see now is Washington setting policy not through Presidents, but by the New Class. It would quite mistake my point, and that of most analysts of the New Class, to associate the cadre with one policy or set of policies. The New Class demands only that there should be a great deal *of* policy, whatever the content might be. Policy is for them what controversy is for lawyers. Presidents resist this. Presidents care more for taxes and government expenditure than their staffs do, and their cabinets. This is understandable. A President gains prestige by being reelected; for a member of his cabinet or staff, prestige lies in getting a new program established. If Lyndon B. Johnson is remembered as an exception, I will testify to the howls that went through his administration when he decreed in late 1963 that his first budget would be *under* $100 billion.

Presidents increasingly find they have staffed their administrations with persons resolutely intent on expanding government *whatever* the President might wish. This is not just a problem for Democrats. Many of the New Class start out far on the left, but generally they end up simply as functionaries.* As the Advisory Commission's statement implies, the surge in federal aid to — and involvement with — local government came under Nixon and Ford. The Republican Presidents *did* try to decentralize authority, but this was prevented by Congress. The congressional staff, as Stephen Hess has shown, became vastly more influential, as against members of Congress. Congress now depends on staff at least as much as the President does, and the staff had recognizably joined the professional-bureaucratic complex. Largely as a result of this new pattern of influence in Congress, huge federal deficits became a fixed feature of government in the 1970s.

President Carter's experience took the development yet farther. He won the presidency in considerable measure by responding to the national mood expressed in the Proposition 13 vote. He arrived in Washington determined to balance the budget, and to break the power of "horrible, bloated" bureaucracy. But when it came to staffing his administration, outside of a half dozen associates from Georgia, he turned, as he had to turn, to precisely this New Class, which had no intention of doing any of the things he proposed, and in fact did none until, in the aftermath of Proposition 13, the President presented his draconian fiscal 1981 budget which proposed a deficit of only $16 billion.

Imprecision is a peril to this kind of theorizing. In what sense, for example, can it be said that the President's appointees as a group did or did not have any "intention" to pursue

---

*I offer lines penned in 1966:

> The S.D.S. will soon desist
> Being so obstructionist.
> Made the City fathers nervous:
> Ended up in the Civil Service.

the President's objectives? I have no response. And yet I "know" that Washington has changed in this respect lately. I have myself been caught up in some of the changes.

In the late 1960s, for example, I argued, again in *The Public Interest,* that we were getting nowhere piling program on top of program, and that what we needed was to focus on *policy.* Ten years afterward, the policy craze is altogether out of hand. Every other week a new national policy announces itself. In 1978, for example, a group of cabinet officers and senior officials met in the Roosevelt Room in the West Wing of the White House to begin plans for a National Cultural Policy.

Go back, let us say, half a century. In what circumstances could a comparable meeting have taken place? There are but two. The first would take place in a world of imaginative satire: A theretofore unknown third act of *Patience* had been discovered. In a swirl of Victorian nonsense and mischance, Bunthorne has entered Parliament and risen to be Prime Minister. He has convened the cabinet for purposes of forming a National Cultural Policy. Enter chorus of Backbenchers denouncing blood sports, demanding gun control, etcetera. The only other setting in which such a gathering could meet a half century ago would have been in one of the two totalitarian states: more likely Fascist Italy than Communist Russia.

In 1978 the consistory in the Roosevelt Room was not made up either of Savoyards or Black Shirts, but rather of mostly young professionals in the new arts of government, trying to do a decent job and to advance their reputations in the process. The problem is that there is so much foolishness and that it costs a great deal of money. In 1969, in *The Public Interest,* Peter F. Drucker wrote:

The most despotic government of 1900 would not have dared probe into the private affairs of its citizens as income tax collectors now do routinely in the freest society. . . . Yet there is mounting evidence that government is big rather than strong; that it is fat and flabby rather than powerful; that it costs a great deal but does not achieve much.

What, for example, will come of the effort to create a National Cultural Policy? If we are lucky, it will be no more than a White House Office entering competition with the National Endowment for the Arts and the National Endowment for the Humanities. But it will cost money and it will extend government farther into areas where government has little business and no competence.

As the New Class grows more influential, it increasingly addresses itself to tasks which only demonstrate its own impotence. If its members would *do* something about oil imports (National Energy Policy) or change something in the South Bronx (National Urban Policy) or stop the water table from receding (National Water Policy), one would not mind if television went on being awful (National Cultural Policy). But mostly they won't because their necessary mode of intervention — government bureaucracy and regulation — doesn't.

What is to be done? Might an analogy from earlier presidencies help? It used to be said that Franklin D. Roosevelt and the New Deal saved the American business class from itself, for that class could not cope with the economic problems it had largely engendered. Franklin Roosevelt did not "betray his class." In this view, he saved it. Nor did Dwight D. Eisenhower betray the "military-industrial complex" when he called attention to the mordant tendencies of that network of interests. Nor will a President (or anyone else) betray the true interest of the professional-bureaucratic complex, which has in so many ways escaped control today, by speaking out. The people involved, the values they represent, the skills they embody are needed. But they must learn the limits of government, and learn (again to employ that useful Marxist term) how to demystify their own conduct. Learn to recognize, for example,

when their high-sounding pronouncements about helping
others can be little more than a justification for helping
themselves. Better yet, invent institutions to impose the
necessary restraints without too much depending on exhorta-
tion and good example. "Thrust ivrybody — but cut th' ca-
ards," said Mr. Dooley. *That* is the art of government.

It is one thing to seize the day when government revenues
have a true surplus. It is quite another to spend an inflation-
generated surplus — the increased revenues that come from
increased prices. It is not a surplus at all: it is a fever.

I persist in thinking that the "promise of social sanity and
stability" persists. This will be lost if we don't insist on
performance more than we have done. As Niebuhr tried to
teach, this involves coming to accept that there are some
things that can't be changed, and learning to recognize which
they are. Not to do so is to be false to a large vocation. In that
sense California's verdict on Proposition 13 partook somewhat
of truth.

In the 1978 general elections a number of states voted on
proposals similar to Proposition 13. None succeeded. California's willingness to make such huge cuts in local taxes shows
up clearly as a by-product of a huge state surplus. (Which
surplus was in turn partly the result of a hugely favorable
"balance of payments" surplus as between California and the
federal fisc, a situation opposite to New York's. In 1976, for
example, California received more than a quarter of the
research and development funds expended by Washington.) In
Michigan, without a surplus, voters chose instead to limit state
spending to a fixed proportion of state personal income.
Everywhere the votes showed a clear disinclination to let
public expenditures float upward with inflation, the way
personal income tax rates do. The political scientist Michael
Barone summarized in *The Almanac of American Politics*:

With clarity unusual for an election year, 1978 . . . [saw] . . . the
emergence of a broad consensus is easily stated: the government

should not get a significantly larger share of the gross national product than it gets now, but it should not get substantially less either.

From the time of the New Deal we have, with respect to the size of government, been on a great *S* curve. It is now flattening out, as sooner or later it had to. The task now is to achieve a steady state of government without immobilizing it.

FOUR

14.
Cold Dawn, High Noon
Salt I and II

IN THE SUMMER of 1978, when it began to be clear that the SALT II treaty would be signed with the Soviet Union, the Select Committee on Intelligence of the United States Senate began to prepare for its role in the procedures by which the Senate would take up a resolution of ratification. As a member of the committee, I journeyed to Geneva to talk to the negotiators of the draft agreement that was taking shape and began to go over the history of SALT I, more formally known as the Interim Agreement on Certain Measures with Respect to the Limitation of Strategic Offensive Arms and the Treaty on the Limitation of Anti-Ballistic Missile Systems, signed in 1972.

It did not take long to establish that, whatever else SALT I might have done, it accomplished little by way of limiting strategic offensive arms. For that matter, it wasn't even an agreement about weapons as ordinarily understood. Rather, it was an agreement to limit the number of launchers each party would have for its long-range ballistic missiles. A launcher (or silo, in the usage of the military) for a land-based missile is a hole in the ground. You could get hurt by falling into one, but it is missiles, and, more specifically, the warheads of missiles, that kill people, and these were not at all limited by SALT I. Nor, it appeared, would they be much limited by SALT II. From the time of the first agreement, the number of American warheads increased steadily, and those of the Soviets more than doubled. It appeared they would double again under SALT II.

This was hardly reassuring. But more troubling still was the realization that this all came as news to me. I had never given great attention to the subject, but from the time of the Treaty Banning Nuclear Weapon Tests in the Atmosphere, in Outer Space, and Under Water, of 1963, I had had the impression that things were going well enough, or at least not badly. I did not have the excuse most persons might have for being vague about the details. I had served in four successive administrations, from that of Kennedy on. I had known virtually all of the principal arms negotiators and, from university life, a good number of the strategic-arms theorists. I had sat at the cabinet table of two Presidents listening to reports on progress. Always they *were* reports on progress. Or such was the impression I took away. I now began questioning my own judgment, then that of others — especially as the Carter administration began to proclaim the virtues of SALT II in terms I could recognize as essentially the same as those in which the Kennedy, Johnson, Nixon, and Ford administrations had presented their achievements in arms control. I began to wonder whether anyone from the most recent administration, or more generally from the world of arms control, would ever describe the agreements in terms that comported with what now appeared to me as a different, even new reality.

I was to wait almost a year, until the morning of Wednesday, July 11, 1979, when Dr. William J. Perry, Under-Secretary of Defense for Research and Engineering, testified on SALT II before the Committee on Foreign Relations. Perry, a mathematician, speaks plainly and, as with many in his rarefied profession, is a man of unassuming appearance and manner.

All the more was the contrast with the Caucus Room of the Old Senate Office Building, in which the hearings were held. The Caucus Room is a place of unashamed exhibition and splendor dating from 1906, when Theodore Roosevelt, having built the West Wing of the White House, commenced to challenge the Congress from his new office, and the Senate decided to get itself an office building of its own. Until that period, Presidents had worked in their living rooms, as it were, and senators at their desks in the Senate Chamber. Neither facility had been much expanded from the time of Jefferson. If the interior of the Capitol can be said to be Palladian and given to republican virtues in design, the Caucus Room, only slightly smaller than the Senate Chamber itself, is Roman Imperial, and make no mistake. It struck me as a not inappropriate setting for Dr. Perry's subject, SALT II.

The Secretary of Defense, Harold Brown, had just finished his prepared statement in favor of the arms-limitation treaty. Curiously, the charts and displays he had brought along to illustrate his points, in the manner of military briefings, were exclusively concerned with recent and prospective improvements in and additions to the nuclear arms of both countries. The capabilities of both the United States and the Soviet Union to destroy so-called hard targets, such as missile silos, were represented as about equal, with the Soviets slightly ahead as of now and maintaining a slight lead through 1990 — when both capabilities would have about trebled.

Perry's testimony began. He had no prepared statement, it being his role to provide answers to technical questions the Secretary's testimony might have raised. But he said a few words anyway, and in doing so made perhaps the best case yet presented for SALT II, while describing with a technician's candor its shortcomings. He said:

SALT I's success was in getting the process started. There was a substantial arms-control success in the [Anti-Ballistic Missile] Treaty, but essentially there was no success in reducing the number of offensive weapons. The best evidence of that is, just look to see what happened to the number of warheads indicated on that chart since SALT I. Both the United States and the Soviet Union have added about 3,000 warheads since 1972.

The Vladivostok agreement [of 1974] was one more important advance in this process. It did specify upper bounds. It included bombers, not just missiles in the forces, but it still permitted substantial increases in warheads as of that time.

President Carter tried to break that upper spiral with his March, 1977, proposal for SALT, and as you well know, that was rejected by the Soviet Union. In fact, it is my belief that any SALT proposal in this time frame that does not preserve the Soviets' right to modernize their ICBM [Intercontinental Ballistic Missile] force would be rejected. My judgment is, they have made a very substantial commitment to that. The ICBM is really the only strong component of their strategic forces, and they seem to be resolutely opposed to making any substantial reduction in it.

Therefore, the SALT II treaty which we have arrived at, while it is a major improvement over the Vladivostok agreement . . . still allows significant upward spiral of the number of nuclear weapons.

I anticipate that the Soviet Union will continue to pursue the modernization of their ICBM program as indicated in the figures which Dr. Brown showed you, and that we will respond to that, so that both sides then will continue to have significant increases in nuclear warheads.

That is the bad news. The good news that comes with that is that SALT II also establishes a process and goals. The most significant goal is the one to achieve a real reduction in nuclear weapons — not in delivery vehicles but in actual weapons. My question then, as a defense planner, is how do we structure our strategic programs in the years ahead to be compatible with that goal — not only to be compatible with it but actually to facilitate the achievement of that goal of getting a reduction, a real reduction, in nuclear weapons in the future.

The master term here is *process*. Clearly, neither the first nor the second agreement did much to limit arms. Weapons and weapons systems on both sides continue to accumulate. But the agreements did establish a forum in which the two nations discussed these matters, and entered into a degree of cooperation concerning them. This was the case, I had understood for some time, in the matter of monitoring — the various means by which each nation keeps track of the activities of the other in order to verify that the SALT agreements are being kept. Whether our abilities here are sufficient was the question the Intelligence Committee faced when it began formal hearings on the issue of verification soon after SALT II was signed by Presidents Carter and Brezhnev in Vienna, on June 18.

Alone of the standing or select committees, the Select Committee on Intelligence normally does its work in closed sessions, which meet in the Capitol dome in a small hearing room that is suspended, you might say, from the cupola. It was built up there for the use of the Joint Committee on Atomic Energy, the first committee of the Congress that routinely did its work in camera. Of the materials the Intelligence Committee deals with, none are more sensitive, because they really are secrets, than those concerning information about Soviet strategic nuclear forces, and, more especially, concerning the means by which that information is obtained. A minuscule fraction of the information comes from agents of one or another sort — HUMINT, in the contraction favored by the intelligence community. Early in the postwar period, it was judged that the Soviet Union was much too closed a society to be penetrated by agents. Machines were put to work, with ever-increasing sophistication; today, by far the greatest portion of our information comes from what are known as "technical collection systems." Basically, there are three such systems. First, a number of satellites continuously circle the earth taking photographs of the Soviet Union, as can now be done with extraordinarily high resolution. (The technicians speak of picking out "the golf ball on the green.") Second, the United

States can monitor the radio signals, known as "telemetry," which the Soviet missiles send back in flight. Third, American ships watch incoming missiles in the Pacific firing zones, establishing distances traveled, the pattern in which multiple warheads land (known as the "footprint"), and other such information. The Russians have comparable systems. Either side can effectively count the number of land-based missiles set in silos and ready to be launched on the other side. The numbers of submarines and launchers are readily enough established, as are the numbers of intercontinental bombers.

Each side, naturally, hopes that the other side will not know when some new advance has been made in detection systems, and on this score there was some difficulty to be resolved as the Senate prepared to consider verification under the SALT II agreement. In recent years, Soviet intelligence in the United States had scored a number of successes that alerted the Russians to the development of new American intelligence technology. In 1975, Soviet agents had obtained information about a major satellite system known as Rhyolite. In 1978, it was learned that agents had also obtained the operating manual for the most advanced of our satellites then in operation, the KH-11. In both instances, the espionage had seemingly been simple and inexpensive; in one case, the materials were acquired, for quite modest amounts of money, from a youthful employee of the TRW corporation, and in the other from an employee of the Central Intelligence Agency itself. This suggested that the Soviets have no great difficulty learning what we are capable of spotting, and can take appropriate evasive action. In addition, the loss to the United States of listening posts in Iran which monitored activity at a missile range near the Aral Sea, in south-central Soviet Asia, involved a considerable loss of information not easily obtained otherwise. Then, on June 28, 1979, the White House leaked to *The New York Times* that the United States had a similar station in Norway. The leak was intentional, to reassure those favorable to the treaty, but at the same time it jeopardized the Norwegian "asset," to use another term of the intelligence community. Thus, the question arose as to whether the United States would be able to be certain that the Russians were abiding by the terms of an arms-limitation treaty that would extend through 1985. The record of SALT I was both reassuring and cautionary. There was no conclusive proof that the Soviets had committed any major violations of SALT I strictly construed. By and large, what they agreed not to do they did not do. But where we said we *hoped* they would not do something they paid not the least attention.

This, as it turned out, was no small matter. One of the principal negotiating objectives on the American side in SALT I was to insure that neither side built any more "heavy" missiles. This is a term for missiles big enough to carry a huge "payload," which can deliver a large number of nuclear warheads capable of reaching and destroying missiles on the other side. They are potential "counterforce" weapons, because they can be used effectively against other forces. (Missiles aimed against cities are called "countervalue" weapons.) As of 1972, the Russians had three hundred and eight heavy SS-9 missiles, while the United States had no modern heavy missiles. In SALT I, it was agreed to freeze both sides, meaning that the Soviets would and we would not have modern heavy missiles. Although this appeared to be an imbalance, American strategic doctrine at that time did not call for counterforce weapons, and we were well enough content. It was understood that the Soviets would replace their SS-9 missiles with a new model, or "generation" — the SS-18. However, the Soviets were then also planning to replace a medium-sized missile, the SS-11, with another new model, the SS-19, which was so much bigger and more accurate as to become, for practical purposes, a new heavy. As the Intelligence Committee stated on October 5, 1979, in the public portion of its report to the Senate on the capabilities of the United States to monitor SALT II:

The Soviets' unanticipated ability to emplace the much larger SS-19 in a slightly enlarged SS-11 silo circumvented the safeguards the United States thought it had obtained in SALT I against the substitution of heavy for light ICBMs.

Similarly, in SALT I the United States conceded to the Soviets the right to build a larger number of missile-carrying submarines than we were permitted, in order to compensate for the Soviets' "geographical disadvantage." (To reach the open Atlantic Ocean, for instance, Soviet submarines must pass through the relatively narrow gaps between Greenland, Iceland, and the United Kingdom; our submarines reach the open ocean at once.) But the range of the SS-N-8, the new Soviet submarine-launched ballistic missile, turned out to be considerably greater than expected, enabling it to be fired at American targets while the submarine remained in the Barents Sea. There is little reason to think the Soviets cheated by misrepresenting the range of their weapon at that time. They simply remained silent about its full potential. But in any case they got an edge on us.

Our monitoring system soon established that the SS-11 had been replaced by the SS-19, although the newer missiles used the same silos, slightly enlarged. The State Department was provided the facts and presented them to the Soviets. It was then that the problem arose. The Soviets agreed, or did not disagree, that they were putting an entirely new strategic-weapons system in place but asserted that nothing in the SALT I agreement prevented their doing this. Nothing did.

SALT I — the Anti-Ballistic Missile Treaty permanently limiting each side's ABM systems, and the "interim" executive agreement that essentially prohibited each side from building additional ballistic-missile launchers for five years — was signed by President Nixon in Moscow on May 26, 1972. In an address to a joint session of Congress on the day he returned to the United States, the President hailed the event, saying, "This does not mean that we bring back from Moscow the promise of instant peace, but we do bring the beginning of a process that can lead to lasting peace." However, two weeks later, in a message transmitting the agreements to the Senate, he stated that while together these were an "important first step in checking the arms race . . . it is now equally essential that we carry forward a sound strategic modernization program to maintain our security and to ensure that more permanent and comprehensive arms-limitation agreements can be reached."

At this time, the Secretary of Defense, Melvin R. Laird, was maintaining that the Congress must go ahead with programs for offensive-weapons systems permitted by SALT I, such as the Trident submarine and the B-1 bomber. In a press conference on June 22, 1972, Nixon stated that Laird was correct in this judgment:

Mr. Brezhnev made it absolutely clear to me that in those areas that were not controlled by our offensive agreement that they were going ahead with their programs. For us not to would seriously jeopardize the security of the United States and jeopardize the cause of world peace.

SALT I, he added, "while very important, is only the first step, and not the biggest step."

SALT II has so far followed precisely this pattern. Just as Nixon had done, President Carter, immediately upon returning to the United States from his summit meeting, delivered an address to a joint session of Congress in June 1979 in which he hailed the agreement, and in the same address (not waiting two weeks) he announced there would be more weapons. Indeed, he asserted that one of the principal advantages of the treaty is that it would enable us to go forward with a new missile system—the MX. This "missile experimental" (one

day it will no doubt be named for a Greek god) is to be a mobile
land-based missile, our first. It will be more powerful even
than the liquid-fueled Atlas and Titan giants of the nineteen-
fifties, the only heavy missiles the United States has ever, so
far, deployed. On September 7, President Carter announced
the "basing mode" and other specifics of the MX. Each would be
placed on a vehicle and moved to a couple of dozen different
launching emplacements around a "racetrack," in random and
presumably unpredictable ways, so as not to be "targeted" by
Soviet missiles. Each would carry ten warheads, each of these
with a yield equivalent to hundreds of kilotons of explosives.
(The Hiroshima bomb was twenty kilotons.) The "racetracks"
would require thousands of miles of road and an area the size of
Massachusetts. The President said the new MX was "not a
bargaining chip," to be bartered away in any future arms
negotiations, but would represent a permanent "unsurpassed"
feature of the nation's strategic nuclear deterrent. Two hundred MX missiles would be deployed in Nevada and Utah. This
mode, the President said, met requirements he had set for a
mobile missile system: survivability, verifiability, affordabil-
ity, environmental soundness, and consistency with arms-
control goals. On this occasion, Secretary Brown, while predicting that the Soviets would respond "negatively" to this
United States announcement, said that if they engaged in "a
fruitless race" to try to overwhelm our new system they would
strain their economic resources, and that if they created a new
land-based missile system of their own they would be vulnerable to United States attack, presumably from the new American system.

The Federation of American Scientists promptly declared
the MX to be "not just an inflationary multi-billion-dollar
strategic mistake, but an arms-control disaster." The F.A.S.,
begun in 1946 as the Federation of Atomic Scientists, has since
that time been a leading advocate of nuclear-arms control. Its
judgment was stern:

The MX missile announced today contains the seeds of its own destruction since, as a counter-force weapon, it will necessarily stimulate the Soviet Union to procure still more warheads which will, in turn, quickly threaten MX quite as much as the Minuteman missiles are presently threatened. In the process, the SALT limits will become untenable. Worse, the Air Force will ask for the right to abrogate the ABM treaty to get anti-ballistic missiles to defend the MX. Thus the ABM treaty will also be threatened and the arms race will really be back with a vengeance.

The F.A.S. warned that there was "no strategic need to imitate the Russian preference for large land-based missiles," and added, "The precipitous quality of the decision to move to match the Soviets in land-based missile throw-weight has been induced by SALT." Induced by SALT? If this seems a contradiction in terms — or, at the very least, "counterintuitive," to use a term of systems analysis — then all the more reason to pay heed. There are systems that exhibit such properties, producing the opposite of their intended outcome, with the consequence that intensifying the effort to achieve the desired one achieves even more of the undesired.

As the summer passed into autumn, attacks on SALT II from arms-control advocates increased. Just two days after the F.A.S. issued its statement, Richard J. Barnet, who served in the Arms Control and Disarmament Agency in the Kennedy administration, described the treaty in an article in the Washington *Post* as "something to stir the hearts of generals, defense contractors, and senators from states brimming with military reservations and arms plants." His tone verged on the contemptuous:

The 100-page treaty, which reads like the prospectus for a bond issue, is neither disarmament nor arms control but an exercise in joint arms management. The treaty has secured the acquiescence of the military in both countries because it ratifies the huge weapons-acquisition programs both are pushing.

In the fall issue of *Foreign Policy,* Leslie H. Gelb began an essay on the future of arms control with the blunt assertion, "Arms control has essentially failed." He had a friendly word for SALT II, which is perhaps not surprising, for, as a director of the Bureau of Politico-Military Affairs from 1977 to 1979, he had had the principal responsibility in the Department of State for conduct of the negotiations once the Carter administration came to office. But he concluded that in the main the process had not worked.

Only a few weeks later, *The New York Times,* with what measure of irony one cannot say, called for ratification by declaring, "SALT II is a sound agreement that will confine the nuclear arms race to specified channels." It is perhaps not fair-minded to press the images of editorialists too far, but it may be noted that when a diffused flow is forced into a confined channel the result is acceleration. Whatever became of arms control?

At each stage of the SALT negotiations, and with each new agreement, the nuclear forces on both sides have increased. Those of the Soviets have increased faster than those of the United States, but this trend was present prior to SALT. When the talks were first proposed, in 1967, the Soviets had 900 nuclear warheads. By 1979 they had some 5,000. At the expiration of the SALT II treaty in 1985, it is estimated, they will have roughly 12,000. During that period, the number of United States warheads will grow from 9,200 to about 12,000 also. By 1985, the Soviets will have four warheads for every county in the United States, and the United States will have four warheads for every *rayon,* a comparable unit of government in the Soviet Union. But the Soviet warheads in total will have more than three times the megatonnage of the American warheads. Although it is possible that these rates of growth would be greater without the treaties, it is also possible that they would be lower.

At the hearings concerning our ability to verify the Russians' compliance with the treaty, men of formidable learning and experience, some passionate, some detached, came before the Intelligence Committee to argue the probabilities and the difficulties of verification, but always in the context of ever-increasing Soviet numbers. It came to me that, with numbers so great, verification couldn't much matter. Suppose that by foul duplicity, compounded by American incompetence, the number of Russian warheads increased in the years immediately ahead from 5,000 to 13,000, rather than to only 12,000. If an additional thousand mattered, surely an additional 7,000 mattered more. Well, not necessarily — only if the increase provided the Soviets some special edge. But they would have an edge on megatonnage in either event. Indeed, they already have that edge. There was something unreal about our inquiry. The possibility that the Soviets might increase their nuclear forces at a pace greater than agreed to was an object of much concern, but almost no heed was being paid to the fact that both they and (now) we are roaring ahead in an arms race, and using the treaty as an argument for doing so.

Was this "the bureaucratic mind at work"? Preoccupied with predictability, but scarcely at all distressed when what seems predictable is disaster? In part, yes. The Arms Control and Disarmament Agency has been in place for almost two decades now, and may be assumed to be as committed to the SALT process as the Bureau of Reclamation is to irrigation, and process can become sufficient unto itself. Jay Forrester, at M.I.T., has contributed the playful maxim that with respect to complex social problems, intuitive solutions are almost invariably wrong. Among the intuitive and the severely logical alike, what is happening is known as a vicious circle.

There was, in any event, a more portentous paradox to be resolved, and as the Intelligence Committee hearings droned on, my attention drifted away from verification toward the subject of doctrine. The SALT process has its premise in the doctrine of deterrence. The MX missile is incompatible with the doctrine of deterrence. It is, as its advocates in the administration like to say, a "hard-target-kill counterforce weapon." But the strategic doctrine of deterrence specifically precludes either side from obtaining counterforce weapons. How, then, could we be building the missile that undermines the doctrine in order to sustain the doctrine?

A paradox? Yes, and the makings also of tragedy beyond human dimension. I had best be out with it directly. Deterrence was a stunning intellectual achievement. It "solved" the seemingly insoluble problem of how to control the use of nuclear weapons. But it was flawed and has been undone by the intuitive but wrong assumption that the Soviets would see the logic of our solution and do as we did. Especially that they would see the meaninglessness of strategic "superiority."

As no other subject, strategic-arms doctrine has been the realm of the intellectual and the academic. This is military doctrine, to be sure, but it has never, in this nation, been formulated by military men. It began with the physicists who created the weapons — men such as J. Robert Oppenheimer, Hans Bethe, and Leo Szilard — who were then joined by other physicists and scientists, and also by social scientists. These latter — men such as Albert Wohlstetter, Herman Kahn, Fred C. Iklé, Alain C. Enthoven, Henry Rowen, and Henry Kissinger — came to be known collectively as "defense intellectuals." They moved in and out of Washington, but in the main they kept to their campuses and think tanks, or almost always returned to them, where their task, in Kahn's phrase, was "thinking about the unthinkable." Indeed, they have been something of a caste apart, even in academia. Oppenheimer at Alamogordo as the first atomic bomb exploded — "I am become death, the shatterer of worlds" — gives something of the aura of it. They ate at their own tables in the faculty clubs, and held seminars to which few were invited. They met with Russians when few others did.

And they developed the doctrine of deterrence — a doctrine of weapon use of which the first premise was that the weapon must never be used first, and of which the principal object was that it never be used at all. The nuclear power was to deploy its forces so that if attacked it could attack back, inflicting assured destruction on the party that had attacked in the first place. This capacity could be achieved by a fairly limited number of missiles aimed at the cities of the potential adversary. Only two developments could undermine the doctrine. If the adversary developed and deployed a defensive weapon — an ABM — that could protect his cities, then his destruction would not be assured and he could become aggressive and threatening. Or if the adversary possessed an offensive weapon that could destroy the missile force aimed at his cities — which is to say a counterforce weapon — then, also, his destruction could not be assured and he could become aggressive and threatening. SALT I blocked the first development. SALT II seems destined to insure the second.

This has come about, in the main, because the Russians did not keep to our rules. There has been nothing academic about their strategic doctrine, or at least not that we know of. They appear to have just gone plodding on, building bigger and better weapons, until, by an incremental process, they are on the point of being able to wipe out American land-based missiles — a counterforce ability. At one level, this achievement has been spectacular; at another, less so. For all the sophistication involved, nuclear weapons today are still nothing more than improved versions of the V-2 rocket with an atom bomb on top. But the improvements have reached the point where the doctrine that was to prevent their use has evidently been utterly undone. It had been the hope of the early arms-control negotiators that we would teach the Soviets our doctrine and they would abide by it. If there was something patronizing in the notion of "raising the Russians' learning curve," as the phrase went, there was also much respect in the belief that once we had come to the correct solution of a complex problem they could be brought to see that we were indeed correct. These were serious American academics, who held their Russian counterparts in full regard. But the enterprise failed. And why? Because the Russian situation is not our situation, the Russian experience not our experience. If intellect must fail, let it fail nobly; and it is in nobly rejecting the notion of failure that intellect fails most often.

Perhaps that is too strong. To state that an enterprise has failed is to suggest that it might have succeeded. Yet from the outset this has somehow seemed improbable. Let it be said for the postwar strategic nuclear theorists that they were not intimidated by their subject, nor immobilized by it. They did not shrink from action in the face of an incredible new dimension of war.

The influence of the theorists was to be seen early on, when the United States government, in 1946, proposed to turn its atomic bombs over to the United Nations — a proposal that the Soviet Union blocked. Then, for a period, the theorists receded from influence as the United States, with the only strategic nuclear force around, adopted, or said it had adopted, a policy of "massive retaliation," which contemplated the use of nuclear weapons in response to aggression by conventional ones. By the late nineteen-fifties, however, the Soviets commenced to have a strategic nuclear force of their own, whereupon the true issue was joined: How to face an adversary with the same powers of destruction?

In one respect, this was an issue as old as the airborne bomb — a development recognized as revolutionary long before it became so. George Quester, in his fascinating book *Deterrence before Hiroshima,* has traced the "prehistory" of nuclear deterrence. In 1899, the First Hague Conference banned bombing from balloons, but the Germans went ahead even so to develop the first strategic bombing force, using dirigibles, while the British may be said to have prepared for them with a theory. In a study, *Aircraft in Warfare,* published in 1916, a British mathematician, F. W. Lanchester, offered a quite contemporary notion of what we think of as the nuclear deterrent:

A reprisal to be effective must be delivered with promptitude like the riposte of a skilled fencer. A reprisal which is too long delayed possesses no moral weight and has every appearance of an independent act of aggression; it may even plausibly be given as an excuse for a subsequent repetition of the original offence . . . The power of reprisal and the knowledge that the means of reprisal exists will ever be a far greater *deterrent* than any pseudo-legal document.

There was much discussion in the prenuclear era of the utility of attacking cities, of the ability to defend cities, of preempting the enemy's offensive air forces, and the like. In a letter written in 1914, Winston Churchill revealed himself a firm advocate of what would be known as "counterforce." "The great defence against aerial menace," he wrote then, "is to attack the enemy's aircraft as near as possible to their point of departure." However, perhaps because the opportunity was so new, most thinking concentrated on attacking cities.

In this respect, the outlines of an enduring argument were apparent well before the technology itself was at hand. It was in the Second World War that technology created opportunities to implement speculation. What to do with a strategic bombing force? What to do with emerging missile forces? We now know from the United States Strategic Bombing Survey, conducted at the war's end, that the bombing of German cities was less effective in weakening Germany than was thought at the time. We also know that Hitler's V-2 rockets might have had significant impact if, instead of being used as terror weapons against city populations, they had been used against the Channel ports — the staging areas for the Allied offensive onto the continent — which is where some of the German generals wanted to send them.

Consideration of these issues in the nuclear era was surely colored by the use of the atomic bomb against Hiroshima and Nagasaki, in what current theorists would call a "counter-value" mode. So awesome was the scale of destruction from what, by today's standards, was a small bomb that the destruction of whole countries could now be envisioned. Had the distinction between military and civilian targets disappeared? It was this possibility, immobilizing to many, that brought forth the doctrine of deterrence. The problem for the United States, as earlier it had been for Great Britain, was to deter aggression. We were the great power, with no need or desire to attack others but wishing to avoid being attacked. We had not succeeded with Germany and Japan. But the nuclear weapon suggested that the power of retaliation had become awesome indeed — enough to inhibit any would-be aggressor who had any sense of the realities involved. Not only awesome but capable, in Lanchester's words, of being "delivered with promptitude," in contrast to the long buildup that had been required for American forces before they could be effectively used in the Second World War.

Albert Wohlstetter conceived the "second strike" as the key concept of deterrence. This is to say, the nuclear riposte. If an enemy strikes, you will strike back with devastating consequences. In addition, Wohlstetter offered two crucial insights. There is an essential requirement for the invulnerability of one's ability to strike back. The design of strategic forces and their emplacement has to insure this. But it is also the case that this can never be insured once and for all. *Any* force becomes vulnerable over time, especially if an adversary is working hard at making it so. Hence, there can be no final deterrent.

It was Wohlstetter's insights that made defense planners aware, in the late nineteen-fifties, that the bombers of the Strategic Air Command were becoming vulnerable to Soviet attack. When the Russians had few warheads and no missiles, two dozen dispersed SAC bases were secure enough. But as Soviet capabilities grew in the nineteen-fifties the airplanes became vulnerable. In response, however, from 1962 to 1967 the United States deployed a thousand Minuteman missiles in the Midwest in "hardened" silos — that is to say, in launchers dug deep and heavily protected. This was then an invulnerable second-strike force. But soon enough this invulnerability was in doubt. Not only did the Soviets acquire more missiles and more warheads, which was predictable, but an unpredictably rapid rise in accuracy also took place. Missiles once meant to hit within miles of a target now possessed accuracies prescribed in hundreds of yards. Hardened silos could be destroyed.

Another technology was also being developed — that of destroying missiles in flight with an antiballistic missile. Whereupon the issue of defense arose. Essential to the doctrine of deterrence was that neither side have any defense. In effect, each side exchanged hostages, whose lives thereafter depended on their side's good behavior. The Russians were given American cities, to be destroyed instantly if the United States launched a nuclear attack on Russia. This was our guarantee to the Russians that we would not launch such an attack. The Russians were deemed to have given us their cities. But now there was talk of hedging. It seemed the Russians might be developing a means to defend themselves against incoming missiles, much as antiaircraft defenses were developed in an earlier period. ABM systems are highly technical in design but simple enough in concept. One bullet shoots down another bullet. But if the systems worked, if our second strike did not assure the destruction of Soviet cities, then the Soviets could contemplate a first strike, and deterrence would fail. In this scenario, the nation that defends its cities can strike first, knowing that its cities are no longer hostage. In another scenario, the nation watching this defense being built strikes first, before it has lost its hostage. This is how SALT began.

They are not impersonal intellectuals who made these calculations. Some are intense and committed as few men of the age. But to share their passion it is necessary to enter their logic. What do you mean, one could ask, when you say that we must not defend ourselves because if we do our enemy will attack? The problem of public perception was not great in the nineteen-sixties. A deference system — a willingness to leave difficult decisions to experts — which had been in place since the bomb was built, continued undisturbed. But then heresy appeared in the midst of the close-knit and almost closed community of experts. Some began to talk of defense, or "damage limitation," as it was termed. If damage limitation was possible, how could it be foregone? Wohlstetter talked of defending the missile sites. The logic was impeccable. The Air Force, understandably, was worried about the vulnerability of our Minutemen, and with a straightforward military logic proposed to double their number: with more targets, a Soviet first strike would have less chance of wiping out our second strike. But with twice as many Minutemen the United States could target the Soviets' missiles as well as cities, and so reduce their capacity for a retaliatory strike. Doctrine has it that, given available technology, two warheads must be aimed at a silo to have a satisfactory probability of a "kill." Given the number of Soviet missiles at the time, one thousand single-warhead Minutemen could not be counted on to "take out" the Soviet strike force, but two thousand could. (There is the ever-present problem of "fratricide," whereby the first warhead to land destroys its mate — but enough.) It was our doctrine to deny ourselves any such capacity, lest the Soviets understandably become alarmed. Better to keep to the one thousand, but to defend them. Not so, said others, most especially Robert S. McNamara, the Secretary of Defense. If we defend anything, the demand will spread to defend everything.

John Newhouse begins *Cold Dawn,* his superb account of SALT I, by likening the debate to the disputations of the Church Fathers:

So much of the substance and vocabulary of SALT are at least as remote from reality, as most of us perceive it, as early Christian exegesis. . . . As in the case of the early Church, contending schools form around antagonistic strategic concepts. The most relevant of these are known as assured destruction and damage limitation, and each can claim broad support and intellectual respectability. Debates between the two schools recall those between the Thomists and the essentially Franciscan followers of Duns Scotus. The Thomists prevailed, as have the proponents of assured destruction, who assert, for example, that ballistic-missile defense of population is immoral because it may degrade your adversary's ability to destroy your own cities in a second strike. His confidence undermined, he might then be tempted in a crisis to strike pre-emptively; in short, knowing you are effectively protected from his second-strike assault and fearing your intentions, he may choose to strike first. Thus, stability, a truly divine goal in the nuclear age, becomes the product of secure second-strike nuclear offenses on both sides.

This is the first thing to know about SALT: The decision to propose talks, and the first agreements, constituted a victory for a specific doctrine — "assured destruction." It was even then a contested doctrine and gave signs of how vulnerable it might be to ideological attack in the form of caricature. In 1969, Donald Brennan, of the Hudson Institute, labeled it "*mutual* assured destruction," so that the acronym MAD came into play, like some new weapons system all its own. But even earlier, in the 1964 film *Dr. Strangelove,* Stanley Kubrick had caricatured a proposal of Herman Kahn, "the doomsday machine," which would automatically produce a second strike, so that the victim of a first strike could never hesitate to retaliate and decide instead to surrender. Making a second strike inevitable in order to prevent a first strike was eminently logical, but its proponents could also be made to seem crazy, like the mad scientist in Kubrick's film — a caricature which suggested that because so many of the defense intellectuals were German, their thinking must also be Teutonically rigid.

Looking back, it seems clear that the urgency with which the

Americans approached the Russians in the hope of obtaining
an arms agreement that would protect the assured-destruction
doctrine arose as much out of concern to secure the doctrine in
American strategic policy as to introduce it to the strategic
policy of the Soviet Union. If it could be codified in an
agreement with the Soviets which committed both sides, then
the argument at home would be more secure. For good or ill,
attacks on MAD had about them a quality of the political left.
If the Russians could be shown to have the same dispassionate
view of nuclear realities, this might mollify such opposition in
the United States. Of course, if Americans of both left and right
persuasions would argue later on that assured destruction is a
strategy that places exceptional reliance on the good faith and
good judgment of quite unreliable adversaries, the adversaries
could well remark that this was our idea, not theirs.

But there was also a technological imperative. In the middle
nineteen-sixties, the Soviets began to deploy their own missiles in hardened silos, which over time might give them a
second-strike capability, and even a first-strike capability, to
destroy U.S. land-based missiles in a surprise attack. No great
technological feats were involved—just a steady creep of
numbers, size, and accuracy. Planners in the Pentagon and
defense intellectuals began to talk of defenses that would
preserve our second strike. Wohlstetter advocated an ABM
defense of the Minutemen. But doctrine decreed that this, too,
would be destabilizing. Once an antiballistic-missile defense
was perfected, the temptation to use it to defend cities as well
as missile silos would grow. And the other side could never be
sure that we weren't planning to do exactly that, as quickly as
possible, at a time of our own choosing.

The decision point came on December 6, 1966 — "the precise
beginning of SALT," as Newhouse has it—at a meeting
between McNamara and Lyndon Johnson, in Austin, Texas.
Instead of going forward with an ABM system, as proposed by
the Joint Chiefs of Staff, McNamara urged that a decision be

put off until the State Department could explore with Moscow the idea of talks on limiting strategic arms.

In these events, as in others, McNamara emerges as a man of deep feeling and utter integrity, but almost too much of the latter. A Captain Vere without serenity. It was his judgment that assured destruction required an ability to destroy 20 to 25 percent of the Soviet population and 50 percent of its industrial capacity in a retaliatory strike. He also judged that the Soviets must be convinced that they could do as much damage to the United States if it fell to them to retaliate. Hence, there must be no American missile defense. In a speech at Ann Arbor, in 1962, he had questioned the prudence, even the morality, of such a targeting doctrine, but thereafter he put qualms behind him and did his duty. He held unflinchingly to the proposition that deterrence "means the certainty of suicide to the aggressor." Through the nineteen-sixties, pressure grew for the United States to develop modern heavy missiles, as the Soviets had done, or to double the Minuteman force. He successfully blocked each effort, asserting, in 1967, when the United States had five thousand warheads, that this number was "both greater than we had originally planned and in fact more than we require." He repeatedly warned against the "mad momentum intrinsic to . . . all new nuclear weaponry," adding, "If a weapon system works — and works well — there is strong pressure from many directions to procure and deploy the weapon out of all proportion to the prudent level required."

In June, 1967, seven months after the meeting in Austin, Soviet Prime Minister Alexei Kosygin arrived in Glassboro, New Jersey, for a summit meeting with President Johnson. Dean Rusk, who was Secretary of State at that time, later recalled for Newhouse that the Americans tackled Kosygin in a "go for broke fashion." The Russians, naturally, wondered what we were up to. When told of the dangers of the ABM, Kosygin replied, in effect, "How can you expect me to tell the Russian people they can't defend themselves against your rockets?" This surely is a recognizable political instinct. At about this time, Senator Richard Russell was saying that if there were a nuclear war and only two persons survived he wanted them both to be Americans.

A year later, on June 24, 1968, the Senate voted funds for the deployment of an ABM system known as Sentinel, which had been developed but not put in service. Three days later, Soviet Foreign Minister Andrei Gromyko announced that his government was ready to begin negotiations. Roger P. Labrie, of the American Enterprise Institute for Public Policy Research, writes that "SALT, like all previous attempts at negotiating limitations on nuclear weapons, stemmed from the interaction of new weapon programs with prevailing strategic concepts."

Then the Russians invaded Czechoslovakia. The first SALT talk, scheduled for September 30, 1968, was put off, and before the atmosphere had cleared Richard Nixon had succeeded Lyndon Johnson. But the two Presidents differed little in strategic doctrine. Nixon, if anything, was the more concerned with the nuclear race. Finally, the talks began. Kissinger took over. SALT I was signed.

What was SALT I? First, agreement was reached that neither side would deploy a general ABM defense. This was a success, surely — at least for doctrine. There would be little defense against strategic missiles. (Each party was to be allowed two truncated ABM sites, but no more.) Second, the Soviets obtained agreement to nuclear parity with the United States. This was a large achievement for them, in both symbolic and real terms, but one that doctrine allowed the United States to concede. At the time the SALT process began, McNamara calculated that the United States had a three- or four-to-one advantage in number of warheads, which he considered the true measure of nuclear power. But the doctrine of assured destruction minimizes the question of advantage. As long as the second strike is devastating, it is sufficient. Superiority, in this perspective, loses its meaning. In July,

1974, after the SALT II negotiations had begun, Kissinger responded to a question in a press conference thus: "What in the name of God is strategic superiority? What is the significance of it . . . at these levels of numbers?" After a point, numbers meant nothing — to us.

The doctrine of assured destruction holds that the curve relating numbers of weapons to strategic power flattens out at a fairly early stage. It may or may not be chance that this stage was seen to have been reached at about the number and extent of the weapons systems the United States already had in the mid-sixties. In 1971, two of the most gifted and experienced defense intellectuals, Alain Enthoven and K. Wayne Smith (the former an official of the Kennedy and Johnson administrations, the latter an official of the Nixon administration), wrote in their book *How Much Is Enough?*:

The main reason for stopping at 1,000 Minuteman missiles, 41 Polaris submarines and some 500 strategic bombers is that having more would not be worth the additional cost. These force levels are sufficiently high to put the United States on the "flat of the curve."

It may be said that this judgment was reached at a time when the atmosphere of the Vietnam War made it pointless to consider any increases. Even so, there should be no question that the view was sincerely held.

Again, looking back, it seems clear that this doctrinal consideration took the edge off the American disappointment that SALT I did not provide for any real arms reduction. The United States had hoped to put a freeze on the development of any further heavy missiles, with their greater capacity to knock out an enemy's ability to retaliate after a first strike. But the Russians were going ahead with both their SS-18 and SS-19, and there was no stopping them. In ballistic-missile-firing submarines, the Russians were accorded a numerical advantage of 62 to our 44 to "compensate" for the greater distances their underwater craft would have to travel to be on station. As noted above, they soon equipped these submarines with a longer-range missile, wiping out their disadvantage, and thus coming out ahead of where they had been. If we were disposed to think that such margins didn't matter, clearly the Russians were not. The United States very much hoped to obtain agreement that neither side would deploy a mobile intercontinental ballistic missile — for example, the MX — but nothing came of this.

The great and debilitating failure of SALT I, however, is that it did not produce any agreement between the two nations on strategic doctrine. It might have seemed that it did, and certainly Americans hoped that it did, but it did not. This failure was made clear in July, 1972 — two months after the treaty was signed — by William R. Van Cleave, a political scientist who has served as an adviser to the SALT delegation. In testimony before a Senate subcommittee headed by Henry M. Jackson, Van Cleave made a point that it was time some political scientist made:

The U.S. arms-control community has always had an academic character and a hyper-rationalistic approach to arms control that assumes arms control to be an intellectual problem rather than a political one.

Van Cleave was critical of the "eagerness" of the American negotiators for an agreement that, he felt, led them repeatedly to change positions. He was scornful of the belief, as he saw it, that we and the Soviets shared an overriding common goal of strategic stability as defined by American strategic and arms-control concepts. The overall evidence, he said, "is persuasive that the Soviet leaders do not share our assured-destruction doctrine. That they do is an unsupportable notion."

What doctrine *did* the Soviets espouse? This seemed evident enough to Van Cleave: "The Soviets — in contrast to the United States — have seen the strategic-force balance as an expression of political power." It had been McNamara's view, and it persisted, "that the strategic-force balance had no important political meaning." Whatever the case, it was clear to Van Cleave that the Soviets thought otherwise. To have the power to blow up the world three times was to have more power than did he who could blow it up only twice. The Soviet military seemed to have a simple notion that more was better than less. There were, at the very least, those among them who were prepared to think of nuclear wars as winnable, in the sense that one side would emerge better off than the other. This sort of thinking, of course, is incompatible with the doctrine of assured destruction.

The Soviet Union's military were, in any event, very much in control. Strategic doctrine in the Soviet Union is not made by professors. In his book *My Country and the World,* Andrei D. Sakharov, the Russian physicist, recounts an event in 1955 in Siberia, where a Soviet hydrogen bomb had been successfully tested:

The evening after the test, at a private banquet attended only by the officials in charge of the tests, I proposed a toast that "our handiwork would never explode over cities." The director of the tests, a high-ranking general, felt obliged to respond with a parable. Its gist was that the scientists' job is to improve a weapon; how it is used is none of their business.

The American negotiators of SALT I were to learn early on just how firmly the Soviet military were in charge when they found that they knew more about Soviet strategic forces than did their Soviet civilian counterparts. Military secrets are not widely shared in the Soviet Union, and at one point in the negotiations a Russian general suggested to an American that it wasn't necessary to talk about such matters in the presence of — what? — unauthorized listeners! Soviet military plans were not, in any significant measure, subject to negotiation with Americans or anyone else. In consequence, the Americans returned home to face a second negotiation with their own military. What seems to happen in SALT talks is that when negotiators have, in effect, agreed with the military forces of another nation that those forces should be increased they are almost required to return and agree with their own military forces that their forces should be increased also. It is a matter of relationships. If the Russians were building a Caribbean fleet, and the United States was either ignoring this or else snarling and snapping and threatening, American admirals, while they would certainly be urging a Baltic fleet or some such countermeasure, could nonetheless be told to stay out of the argument and leave foreign affairs to the President. But once the President had agreed with the Soviets that it was quite acceptable for them to have a flotilla in the Caribbean he simply would not be in a position to tell his own admirals that they would be allowed no compensatory increases. He could, of course, but he would be discredited as a man who preferred the interests of other people's military to his own. In a situation where the Soviet military always insists on more, the process will always end with the American military insisting on more as well.

One display Secretary Brown brought to the Senate Foreign Relations Committee last July (1979) compared the Poseidon missile, now deployed in the Poseidon nuclear submarines, with the Trident missile that has been designed for the new Trident submarines, the first of which will go to sea sometime this year. Secretary Brown's display ticked off the revelant information:

TRIDENT IMPROVEMENTS OVER POSEIDON
* Weight — 15% greater
* Fuel — advanced technology, more efficient
* Accuracy — ⅓ more accurate at same range
* Range — twice as great
* Explosive power — twice as great

Those who follow weaponry would have noted that the new missile, with far more destructive power, is nonetheless about the same size as its predecessor. In fact, Trident I missiles can be fitted in the launchers of the Poseidon submarine. (This is now being done, with the result that our submarine fleet will have much greater megatonnage in its warheads even before the new Tridents begin to be commissioned.)

As one thought connects to another, I found my attention drifting away from Secretary Brown's exhibit and back to a sunny June day in 1977, my first year in the Senate, with many things still unfamiliar. The Navy was launching a new submarine, the U.S.S. *New York City* — the first warship ever named for our town — and I had been asked to speak at the ceremonies in the shipyard of the Electric Boat Company, in Groton, Connecticut, where it was to be launched. I had done a spell in the Navy at the end of the Second World War, and shipyards were familiar. But as the official party walked along to the ways where the modest *New York City* awaited us, a never equaled leviathan hove in sight. There, broadside to the river — for it would fair stretch to the opposite bank if launched in the conventional manner — was the hull of the first Trident submarine. There has never been such a thing, and anyone who has been to sea would know it. My U.S.S. *Quirinus,* 40mm. gun mounts and all, could have been taken on board as a ship's launch. James R. Schlesinger, then Secretary of Energy, was walking beside me. He had been Secretary of Defense during the period when the Trident program was getting under way, and he recalled expressing misgivings about it, saying that the boats were too big, too vulnerable — that smaller ones would have done better. What had possessed us? I asked. It was the price of SALT I, he replied.

And so an American buildup of sorts commenced, ending the long freeze of the late nineteen-sixties. But we hadn't our heart in it; we just did it. We never admitted to ourselves that the

Russians did not accept deterrence as doctrine; that, unless
stopped by the most forceful intervention, they would build
until they achieved superiority. They might, for example, have
been told in 1969 that this would be a wholly unattainable
goal. That we would outspend them two to one. That we would
still be spending when they were bankrupt. But this was a
threat we could not make, even though, ironically, it is one we
could have carried out. I fear that those may turn out to have
been the days when the peace of the world was irretrievably
lost.

They did not seem so. Nixon deeply desired that a SALT II
agreement — a permanent treaty this time — would put an
end to increases in nuclear weapons and possibly bring about
actual decreases. But he fell, and negotiations made no
progress in that direction under President Ford, although he,
too, was altogether committed to the process. Then came the
new Carter team, including many old faces from the Johnson
years. They were hopeful, even exhilarated by the opportunity
they now had, and they moved quickly with a bold proposal.

In March 1977, the Carter administration, in the person of
Cyrus Vance, who had been Deputy Secretary of Defense under
Johnson and was now Secretary of State, proposed to Moscow a
significant reduction in nuclear weapons. This Comprehensive
Proposal would have reduced the number of launchers for
MIRVs (multiple independently targetable reentry vehicles)
from 1,320, which had emerged as the lowest level the Soviets
would accept, to between 1,100 and 1,200, with a separate
sublimit of 550 on the number of MIRVed ICBMs, the most
accurate and worrisome kind. (A MIRVed missile has more
than one warhead, each of which can be independently aimed
at a different target. As the "bus" travels through space, it
ejects first one warhead, then another, in different trajectories
and at different velocities.) Five hundred and fifty is the
number of MIRVed ICBMs the United States has deployed.

Paul Nitze, who has been officially involved in arms negotiations under Presidents Kennedy, Johnson, and Nixon (there are not many qualified persons in this field, and careers show greater durability than in any other field of policy), has testified that Vance's 1977 proposal offered the Soviets "complete assurance against any significant counterforce threat from the United States." But the Russians abruptly turned it down. Gromyko was scarcely polite. He all but suggested that to propose to the Soviets that they reduce strategic arms was an insult. (To be sure, his actual remarks were addressed to the suddenness with which the proposal was made.) In any event, with significant reductions dismissed, the SALT II negotiations proceeded to a wan conclusion, the basic numbers almost unchanged after two and a half years of negotiations by the new team. At Vladivostok, in 1974, President Ford and General Secretary Brezhnev had agreed that each party should have 2,400 strategic nuclear delivery vehicles (missiles and bombers), with a sublimit of 1,320 MIRVed missiles plus bombers capable of carrying cruise missiles. (A cruise missile is essentially a pilotless plane. Unlike a ballistic missile — which simply goes where it has been aimed, like a bullet — a cruise missile can be directed in flight.) SALT II would reduce this overall limit to 2,250 by 1981, but without any consequence. The Soviets would scrap some antiquated missiles they have probably kept around only for bargaining purposes. We would hold on to our B-52s — planes that are now as old as the pilots who fly them. SALT II limits the number of warheads per MIRVed ICBM, but each side is to be permitted an entirely new ICBM and to improve its existing ones within limits that may or may not permit fundamental advances. There are no limitations of significance.

Once again, a second negotiation took place back in Washington. The result was the MX. Recall that a principal American objective in SALT I was to prevent the Soviets from building any more heavy missiles, which they proceeded to do regardless. Again, no reduction in modern heavy missiles could be agreed to; thus SALT II provided that the Soviets should continue to have 308 and we should continue to have none. Opponents of SALT II make much of this "imbalance." But, as Ambassador Ralph Earle II, chairman of the American delegation to SALT, told the Senate Foreign Relations Committee in July, the MX, while not a heavy missile, does have as much "equivalent effectiveness as Soviet heavy ICBMs." In a word, the MX is a counterforce missile. And that is what the issue has been from the first. The United States would now do what we vowed we would never do. And so SALT II produced precisely the advance in counterforce weaponry which SALT I had hoped to prevent. Spokesmen for the Carter administration began to stress that the content of the treaty really didn't matter much, that it was the process that had to be preserved.

But if the process meant anything, it had to be one that protected assured destruction as a strategic doctrine. The proposal to go ahead with the MX implied that we ourselves were abandoning that doctrine. Of course, by 1979 assured destruction was already in ideological danger in its own sanctuaries. Newhouse, likening much of the debate in the nineteen-sixties to earlier debates about heresy, also notes that heresies somehow never die out. However much orthodoxy always asserted itself in the end, McNamara continued to have doubts. In 1964, less than two years after his Ann Arbor speech, he declared in a Defense Department "posture statement" that "a damage-limiting strategy appears to be the most practical and effective course for us to follow." Such a strategy would involve trying to destroy some of an adversary's missiles in order that his retaliatory strike would not be so devastating. (Of course, implicit in this concept is the possibility that the United States might, after all, strike first — in response, for example, to a Soviet invasion of Europe.) At this time, United States missiles were presumably aimed at Russian cities. McNamara acknowledged that a damage-limiting strategy would require greater forces than the "cities only" strategy, but he thought it would be worth it, especially with a Chinese nuclear force coming on line. In 1966, he appeared to favor an anti-Chinese ABM system. This would be a "thin" system, designed to defend against only a few missiles. The Russians would know that such a system was not directed against their large and growing force, simply because it would offer no effective defense. The proposal is worthy of note as an example of logic producing illogic. The reasoning that led to the decision was flawless, save that the Chinese had no missiles. McNamara soon enough recanted. In the middle of the Vietnam War, he could scarcely ask for more nuclear weapons, but his doubts were on record. He was not alone.

In the spring of 1968, just as the first SALT talks were about to begin, Harold Brown, then Secretary of the Air Force, told the Senate Preparedness Subcommittee:

In addition to the basic deterrent capability, our measurement of deterrence should include two other criteria, less central but still important: (1) ratios of surviving population and industry must not be badly adverse to the United States, and (2) the surviving military balance should remain in our favor . . . if deterrence should fail, a favorable surviving military balance could make it easier for us to negotiate an end to the war and limit further damage to the United States.

At this time, Schlesinger, still at Rand, commenced to argue that the United States could not allow the Soviets to develop an "asymmetric capacity against us." That is to say, they should not have a counterforce capability greater than our own. For either side to have such a capacity would be fatal to the doctrine of assured destruction, properly construed; for both to have it would be doubly fatal. Schlesinger persisted, and in 1973, as Secretary of Defense, he proposed that the United States develop a "heavy throw-weight" missile to offset Soviet developments. This missile became the MX.

More to the point, in the course of the nineteen-seventies

Pentagon officials began to talk openly of targeting Soviet military facilities in terms of "limited strategic options." The Trident II missile, to be deployed aboard the giant submarine, would verge upon a counterforce capability. (Submarine-launched missiles are still not as accurate as land-based missiles. Thus, while they are fully effective in an assured-destruction model — they can be sure of hitting Leningrad, for example — they are less so in a counterforce mode, where the target is a hole in the ground ten or fifteen feet in diameter, requiring that a warhead land within several hundred feet or so in order to "kill.") Nothing dramatic by way of a great debate ending in a break with previous policy occurred. Rather, as the Soviets crept toward a first-strike capability, American strategic doctrine slowly changed also. This was never really acknowledged, except in the edginess and growing anxiety of those who could sense the drift of events but could not arrest them.

An episode in the fall of 1976 revealed the depths of this anxiety. Once each year, the intelligence community produces the National Intelligence Estimate, known locally as the N.I.E. A measure of grumbling began about the relative optimism of the assessment of Soviet intentions. Leo Cherne, of the President's Foreign Intelligence Advisory Board, had the inspired notion to set up competing teams, one to defend the official estimate and one to challenge it. George Bush, as director of the Central Intelligence Agency, had the self-confidence and good grace to agree. The exercise went forward and was concluded. The B Team made a powerful case — more so than had been anticipated. In October, word of the exercise leaked; in December, *The New York Times* reported the results. The B Team, headed by Richard Pipes, of Harvard, had come to the conclusion that the Russians were seeking strategic superiority.

The indignation in Washington was palpable. The very suggestion was greeted with horror, as will happen when a doctrine grows rigid. The B Team members were near to anathematized. They had been invited to challenge the conventional wisdom, but they had made too good a case. Senator Malcolm Wallop subsequently observed:

While consciously refusing to entertain the Soviets' own conception of what they are about militarily, the authors of the NIE's over the years have evaluated Soviet strategic forces using indexes which tend to stress our own doctrine of MAD.

The 1976 N.I.E., Wallop noted, did mention that the Soviets seem to think in terms of ability to win nuclear wars. Nevertheless, the estimates continued to interpret both United States and Soviet forces according to the criterion of assured destruction. But how could this interpretation be reconciled with Soviet conduct? By 1976, they were (as they still are) spending 12 to 14 percent of their gross national product on defense — the sign, if the nineteen-thirties offer any evidence, of a country planning to go to war. "Bureaucratic inertia" was an explanation put forth, and it could well be the right one, although "momentum" might be the better term. But after a point larger possibilities had to be confronted. In his 1978 annual report as Secretary of Defense, Brown said that because of "a substantial and continuing Soviet strategic effort," the strategic balance "is highly dynamic." Although puzzled as to "why the Soviets are pushing so hard to improve their strategic nuclear capabilities," he noted that "we cannot ignore their efforts or assume that they are motivated by consideration either of altruism or of pure deterrence." Then, in May 1979, in the commencement address at Annapolis, Brown asserted that Moscow had long sought to threaten American land-based missiles and would probably be able to achieve this capability in the early nineteen-eighties. In an analysis of the speech, Richard Burt a formidably well informed and well connected journalist, offered the judgment that Brown had accepted the B Team's analysis.

As perspectives on Soviet conduct began to change, American conduct began to be seen in different light also. Was it the case that the Soviets were "catching up"? Were we "falling behind"? It must be understood that these were new questions. In the McNamara era, it had been assumed that American strategic superiority was as certain as was the validity of American strategic doctrine. But now it began to be noted that while the United States budget for strategic arms had been level for a decade and a half, that of the Soviets had continued to rise. In rough terms — they can only be that — the Soviets since 1968 have been outspending the United States in strategic forces by a margin of two to one. Dr. Perry reported to the Foreign Relations Committee that current United States spending on strategic forces is about $12 billion a year, while the Soviets spend on the order of $25 billion. (More recently, the Arms Control and Disarmament Agency reported that the Soviet Union spent a total of $140 billion on all its armed forces in 1977 — almost one third of all military spending in the world. The United States spent $101 billion. Wohlstetter calculates that American strategic spending, in constant dollars, actually peaked back in fiscal year 1952.) The Soviet buildup has been steady over a generation now, leading an arms-control expert from the Kennedy era to remark recently that if the familiar man from Mars were to be presented with a chart showing the rise of Soviet weaponry over the past three decades and told that somewhere during that period an arms-limitation agreement was signed with the United States, the visitor would be quite unable to pick the year.

The result is to be seen in numbers of warheads. If plotted, it would be seen that the Soviet curve has been steeper for some time now — up from a more than five-to-one disadvantage in 1967 to less than two-to-one today, on to parity in 1985 and to superiority thereafter, if the trends persist.

Number of warheads, however, is not the only measure of nuclear power. Size matters, and accuracy matters even more. It is not a question of projecting a time when the Soviets will have attained superiority; they have already done so. In this area, Nitze's estimates are indispensable, both because they are his and because they are public. In throw-weight — the pounds of "payload" that can be sent aloft — Nitze estimates that the Soviets by 1977 had an advantage of 10.3 million pounds to the United States' 7.6 million, this being the effect of the Soviet heavy missiles. By 1985, he projects a widened gap: 14.5 million for the Soviets, 8 million for the United States. The gap is even more dramatic in the critical category of explosive power — in what is called "equivalent megatonnage." Nitze gives the Soviets a two-to-one advantage for 1977: 6,160 equivalent megatons for the Soviets, 3,370 for the United States. For 1985, he projects a slightly widened gap with increases of near 30 percent on either side.

How did this come about? As near an answer as we are likely to get is that a synergistic relationship developed between the doctrine of assured destruction and the combined restraints on the United States imposed by the experience of Vietnam and the hopes aroused by détente. If this seems complicated, let it be said that nothing simple is likely to explain how the world's most powerful military nation lost its advantage over an economically and technologically inferior competitor in the course of a decade — and with almost no one noticing.

The doctrine of assured destruction, as I have noted, holds that the curve relating numbers of weapons to strategic power flattens out at a fairly early stage. One of the virtues of the assured-destruction doctrine was that it permitted the civilians in the Pentagon and in the Bureau of the Budget to form an estimate of what the military really needs. How many warheads, for example, were required to insure that 50 percent of the industrial capacity of the Soviet Union would be destroyed in a second strike? The doctrine fitted in surprisingly well with the management ethos that McNamara and others brought to defense issues. It suited even better the needs of the government leaders of the later nineteen-sixties who, while seeking strategic-arms limitations, were also waging war in Vietnam. Holding back expenditure in the strategic area eluded the fury that would have arisen had they proposed otherwise, and may have moderated opposition to the war. (An interesting aftermath: those most bitter about the Vietnam policies of the Johnson era are today likely to be most supportive of the strategic policies put in place by that administration, while those who supported Johnson in Vietnam are likely now to be suspicious of SALT.)

These considerations were, if anything, even more intensive in Nixon's first term. Certain defense intellectuals of the Johnson era began to assert that Soviet strategic behavior was basically imitative of ours — two apes on a treadmill, as the image went — overlooking, presumably, that the fondest hope of the community in the early sixties was that Soviet behavior *would* become imitative. In any event, this was presented as an argument against increasing American forces. Then Nixon embarked on the policy of détente with the Soviets, which added further grounds for allowing United States force levels to remain frozen. And that is what happened.

The irony of all this was nicely illustrated in an article in *The New Republic,* in August 1979, by the journalist Morton Kondracke. At the end of July, Henry Kissinger had testified before the Foreign Relations Committee, declaring himself not so much opposed to SALT II — he allowed he would have initialed the treaty — as in favor of great new military expenditures to prevent a further weakening of the United States of a sort that, he said, had brought about a "crisis situation threatening the peace of the world." Kondracke interpreted this as the familiar (although puzzling) charge that Democrats are somehow soft in these matters. He seems to have taken the charge personally. In any event, he retorted with some vehemence:

According to Kissinger, when the US left Vietnam, the Republican administration of which he was a part planned to build major new strategic weapons systems: the B-1 bomber by 1981, the MX missile by 1983, the Trident submarine and missile by 1979, and various kinds of cruise missiles in the 1980s. These weapons would have reversed the trend toward Soviet superiority, "but every one of these programs has been canceled, delayed, or stretched out by the current administration."

Kissinger's version of history scarcely squares with the facts or with Pentagon figures. Far from trying to reverse the strategic doctrines of the Johnson administration, Kissinger and President Nixon accepted them completely. The US land-based missile force was not increased by a single launcher during eight years of Republican administration. In fact, the Nixon and Ford administrations cut back on strategic spending from the levels reached in the closing Johnson years. Johnson's last budget called for $22 billion in strategic outlays, but the Ford and Nixon administrations averaged $10 billion a year in comparable dollars. Some cuts were imposed by Congress, but most were called for in Nixon-Ford budgets. It's true, few liberals were impressed when Republican officials boasted that they were continuously cutting defense spending, but they really were.

All true enough. The Nixon-Ford years were a time of unprecedented increase in social spending, and of decline in military spending. Rather like the Hitchcock film in which the diamond is hidden in the chandelier, this information was effectively concealed from the American people by publishing it in the budget. It may well prove that the historic mission (as Governor Jerry Brown might say) of the Carter administration is to increase defense spending and cut social spending. There is a mild law of opposites in American politics. Republicans frequently do what Democrats promise, and the other way around. President Carter was the most dovish of candidates in

1976, promising to cut the defense budget by $5 to $7 billion a year. Nothing of the sort happened, however. Social spending was effectively frozen, but defense spending began immediately to rise. In an address in Washington on September 27, 1979, Zbigniew Brzezinski, Assistant to the President for National Security Affairs, made a good deal of this:

> While our critics say they would have been strong for defense if they had remained in office, in fact, defense spending in constant dollars declined in seven of the eight years of the Nixon-Ford Administration. For the past decade, there has been a steady decline in the level of the defense budget in real dollar terms. We began to reverse that trend in the first three budgets of the Carter Administration, and President Carter is the first President since World War II to succeed in raising defense spending for three straight years in peacetime.

Brzezinski was not just taking credit for increasing defense spending. He was asserting that his administration, unlike its predecessors, was awake to the Soviet challenge. It has been a quiet development, this emergent challenge. Those who espy some special cunning at work have a difficult case to make. The plain fact is, as Van Cleave testified in 1972, that the Soviets never gave any indication that they accepted assured destruction as a strategic doctrine and would not seek nuclear superiority. How does the proverb go? The fox knows many things, the hedgehog knows one thing. The one thing their hedgehog generals seemed to know is that more is better. So they kept getting more. In this manner, the Soviets have acquired, or are about to acquire, a first-strike capability against our land-based ICBMs. We hope to do the same to theirs. Everything the SALT process was designed to prevent has come about.

The Soviets did not do this by cheating or by startling technological breakthroughs. They did it by the steady accumulation of more missiles (an additional thousand in the course of the nineteen-seventies) with greater accuracy, and more warheads with greater explosive power. They aimed them, as evidently they have always done, at our silos — in violation, that is, of our doctrine that they should be aimed at our cities, so that they could retaliate with vast destruction in case we attacked first. They either now can or soon will be able to take out our silos, leaving the United States with a much reduced second-strike capability. Not enough, it is generally thought. Besides, Nitze writes, the Soviets now have a third and fourth strike — an ability to deter our retaliatory strike by threatening our surviving cities and population. If it is all unthinkable, the Soviets seem nonetheless to have been thinking about it.

As have we. Heresy and recantation abound, and one of the more striking events of the SALT II debate so far is that both Secretary Brown and Kissinger appear to have joined Schlesinger. In his testimony before the Foreign Relations Committee on July 11, 1979, Brown said that the administration's primary goal was maintaining essential equivalence with Moscow in nuclear forces, but that to do it "we need to show the Soviets that they do not have an advantage in attacking military targets — that we, too, can do so." And he elaborated a bit, in response to a question from Senator George McGovern: "It is not a matter of us pushing the Soviets into being able to destroy our silo-based missiles. They have gone that route." Brown stressed that the mobile MX missiles, in addition to being able to survive attack, had another attribute: "Because of their accuracy and their warhead capability they will be able to hit Soviet silos, and that will, indeed, give the Soviets a motive for going away from silo-based missiles."

A month after testifying before the Foreign Relations Committee, Henry Kissinger spoke in Brussels at a meeting of military experts. As reported, he said he now believed that successive United States administrations, including the Nixon and Ford administrations, were wrong in thinking they could adequately protect the United States and Western Europe against Soviet attack with a strategic nuclear force primarily designed to wipe out Russian cities and factories rather than to strike at missile silos and other military targets. The policy of mutual assured destruction had created a "paradoxical world [in which] it is the liberal, humane, progressive community that is advocating the most bloodthirsty strategies." It was absurd, he continued, "to base the strategy of the West on the credibility of the threat of mutual suicide." It was necessary for the United States to develop a new nuclear "counterforce capability" consisting of missiles designed to be used against military targets rather than civilian ones.

Herein resides the final irony of the SALT process. Not only has it failed to prevent the Soviets from developing a first-strike capability; it now leads the United States to do so. The process has produced the one outcome it was designed to forestall. And so we see a policy in ruins.

What are we to do? First, we must try to get some agreement on what our situation is. Is it wrong to think that something of the sort is emerging? The Washington *Post* noted on August 1, 1979, "Here it is barely midsummer, and a growing chorus of important voices (whose opposition had been most feared) is saying that the treaty itself is no villain, that its ratification is almost a matter of indifference, that the fundamental strategic problems that most concern them are in fact beyond the power of the treaty, *as such,* either to remedy or even make much worse."

Jimmy Carter was the exception. On July 31, the same day Kissinger testified before the Foreign Relations Committee, the President declared, in Bardstown, Kentucky, that SALT II would "stop the Soviets' buildup." It will not do anything of the sort. Nor does anyone in the Carter administration who is in a position to know argue any longer that it does. In the spring and summer of 1979, the Joint Chiefs of Staff, testifying before the Senate Armed Services Committee, were unanimous in their conclusion that Soviet strategic power, under the agreement, would expand beyond what it is now. At the July 11 meeting of the Foreign Relations Committee, the Chairman of the Joint Chiefs, General David C. Jones, said, "Some may conclude that the agreement, by itself, will arrest the very dangerous adverse trends in Soviet strategic forces, including current and projected qualitative improvements. This is simply not the case." And later: "Similarly, the focus on constraining what the Soviets could do without a SALT agreement had obscured the more fundamental recognition of what they have done, are doing, and can do within the SALT framework." The director of the Arms Control and Disarmament Agency, George M. Seignious II, has stated that the Soviets will continue to engage in a "relentless" strategic-arms buildup with or without the SALT II treaty.

The SALT II treaty is in trouble, because it has been misrepresented. A profound change could take place if its administration advocates were simply to say that it is a chilling agreement but the best we could get, and that it is in our interests only if SALT III brings true reductions. Secretary Vance, in his letter of June 21, 1979, submitting the treaty to the President for transmission to the Senate, said, candidly enough, "For the first time, we will be slowing the race to build new and more destructive weapons." If the President were to say only as much — that we are at most slowing the race — things could be different. If he does not, there is no alternative save to oppose him on the facts, and try to develop a national policy without him. This is not easily done *with* a President engaged. But, in my view, it must be done. For those in charge of American strategic policy — including the President, whether or not he has thought it through — are now advocating a course of action which, if successful, will bring about the very nuclear face-off that not ten years ago was unhesitantly defined as the worst-case condition. This is to say that the United States and the Soviet Union will be confronting each other knowing that both have the capacity to attack and destroy the other's land-based missile forces, and can do so in forty-five minutes.

If still further irony is desired, it may be noted that, in the most explicit way, American behavior has turned out to be imitative of the Soviets. This was implicit in the aftermath of SALT I, when the Trident submarine and the B-1 bomber were agreed to. But these weapons were at least compatible with an assured-destruction doctrine. The price of SALT II, negotiated within the administration before the treaty was even signed, was the MX missile. From the time Schlesinger first proposed it, it has been understood that the MX is a counterforce missile. In other words, after only two rounds of negotiations, acquiring a counterforce capacity has become the condition of salvaging the very negotiations that were begun with the object of preventing either side from obtaining a counterforce capacity.

In any event, the world is sure to be different for the United States, and considerably less secure. Early in the 1980s, the Soviet Union will have the capacity to destroy the Minutemen, our land-based deterrent. These are the missiles that were meant to deter the Soviets from initiating any nuclear exchange. Following such a first strike by the Soviets, an American President could send in bombers and launch our submarine missiles. No one can estimate the horror that would follow in the Soviet Union and then, of course, in the United States. It may be that this prospect will be sufficient to deter the Soviets from launching a first strike, whatever the degree of provocation or panic. But is there reason to suppose that nuclear superiority will have no effect on their international behavior? Certainly men such as Nitze think otherwise. On July 30, 1979, he stated, in testimony before the Senate Select Committee on Intelligence,

To some of us who lived through the Berlin crisis in 1961, the Cuban crisis in 1962, or the Middle East crisis in 1973, the last and key judgment in this chain of reasoning — that an adverse shift in the strategic nuclear balance will have no political or diplomatic consequences — comes as a shock. In the Berlin crisis of 1961 our theater position was clearly unfavorable; we relied entirely on our strategic nuclear superiority to face down Chairman Khrushchev's ultimatum. In Cuba, the Soviet Union faced a position of both theater inferiority and strategic inferiority; they withdrew the missiles they were deploying. In the 1973 Middle East crisis, the theater and the strategic nuclear balances were more balanced; both sides compromised.

It is hard to see what factors in the future are apt to disconnect international politics and diplomacy from the underlying real power balances. The nuclear balance is only one element in the overall power balance. But in the Soviet view, it is the fulcrum upon which all other levers of influence — military, economic, or political — rest.

In any international crisis seriously raising the prospect that the military arms of the United States and of the USSR might become engaged in active and direct confrontation, those directing U.S. and Soviet policy would have to give the most serious attention to the relative strategic nuclear capabilities of the two sides.

Unequal accommodation to the Soviet Union would then have resulted not in coöperation and peace but in forced withdrawal.

It has been said that the Soviets have learned to live with American nuclear superiority and that we can learn to live with theirs. No doubt we can. But will anyone assert that in such circumstances we will not be living differently? And if one is drawn to the unhappy conclusion that the SALT process has not limited the number of weapons in the United States and the Soviet Union, what are we to think about the nature of world politics when many nations possess the nuclear weapon? What will be *their* views — the views of India, Pakistan, South Korea, Israel, South Africa, Libya, Argentina, Brazil, perhaps others — on deterrence, assured destruction, and the rest? Kissinger suggests that once the present state of affairs is understood, "panic" will spread through the world.

The decisive technological event that led to the shift in the balance of power, or so it seems to me, was the deployment of MIRVs — a term first used in public in 1967. Packing a number of warheads on each missile no doubt seemed an elegant and economical solution to the problems that the Johnson administration faced. (In the United States, development of MIRV began in 1965. The first flight tests took place on August 16, 1968. The first Soviet test took place five years later, in August 1973.) But it profoundly transformed the significance of the Soviets' huge rockets, with their tremendous throw-weight. Once the Soviets could install MIRVs, they were bound to be "ahead." As viewed in hindsight, it might have been perceived that the MIRV technology would work ultimately to the Soviet advantage. If it were the case that the American interest in MIRV was related to a desire to overcome a putative ABM system in Russia, the elimination of ABM should have argued simultaneously for the elimination of MIRV as well. But this assuredly did not happen. So long as no one had a defense, deterrence doctrine tended to ignore the proliferation of offensive weapons.

In what sense, it is asked, do the Soviet heavy missiles mean that the Soviets are "ahead"? This is the question with which adherents to assured destruction automatically respond when the Soviet superiority is mentioned. President Carter, in his 1979 State of the Union message, reported that "just one of our relatively invulnerable Poseidon submarines . . . carries enough warheads to destroy every large and medium-sized city in the Soviet Union." His proposal that the giant new mobile missiles be deployed on a racetrack system was openly a response to those who question whether submarines alone provide assured destruction. *The New York Times,* on September 11, stated that "President Carter's choice of a new basing system to make American missiles mobile and invulnerable to surprise attack removes the only real obstacle to ratification of the SALT treaty." This is, of course, the administration's view also; as long as a second strike is assured, received strategic doctrine remains valid, and technicalities such as the size of an adversary's forces are not relevant. This is to say that if the Soviets are "ahead" merely in the sense that they have more, it just doesn't matter that much.

And what happens if we don't, in fact, build the MX? The deference structure that previously surrounded nuclear strategy is no more. (Who, reading this chapter, can remember noting that the Johnson administration had decided to develop a multiple independently targetable reentry vehicle?) In a nation where nuclear power plants can no longer be built, does anyone seriously suppose that the government can dig up Utah and Nevada to put in place our largest missiles without arousing passionate opposition, of which the statement of the Federation of American Scientists is merely a foretaste? The opposition to the Alaska pipeline will be recalled; a key amendment protecting the pipeline from court challenges by environmentalists passed the Senate by one vote. The Air Force has identified thirty-eight federal laws that could have bearing on the MX and on the vast network of shelters that will have to be dug in Utah and Nevada in order to hide it. (This list still overlooks the Wild, Free-Roaming Horse and Burro Act of 1971.) In Washington, it was plain that a considerable body of opinion is remaining muffled on the MX so as not to jeopardize SALT II. With SALT II in jeopardy, opposition will become open, and will find leadership in the political world.

If environmental obstacles fail, opposition will surely arise to the spending involved. Indeed, it already has arisen. Early in the debate on SALT II, it was reasonably safe to assume that there was a high correlation between support for the treaty and opposition to defense spending. The correlation was not perfect, but it was significant. Thus, in January, 1979, Senator Edward M. Kennedy, a dependable critic of military spending, said, in a detailed statement fiercely attacking the Carter administration's 1980 budget, "Only defense receives a real increase in funding." He said these increases should be given the closest scrutiny:

First, in the strategic field, we should not reorient our defense posture more to fight a nuclear war than to prevent it. We should not develop weapons systems that increase the threat of nuclear war. We should not buy weapons to appease the opponents of SALT.

Here our number one concern ought to be the MX missile and its basing system. The Administration plans to spend nearly $1 billion in the FY 1979 Supplemental and the FY 1980 budget. This billion is but a foot in the door for many additional billions. Even without cost overruns, the system will cost us at least $30 billion to build and deploy.

The MX missile is highly accurate and devastating. It is so threatening to Soviet nuclear forces that it could tempt Soviet leaders to strike us first in a crisis. The result will be unparalleled destruction to both societies.

But President Carter went ahead in any event. And then went beyond that. Carter had accepted increases in defense spending; he now began to advocate them. Public-opinion polls showed that the strongest argument for SALT II was that it would improve our strategic position. The public felt strongly that we should not cut defense spending if there was a new SALT treaty, and many seemed to think the right course was to have both — SALT II and a bigger defense budget. Whatever the case, SALT II was no more than signed when the President — "to the consternation of liberals," as the political scientist William Schneider observed — began to argue that the new treaty allows for higher United States military spending in order to reach parity with the Soviet Union. More immediately, a number of senators, such as Sam Nunn, began to state that they could not support any treaty unless there was such an increase in military spending. The administration agreed, and before long the SALT debate had produced what

Richard Falk, of Princeton, who does not at all approve, has called "a mood of bipartisan militarism." Senator Ernest F. Hollings said:

The SALT hearings did have a shocking effect on this Congress and on the people of the United States. . . . Rather than a disarmament arms limitation, we had, in contrast, rearmament hearings and a rearmament conference and a rearmament treaty between the American people and our leadership.

In the course of all this, the Senate doves of a sudden found themselves in a hawk trap. In 1972, the SALT I ABM treaty passed easily, by a vote of 88 to 2, but by the autumn of 1979 it was hard to count 35 votes for SALT II. If a resolution of ratification were to pass, a great many undecided votes would have to be obtained, and many of these set as their price an increase in defense spending. Senator Nunn called for a true increase of 5 percent per year for the coming five-year period. In September, 1979, the Senate, by an overwhelming 78–19 vote, agreed to a true increase of 3 percent for the coming fiscal year. (Kennedy voted for the increase, and has come out in favor of development, but not deployment, of the MX.) Next, by a surprising 55–42 vote, a 5 percent true increase was agreed to for fiscal years 1981 and 1982. The 1982 defense appropriation would be in the neighborhood of $170 billion. The total outlay for fiscal 1976 was $87.9 billion.

A case can be made for increases. (I supported both.) But not for the blindness with which the administration and its supporters have gone about it. The dominant mood in the 95th Congress was to bring a halt to increases in federal spending. This culminated in an amendment to a tax-cut bill in 1978 which was sponsored by Senator Nunn and Senator Lawton Chiles, both Democrats. The amendment, which was passed by the Senate but failed of adoption in the House, would have required that total federal outlays as a proportion of the gross national product decline by stated intervals from 21.5 percent in 1979 to 19.5 percent in 1983. Very simply, if the country wants the overall budget ceiling to come down and the military budget floor to rise, social spending will be crushed. A pretty price for an arms-limitation treaty that increases arms.

Of course, advocates of social spending are at least as influential as those who want to see military outlays increased. The record over the decade, as Dr. Brzezinski's speech of September 27, 1979, suggests, is that they are more powerful. There is every reason to think that if SALT II is ratified they will withdraw their support for the military increases, having realized what such costs — the defense budget would about double, to $250 billion by fiscal 1985 — will mean to domestic outlays. There is room for much misunderstanding and not a little bitterness in all this.

And if these pressures are not sufficient, the Soviets will surely launch a determined propaganda campaign. The MX, they will say — have said! — is contrary to the "spirit of SALT." Those who supported SALT will be rallied to oppose this abandonment of SALT principles. In 1978, the Soviets demonstrated that they could reverse with relative ease the United States' decision to deploy the neutron bomb — the "capitalist" bomb that "destroyed people but not property." The MX missile will certainly arouse yet fiercer passions.

For two decades now, the doctrine of deterrence has led us to believe that strategic superiority doesn't matter. "What in the name of God is strategic superiority?" Kissinger asked. There is a simple answer. Strategic superiority is the power to make other people do what you want them to do. Already, the Soviets, approaching a palpable strategic superiority, give signs that it is their intention to control our defense policy. They set out to block the deployment of the neutron bomb in Europe, and they did. They evidently intend also to try to prevent our deployment of intermediate-range Pershing II missiles in Europe. They have given plain notice that they will not permit the United States to deploy an MX missile that would in fact be an "invulnerable" counterforce weapon. In the best of circumstances, the missiles could not be in place until late in the nineteen-eighties. SALT II, if ratified, expires in 1985. By then, the Soviets will know all there is to know about the capabilities of the new American weapon. They know enough already to be certain that it is a counterforce missile, and we do not pretend otherwise. It will have a combination of yield and accuracy that gives to each warhead a kill probability against a Soviet silo without precedent in our missile force. In response, the Soviets need only say that if we go ahead they will have to abandon the "fractionation" limits of a maximum of ten warheads per land-based missile which are imposed by SALT II. President Carter has said that it is these limits which make the MX viable. If the Soviets went to, say, thirty warheads per missile, as the size of their heavy missiles permits, they would effectively have a first-strike capability against the MX. Tom Wicker, writing in *The New York Times,* states:

Without the limit of 10 warheads per missile . . . the treaty would impose, the Soviets could put so many warheads on their giant SS-18 missiles that not even the mobile MX missile system could be made safe.

This, alas, is not the likely "scenario." When the Soviets announce that they are increasing the number of warheads per missile, as they will be permitted to do once SALT II expires at the end of 1985, the President of the United States, whoever he is, will announce that in view of this Soviet action our reaction must be to double the size of the MX. Whereupon the Soviets will announce that they are putting mobile missiles on highways. (A trench system will be too expensive for them.) SALT II will have effectively brought an end not only to the hope of arms limitation but to the SALT process itself.

Is there no hope? There is some, if not much. We should be clear that we are in for a very bad time, and that the longer we put off recognizing our condition the worse it will become. It may just be possible to join hawk and dove, liberal and conservative (hopeless, deceitful terms!) in recognizing that we have held to a strategic doctrine that cannot be sustained. It would work only if the Russians shared it, but evidently they do not, and neither do a growing number of Americans. The physicist Freeman Dyson has argued most vigorously that only defense weapons are moral in a nuclear world, making the nice point that we don't have such defenses in part because there is no elegance in their development. In his memoir, *Disturbing the Universe,* Dyson writes, "The intellectual arrogance of my profession must take a large share of the blame. Defensive weapons do not spring, like the hydrogen bomb, from the brains of brilliant professors of physics. Defensive weapons are developed laboriously by teams of engineers in industrial laboratories." Engineers!

Dyson continues:

Mutual assured destruction is the strategy that has led the United States and the Soviet Union to build enormous offensive forces of nuclear bombers and missiles, sufficient to destroy the cities and industries of both countries many times over, while deliberately denying both any possibility of a defense. . . . The basic idea of mutual assured destruction is that the certainty of retaliation will stop anybody from starting a nuclear war.

Dyson is a believer in damage limitation:

The ground on which I will take my stand is a sharp moral distinction between offense and defense, between offensive and defensive uses of all kinds of weapons. The distinction is often difficult to make and is always subject to argument. But it is nonetheless real and essential. And at least its main implications are clear. Bombers are bad. Fighter airplanes and anti-aircraft missiles are good. Tanks are bad. Antitank missiles are good. Submarines are bad. Anti-submarine technology is good. Nuclear weapons are bad. Radar and sonar are good. Inter-continental missiles are bad. Anti-ballistic-missile systems are good.

Just as Dyson's views were being published in *The New Yorker,* the political scientist Karl O'Lessker was making almost precisely the same point in *The American Spectator,* an organ of pronounced conservative views:

Older readers will recall that most notorious of all presidential campaign television commercials, the one in 1964 that showed a little girl plucking the petals from a daisy while the voice-over recited the countdown to an all-obliterating nuclear explosion. Paid for by the Democratic National Committee, it was designed to impute to Senator Barry Goldwater a degree of recklessness, bordering on insanity, that would, were he to be elected President, in all likelihood lead to a nuclear holocaust killing tens of millions of little children around the world. The ghastly irony of that commercial is that at the very time it was receiving the personal approval of President Johnson, his own Secretary of Defense, Robert McNamara, was fixing in concrete an American military strategy that had no options other than this nation's surrender or the indiscriminate slaughter of countless millions of civilians here and in the Soviet Union in a militarily pointless nuclear exchange. What makes it all the more appalling is that the Russians, by contrast, were then elaborating a strategy designed to gain victory by destroying Western armed forces while minimizing civilian casualties: an application of classic Clausewitzian doctrine. . . .

It is this reality that underlies the anti-MAD, anti-SALT partisans' call for the development of city-protection systems, from fallout shelters to anti-ballistic missiles. And it is one of the sovereign ironies of our age that the proponents of MAD have succeeded in portraying the anti-SALT camp as being indifferent to the horrors of nuclear war, while in point of fact it is MAD, and MAD alone, that postulates the nuclear annihilation of great cities as the logical culmination to international conflict.

Andrei Sakharov, a fervent supporter of SALT II, in a review of Dyson's book in the Washington *Post,* made a similar point. Sakharov repeats Dyson's words "Somewhere between the gospel of nonviolence and the strategy of Mutual Assured Destruction there must be a middle ground on which reasonable people can stand — a ground that allows killing in self-defense but forbids the purposeless massacre of innocents." Sakharov then comments, "With all my heart and soul, I support this thesis," adding his agreement with George Kennan that first-strike nuclear weapons are both amoral and, in the West, can lead to, in Sakharov's words, "dangerous complacency with regard to conventional weapons." (He refers to the decline of Western conventional arms.)

Moving and humane as such a comment may be, it ignores the fact that, in principle, assured destruction was not an offensive strategy. Cities would be leveled only as a response to aggression: the very terribleness of the response to aggression was supposed to prevent it. It were well that, before abandoning the doctrine, we remember why we adopted it in the first place. But that, in a way, is the most telling point. It is *hard* to remember just why we did it. As a set of ideas, deterrence theory was perhaps not very complex; but it was too complex.

Political ideas must be simple. Which is not to say they must be facile. To the contrary, the most profound propositions are often the simplest as well. Whitehead's rule to "seek simplicity and distrust it" is appropriately cautionary, but he did first of all say: Seek simplicity. Imagine explaining assured destruction to a rally. There was a time when no one had to do that, when the essential information was held in a few hands and a deference system made it possible for decisions to be made without much being questioned. That was the political situation in which assured destruction was adopted as national strategy. That situation no longer exists. We will never knowingly agree to start building the MX merely as a bargaining chip, as some have suggested, intent on stopping as soon as a bargain is reached. A shift in American strategy to defensive modes that the Soviets could not think aggressive or destabilizing would now require an open debate on strategic doctrine of the kind we have not had. For what it may suggest, let me note that after some immersion in the subject I have no view of my own, save the disposition to think that political ideas, in order to be viable, must be simple. Assured destruction is the kind of idea that wins acceptance in a faculty seminar. Damage limitation, by contrast, is instinctive — the idea of defending oneself is easy to grasp.

But, above all, is it not possible to return to the simplicity of the idea that nuclear arms should be controlled? Wohlstetter has remarked of SALT that it is a problem posing as a solution. Part of the problem has been the attachment of the process of negotiation to the specific assumptions of a strategic doctrine that only one side entertained. Yet a further problem has arisen from the unreal notion that there is somehow a distinction between "strategic" nuclear weapons and other kinds. The Pershing II missile, which the United States would like NATO to deploy in Western Europe, is as much a strategic weapon as far as Britain and Holland are concerned as is the Trident in the United States. Almost the best case for SALT II is that SALT III could engage the whole panoply of nation-busting nuclear arms. The United States and the Soviet Union today have far too many nuclear weapons. They ought not to have any. Yet while the other does, both will. But need we have more and more? Need we sign treaties to legitimate an arms race that neither side might be willing shamelessly to go forward with unilaterally?

An agreement on principles accompanying SALT II asserts that it is the intention of the parties to achieve in SALT III what are called "significant and substantial reductions in the numbers of strategic offensive arms." But the Carter administration — the strangely ambivalent administration whose pronouncements Senator Charles McC. Mathias, Jr., has described as "an antiphonal chorus of hawk and dove" — warned us not to expect anything of the sort. Gelb, in his *Foreign Policy* article, noting that "many people insist that only through reductions can one achieve 'real arms control,'" warned against "a fascination with reductions." Not many weeks after the article appeared, this became a distinct administration line. When the Foreign Relations Committee began in mid-October to "mark up" the SALT II treaty, "highly placed" sources were all over Capitol Hill warning against the very thought that SALT III might produce arms reductions. Vernon A. Guidry, Jr., reported in the Washington *Star:*

One key SALT analyst still in government, who did not want to be named, says any new treaty will have to include reductions because they have come "to represent strategic seriousness."

But as for making "deep cuts" the test of any new agreement, he says, "we've got to get our arms control constituency thinking in a more sophisticated and mature way about these things."

Gelb and other analysts point to the need to look more closely at elements within the over-all total of strategic weapons, such as agreements that would help keep missile submarines safe.

Within government, thorough examination of these questions has only recently begun. There is no expectation of breakthrough negotiations next time. "The next SALT agreement will indeed be modest," said one knowledgeable Pentagon official.

Is it truly not possible to propose to the Soviets that some reductions be negotiated forthwith? So that the world, ourselves included, will know that the time is coming when the strength of our respective forces will at last begin to decline? And if the Russians refuse then, at least we will know what we are in for.

A senator can take refuge in what the body calls the "pending business." And that is the SALT II treaty. The debate over its ratification ought to be an opportunity for the illumination of our situation, an opportunity to examine the quality of the ideas that have brought us to our present pass. On August 1, 1979, I proposed an amendment to the treaty in the hope that it might prove clarifying. I have taken the language about "significant and substantial reductions in the numbers of strategic offensive arms" from the Joint Statement of Principles and Basic Guidelines for Subsequent Negotiations which accompanies the treaty and inserted it as the last paragraph of the treaty and specified that unless such reductions are agreed to by December 31, 1981, the treaty terminates.

This date corresponds to the period of a protocol accompanying the treaty which prohibits either side from deploying mobile ICBM launchers — an MX, for instance — or deploying sea-launched or ground-launched cruise missiles with a range in excess of six hundred kilometers, of the sort we now contemplate placing in Western Europe. The Joint Statement of Principles provides that these issues will be discussed in SALT III. But in October, 1979, President Carter assured Senate Majority Leader Robert C. Byrd that he was utterly and irrevocably committed to going forward with both the MX and the cruise missiles and would never bargain them away in return for Soviet reductions. And so it has come to this. Determined above all else to win Senate approval for a treaty with arms limitation in the title, a President pledges himself never to limit arms but rather to raise them to unprecedented levels. This, of course, will mean the collapse of SALT III — unless we agree now that by a time certain in the near future actual reductions will be agreed to. This is to say, before the MX momentum is so great that the Russians shift into a yet higher gear in order to outrace us, while we become ever more panicky as the realization spreads that two decades of deterrence have left us desperately exposed to Soviet threat.

I expect all manner of criticism of my particular initiative. It will be argued, by defenders of the SALT process, that two years is too short a time to complete the task. I will be told that wisdom dictates that the pace of arms-reduction negotiations not be forced. Yet one wonders whether such objections by defenders of the process do not indict that very process — by pointing out the futility of trying to make it do what it is supposed to. I will be reminded that the Soviets resisted the proposals for armed reductions offered by Secretary Vance in March of 1977. If they would not agree even to discuss them in 1977, why should they do so now? I believe this question needs to be answered, and as soon as reasonably possible. I think it best that the SALT II treaty itself oblige the Soviets to give us their answer — one way or the other — so that we are no longer able to delude ourselves about our prospects.

We *did* delude ourselves after SALT I. An amendment by Senator Alan Cranston to the Joint Resolution of Congress that endorsed the Interim Agreement called on the President at the earliest practicable moment to begin "Strategic Arms Reduction Talks (SART)" with the Soviet Union, the People's Republic of China, and other countries. In a prescient speech on the Senate floor on September 14, 1972, Cranston said:

As I look ahead, I see what looks like endless series of escalators broken only by occasional landings which lead in turn to other escalators. A partial limitation will be followed by a new build-up, which may in turn be limited by a new freeze and superseded by new and sophisticated forms of escalation. And so it will go.

An amendment by Senator Edward S. Brooke declared:

Congress considers that the success of the interim agreement and the attainment of more permanent and comprehensive agreements are dependent upon the preservation of longstanding United States policy that neither the Soviet Union nor the United States should seek unilateral advantage by developing a first-strike potential.

Clearly, neither expression of congressional intent and desire had the least effect on the outcome of SALT II.

But have we ever probed deeply into Soviet feelings on this matter? We have never asked them to face, directly, the intellectual dilemma of an arms-limitation negotiation that produces arms expansion. Or is this what the Soviets have wanted all along? Is the question naïve? Surely, they have prospered militarily and geopolitically during the life of the SALT negotiations. Has that been their purpose? But we have nothing whatever to lose if we try to find out. At the least, I have been convinced that the SALT process is not self-corrective, and that, accordingly, the energy necessary to change its present direction must be generated from outside the SALT process. It is a process grown unreal, producing results opposite to those intended but thereupon defended as valuable in their own right. Gibbon has been described as detecting a "leakage of reality" in the late Roman Empire. There was a pope then, and it didn't help, and it may not help that there is one still. But John Paul II certainly had a point when he said, at the United Nations, that the nuclear buildup shows there is "a desire to be ready for war, and being ready means being able to start it."

In January, 1980, as almost the first executive act of the decade, President Carter asked the Senate to put off consideration of the SALT II treaty. His nominal concern was that the Soviet invasion of Afghanistan had created a political climate hostile to cooperation with the Soviet Union, even on so crucial a matter. But there was a measure of disingenuousness — *avoidance* is a gentler and perhaps more appropriate term — in the President's request. Half a year had passed from the time the treaty was signed, and there were still not thirty-five votes for it in the Senate, which had been startled to learn how little arms limitation there had been, and how fast the Soviets had moved up. In February, 1980, General David C. Jones, Chairman of the Joint Chiefs of Staff, testifying for increased military spending, told the Senate Budget Committee more perhaps than he intended:

The extensive SALT II hearings last year dramatically illuminated the facts of the deteriorating strategic balance for the Congress and the American public. . . . There is no question that Soviet momentum has brought them from a position of clear inferiority to their present status of at least strategic equality with the United States and the trends for the future are adverse.

It is important to realize that these trends are the consequence of more than 15 years of unequal and diverging rates of investment in force modernization — the product of unilateral choices rather than an outcome of negotiated arms control.

The shock will wear off, but the dilemma will remain. If the Soviets will not act as we do, must we act as they do? It is an awful choice, but at least we know it is there. A period of profound delusion is past; and the future is now at issue.

Index

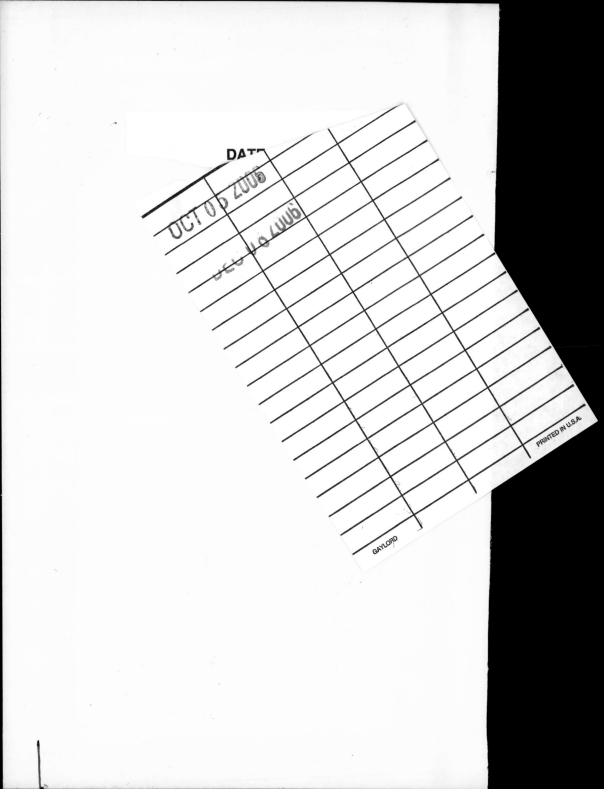